JESUS
is the
CHRIST

Studies in the Theology of John

by

LEON MORRIS

WILLIAM B. EERDMANS PUBLISHING COMPANY
Grand Rapids, Michigan

INTER-VARSITY PRESS
Leicester, England

ACKNOWLEDGMENTS

In writing this book I have made use of my contributions to the Festschriften for Bo Reicke and G. E. Ladd. In Chapter 2 I have embodied most of my article "The Relation between the Signs and the Discourses in John," published in Volume II of *The New Testament Age,* edited by William C. Weinrich; I am grateful to the Mercer University Press for permission to use this material. And in Chapter 3 I have made use of my article "The Jesus of Saint John," originally published in *Unity and Diversity in New Testament Theology,* edited by Robert A. Guelich; I express my indebtedness to the William B. Eerdmans Publishing Company for permission to use it here.

Copyright © 1989 by Wm. B. Eerdmans Publishing Company
255 Jefferson Ave. S.E., Grand Rapids, Michigan 49503

First British Edition 1989 by Inter-Varsity Press
38 De Montfort Street, Leicester LE1 7GP, England

Library of Congress Cataloging-in-Publication Data

Morris, Leon, 1914 –
Jesus is the Christ: studies in the theology of John / by Leon Morris.
p.   cm.
ISBN 0-8028-0452-7
1. Bible. N.T. John—Theology. 2. Jesus Christ—Person and
offices—Biblical teaching. 3. Jesus Christ—History of
doctrines—Early church, ca. 30–600. I. Title.
BS2615.5.M67   1989
226'.506 — dc19   89-30624
                                                              CIP

British Library Cataloguing-in-Publication Data

Morris, Leon, *1914* –
Jesus is the Christ.
1. Bible. N.T. John. Devotional works
I. Title
242'.5
IVP ISBN 0-85111-574-8

Contents

v

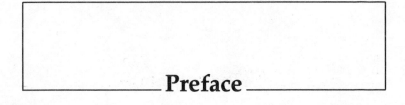

Preface

I N 1976 I HAD THE HAPPY EXPERIENCE OF BEING GUEST professor at Trinity Evangelical Divinity School in Deerfield, Illinois. Among other things I was asked to teach a class in Johannine Theology. This proved to be one of the most stimulating classes it has ever been my privilege to teach. I do not know whether my students learned anything, but they certainly taught me a lot. And they did more. They instilled in me the desire to write something on the theology of John. Throughout the years I have had the pressure of other commitments and have not been able to get round to it. But now, after all too long a time, I want to pay my tribute to my class of 1976 and to express something of what I have learned from the teachings of John.

It would have been possible to take in all the Johannine writings and say something about what most modern writers see as the Johannine school. But that would have involved discussion of questions of authorship and the like, and I do not care at this time to be sidetracked into such questions, important though they undoubtedly are. This book is simply a series of essays concerned with some of the teachings of our Fourth Gospel. I have not tried to make it exhaustive, and doubtless many of my readers will think of things that I should have included. I have simply taken John's declared aim (20:31) and tried to show a little of the way that aim was accomplished.

Here then is my little tribute to the class of '76. I trust that it will prove of interest to other students of the Johannine writings.

LEON MORRIS

Abbreviations

ANF	The Ante-Nicene Fathers
BAGD	W. Bauer, W. F. Arndt, F. W. Gingrich, and F. W. Danker, *A Greek-English Lexicon of the New Testament and Other Early Christian Literature*
BDF	F. Blass, A. Debrunner, and R. W. Funk, *A Greek Grammar of the New Testament*
CBQ	*Catholic Biblical Quarterly*
DB	James Hastings (ed.), *Dictionary of the Bible* (rev. by F. C. Grant and H. H. Rowley)
ET	*Expository Times*
GNB	Good News Bible
IB	*Interpreter's Bible*
IBD	*Illustrated Bible Dictionary*
IDB	*Interpreter's Dictionary of the Bible*
ISBE	*International Standard Bible Encyclopedia*
JB	Jerusalem Bible
JBL	*Journal of Biblical Literature*
JTS	*Journal of Theological Studies*
LB	Living Bible
LXX	The Septuagint
NEB	New English Bible
NIDNTT	*New International Dictionary of New Testament Studies*
NIV	New International Version
NovT	*Novum Testamentum*
NTS	*New Testament Studies*
RSV	Revised Standard Version
SBk	H. Strack and P. Billerbeck, *Kommentar zum Neuen Testament*
SE	*Studia Evangelica*
TDNT	*Theological Dictionary of the New Testament*

vii

CHAPTER 1

John's Theological Purpose

WE ARE NOT LEFT TO GUESS AT WHAT JOHN WAS aiming to do in writing his Gospel. He tells us explicitly: "Jesus did many other signs before his disciples, which have not been written in this book; but these have been written in order that you may believe that Jesus is the Christ, the Son of God, and that believing you may have life in his name" (20:30-31). This statement of purpose directs our attention to the "signs" that Jesus did, to the fact that John has made a selection from "many" of these, and to the evangelistic and theological aim that directed all that he has written. John has written about many things in his Gospel: the ministry of John the Baptist, the discourses of Jesus, the magnificent account of what went on in the upper room on the last night of Jesus' life, stories of events both heartening and disappointing, reaching their climax in the passion and the resurrection.[1] But when he comes to put in a sentence the purpose of it all, John singles out the "signs". This does not, I think, mean that for John the signs were the most important part of the Gospel. But it does mean that when he wanted to

---

1. This variety of topics has brought about a wide variety of approaches to the study of this book. Brevard S. Childs remarks: "J. A. T. Robinson and van Unnik have argued that the Gospel served as a missionary handbook to convert the Diaspora Jews. Baldensperger saw an apologetic purpose to counter the sectarianism of a group around John the Baptist. Wilkens finds the Gospel's intention to be primarily one of opposing gnostic heresy and docetic teachings. R. E. Brown, Martyn, and Meeks agree in focusing on the book's role in establishing a community's social identity in the context of conflicting group struggle. Finally, Barrett, as a reaction to the stress on external factors, argues for the primacy of the author's internal reasons which were independent of whether the book was ever read by others" (*The New Testament as Canon*, London, 1984, pp. 123-24). I have not tried to deal with this immense variety of opinion, but simply to follow the text of the Gospel as well as I can.

1

make clear the purpose of it all, it was the signs to which he turned.[2]

The Signs

John has his own distinctive way of using the word "sign". It is an important word which points to something beyond itself.[3] When a miracle is designated by this term, it is seen as a happening that is not self-contained, not an end in itself. It has a meaning that is fulfilled elsewhere than in the miracle. The term is, of course, not confined to John. The Synoptists use the expression quite often (Matthew has it 13 times, Mark seven times, and Luke 11).[4] But they use it for such things as the "sign" the angels gave the shepherds that they would see a baby wrapped in baby-clothes and lying in a manger (Luke 2:12), or the "sign from heaven" that the Pharisees asked Jesus to produce (Mark 8:11). Jesus condemned the people of his day as "an evil and adulterous generation" for their seeking for a sign, and went on to say that the only sign they would be given was the sign of Jonah the prophet. God had been at work in Jonah, and thus he was a "sign." As that reluctant prophet was in the sea monster's belly three days and three nights, so, Jesus said, would the Son of man be "in the heart of the earth three days and three nights" (Matt. 12:38-40). On another occasion when the Pharisees and Sadducees combined to ask for a sign Jesus complained that they knew how to interpret the weather, discerning from the sky the signs of fair weather and foul, but they could not handle "the signs of the times". Again, he says that "an evil and adulterous generation"

2. This point is sometimes overlooked. Some scholars write on the theology of the New Testament and specifically on that of John without giving attention to the signs. But on Johannine premises I do not see how the purpose of the Fourth Gospel is to be understood without reckoning with the signs.

3. K. H. Rengstorf rightly comments that in Johannine usage "*sēmeion* is a key word in theological interpretation, and in this respect there is a fundamental difference from its use not only in the Synoptic Gospels . . . and Acts . . . but also in the surrounding world" (*TDNT*, VII, p. 247). John has his own way of using "sign", and he is not to be explained by the way other people use the term.

4. Perhaps we should add to Luke the 13 he has in Acts. Paul uses the term eight times, Hebrews once, and Revelation seven times. The New Testament total is 77.

is looking for a sign, but none will be given other than "the sign of Jonah" (Matt. 16:1-4).

Jesus' disciples could look for a sign. They asked Jesus, "When will these things happen, and what will be the sign when all these things will come to their fulfilment?" (Mark 13:4; cf. Luke 21:7).[5] Matthew has this in the form "When will these things happen, and what will be the sign of your coming. . . ?" (Matt. 24:3). In the discourse that followed, Jesus spoke not of "the sign" that they had asked for but of a multiplicity of great signs and wonders that would in due course appear (Matt. 24:24; Mark 13:22; Luke 21:25- 28), though Matthew speaks specifically of "the sign of the Son of man" which would appear in heaven (Matt. 24:30).

It may be significant that the demand is always for a sign, not for signs. Nobody asks that Jesus perform a multitude of miracles. The reasoning behind this seems to be that the "sign" would be an unmistakable proof that he came from God. Nobody says what the sign was expected to be, so apparently there was no expectation of some specific happening that would constitute *the* sign. But people thought that if there was just one incontrovertible happening that showed in a blaze of light that Jesus was a heavenly being, all would be made clear. It was this kind of sign that Jesus steadfastly refused to produce. He was to be recognized by who and what he was[6] and what he habitually did. There were signs there for those who had eyes to see, but there was to be no dazzling performance that would compel belief of some sort from everyone who saw it. The demand for such a sign is basically a demand that God should act in accordance with the ideas of the scribes and Pharisees, that God be a god made in the likeness of

---

5. "Their question is one that pervades all biblical and extra-biblical apocalyptic. They want to be told what will be 'the sign'—that is, they want an infallible means of recognizing the approach of the End; they want in fact to be relieved from having to 'watch'. But instead of a single sign Jesus gives them a baffling multiplicity of signs. The purpose of his reply is not to impart esoteric information but to strengthen and sustain faith" (C. E. B. Cranfield, *The Gospel according to Saint Mark*, Cambridge, 1959, p. 394).

6. In the Old Testament Isaiah and the children God gave him are said to be signs in Israel (Isa. 8:18), and more than once Ezekiel is said to be a sign (Ezek. 12:11; 24:24). Perhaps we should understand that Jesus was himself a sign to the people of his day.

humankind. So Jesus calls those who asked for this kind of sign "an evil and adulterous generation."

Signs in John's Gospel

John uses the word *sēmeion* 17 times, of which 11 refer to the miracles of Jesus. It may be a general reference such as Nicodemus had in mind: "Rabbi, we know that it is from God that you have come as a teacher, for no one can do these signs that you do unless God is with him" (3:2). Notice that Nicodemus both discerns that the miracles are not ends in themselves (they are "signs") and sees this as showing that Jesus is "from God" (he correctly discerns what "signs" mean). We find a somewhat similar attitude in some of the Pharisees when Jesus gave sight to the man born blind. One Pharisaic opinion was, "This man is not from God because he does not keep the Sabbath," but others of this party asked, "How can a man that is a sinner do such signs?" (9:16). This opinion was not refuted, but neither did the holders of the other view change their verdict. But the second opinion shows an insight into the signs. Those who uttered the words discerned that God was at work in Jesus, and this outweighed what the Pharisees in general could not but regard as a breach of Sabbath regulations.

The signs could lead people to come to Jesus, as those did on the day he fed the 5,000 with a few loaves and fish (6:2).[7] Coming with such a motive is perhaps not ideal, but Jesus does not reject those who came in this way. Indeed, a little later he complains about some who came to him with a lesser motive than the signs: "you seek me out," he said, "not because you saw signs, but because you ate of the loaves and were filled" (6:26). Faith that rests on signs may not be the highest kind of faith, but it is better than none and certainly much better than coming to Jesus on the basis of a good meal. Signs are meant to elicit faith, and Jesus welcomes those who react to signs by believing in

---

7. We should bear in mind that John uses a succession of tenses with continuous force: "A great crowd kept following him because they continually saw the signs which he habitually did on the sick people." John leaves the reader with the distinct impression that Jesus did a great many signs. He has chosen to record only a few of them, but we should not overlook Jesus' continuing healings.

him.[8] This does not mean that he worked the kind of sign that leaves no possibility for people to reject him. A little later in the same incident people asked, "What sign do you do, then, so that we may see it and believe you?" (6:30). But the Jesus of the Fourth Gospel just as consistently refused to produce this kind of sign as did the Jesus of the Synoptics. The signs could and quite often did lead to faith. But they were never the kind of thing that smashed down all opposition so that no alternative was left.[9] There was always the possibility that people might refuse to see the hand of God in them and accordingly that they would not believe. Only people who were open to what God was saying would respond in faith. But those people would and did respond in this way.

The word "sign" in itself has no necessary connotation of the supernatural. It can be used "of marks in the landscape showing direction.[10] Using the word in a sense like this, Paul tells the Thessalonians that the greeting in his own handwriting "is the sign in every letter" (2 Thess. 3:17). He can also speak of circumcision as a "sign" (Rom. 4:11), and of course this is a divinely instituted sign: God had long ago established circumcision as a sign of the covenant he made with Abraham and his descendants (Gen. 17:10-14). This brings us to the more characteristic use of the term in the

8. J. T. Forestell holds that "a peculiar Johannine theology of miracle can be uncovered from the present text of the gospel. The miracles are works of God which reveal Jesus' glory as the glory of the only Son of the Father. They were a normal way to faith for the first disciples. Properly disposed and drawn by the Father, a man should pass from wonder at the marvellous to recognition of Jesus as a prophet and to faith in his word" (*The Word of the Cross*, Rome, 1974, p. 70). This draws attention to an important aspect of the signs, but I wonder whether seeing the signs as "a normal way to faith" allows sufficiently for the facts that (a) people could come to Christ by other ways than seeing the miracles, (b) many who saw them did not respond to the signs, and (c) John does not regard faith on the basis of the signs as the highest kind of faith.

9. R. Bultmann remarks that Jesus' signs, like his works, "are misunderstandable" (*Theology of the New Testament*, II, London, 1955), p. 44.

10. BAGD, *sub sēmeion*, 1. K. H. Rengstorf notes its use as "a visual sign by which someone or something is recognised" and mentions the "symptom" of illness or of health, the "scent" that shows the presence of an animal, the ensigns by which ships are known, and other examples. "In all the examples given someone or something is to be recognised and a fact or object perceived with a view to conceptual assimilation and correct classification" (*TDNT*, VII, pp. 204-205).

Bible, its use in connection with the presence of God. This may, as with circumcision, refer to something that God has commanded and which is of importance in the practice of religion, or it may be something that God himself is doing. An important and characteristic example is the use of the expression "signs and wonders" to describe what God did in bringing Israel out of Egypt (e.g., Deut. 26:8). While the term did not lose its ancient secular connotation as a general term for all sorts of things in which significance may be discerned, it came to have special relevance for religious people; a "sign" could show the activity of God.

It is this "presence of God" that is looked for in some of the passages in which the term is used in John.[11] Nicodemus recognized this, for when he came to Jesus he greeted him with the words, "Rabbi, we know that it is from God that you have come as a teacher, for no one can do these signs that you do unless God is with him" (3:2).[12] We do not know to which signs Nicodemus was referring at this point in his narrative.

Since John has mentioned only the changing of the water into wine at the marriage in Cana of Galilee, it is unlikely that the Pharisee from Jerusalem would be referring to this rustic happening. But John has let us know that Jesus had done a plurality of signs known to the inhabitants of Jerusalem (2:23), and evidently Nicodemus had heard of them. And he had not only heard of them but recognized them for what they were. Thus he was ready to acknowledge Jesus' heavenly origin.

I want to go on to speak of things John says about Jesus and what the signs tell us about him, but before I do, let us notice that the signs tell us a lot about God. No one in his senses is going to minimize the place of Jesus in the Fourth Gospel, but we should

11. "The Johannine miracles are revelations" (Ethelbert Stauffer, *New Testament Theology,* London, 1955, p. 122). D. S. Cairns says of the Gospel miracles in general (not specifically of those in John), "These signs, therefore, are integral parts of the revelation, and not adjuncts to it. They are revelations of the ideal purpose of God for mankind, and therefore of His character" (*The Faith that Rebels,* London, 1933, p. 98).

12. This beginning "represents open-mindedness on the part of an authority, who might be expected to resent the position which Jesus is gaining for himself among the people. It also has a deeper relation to the following dialogue, in that the argument will turn on Jesus' unique function as the bringer of revelation from God (11-13)" (Barnabas Lindars, *The Gospel of John,* London, 1972, p. 150).

be clear that this Gospel puts the Father in the highest place. In the signs none less than the supreme God is at work and makes himself known. C. K. Barrett draws attention to an important difference between writers like Philo and the Gnostics on the one hand and John on the other. Philo and the Gnostics both began with an understanding of the nature of God: he is to be understood as pure goodness or pure being, as omnipotent and thus able to bring his purposes to pass. They ask questions like, "How can such a God love and redeem creatures who are manifestly unworthy to be loved and on the whole unwilling to be saved?" So they develop "elaborate systems of mediation" as to how the God they postulate can do all this. But John begins with the Mediator, the Mediator who brings people to "the God of the biblical tradition, who, high and lifted up though he was, was the Creator of all things, an active participant in human affairs and ready at all times to dwell with him that is of a lowly and contrite spirit."[13] We should be clear that behind the Fourth Gospel is not some high-flown theory about the nature of God and how such a God might span the gap between creation and himself. There is a Mediator, one who in what he is and what he does reveals none less than God himself. And the God we find in this Gospel is a God who is interested in his creation, who loves his people, who never forsakes those he has made. In Jesus it is this God who is active and who is effecting his purpose. At the tomb of Lazarus Jesus prayed, "that they may believe that *you* (emphatic *sy*) sent me" (11:42). He was not looking for something for himself to emerge from the "sign" that was about to take place, but for people to see that God had sent him. John paints a vivid picture of Jesus, to be sure. But he also confronts his readers with the living God.

The signs tell us something about the way God works and the way the hand of God is to be seen in them. But the signs also tell us something about Jesus. As John tells the story, the signs were not such as could be performed by any godly man; they could be performed only by one who stood in a special relationship to God. They are a mark of Jesus' superiority to godly men, not an indication that he belonged among them. R. Schnackenburg, having looked at the theological significance of the signs, holds that "we

13. *Essays on John* (London, 1982), p. 9.

are led finally to assume an intrinsic connection between the incarnation and the revelation of Jesus Christ in 'signs' which it introduces and renders possible."[14] The signs point us to what God is doing certainly, but it is what he is doing in Jesus, not what he is doing in the human race at large, that is their object.

And what God is doing in Jesus is accomplishing the decisive act for the salvation of sinners. He is making a revelation—it is because of what he did in Jesus that we know that "God is love" (1 John 4:8, 16). But he is also bringing about atonement, for his love issued in the giving of his only Son "so that everyone who believes in him should not perish but have life eternal" (3:16). The signs point to this decisive act. Thus Alan Richardson can say of the first sign John records, the turning of the water into wine, that it "carries some highly suggestive symbolism, and there is a sense in which the whole Gospel is a commentary upon it." He points out that in chapter 3 Nicodemus "is shown the inadequacy of Judaism and the necessity of a re-birth through Christ. The meaning of the miracle at Cana is that Judaism must be purified (cf. ii.6) and transformed in order to find its fulfilment in Christ, the bringer of new life, the eternal life of God, now offered to the world through His Son."[15] The meaning of the individual signs is to be discerned only in the light of the great work of salvation God is doing in his Son. J. D. G. Dunn insists on this. He can say, "The real significance of the miracles of Jesus is that they point forward to Jesus' death, resurrection and ascension, to the transformation brought by the new age of the Spirit, and thus lead to a faith in Jesus the (crucified) Christ, the (risen) Son of God."[16] This may be

14. *The Gospel according to St John*, I (New York and London, 1968), p. 524. Cf. Stephen S. Smalley, "The principle which makes these six signs what they are is announced in the introduction to the Fourth Gospel, John 1 (the whole chapter). There we learn of the incarnation . . ." (*John: Evangelist and Interpreter*, Exeter, 1978, p. 87).

15. *The Miracle Stories of the Gospels* (London, 1941), p. 121. He goes on: "The truth is known only to those who do His will ('the servants who drew the water knew,' ii.9; cf. vii.17)."

16. *IBD*, III, p. 1450. Cf. O. Hofius, "The Gospel itself stresses the historical reality of the events. At the same time the miracles are understood as signs pointing beyond themselves to the One who performs them. They prove Jesus' identity as the Christ of God (20:30), who brings the fullness of eschatological salvation. . ." (*NIDNTT*, II, p. 632).

seeing a little more in the signs than others would be prepared to admit, but that they point beyond themselves to Jesus' saving work is surely beyond dispute.

It is not without its importance that sometimes John records that people believed simply on the basis of the signs. This happened in the case of the first of them, the miracle at Cana in Galilee. After this sign we find that "his disciples believed in him" (2:11). There is no discourse, no teaching about the significance of what had been done. There is just the sign and then faith. The same is true of the healing of the nobleman's son. When the nobleman found that the boy had recovered in Capernaum at the very time Jesus spoke the healing words in Cana, "he believed, and his whole household" (4:53). Again there is no discourse; Jesus does not explain that God is in it all, nor does he ask for faith. He just does the sign and faith follows.

It was different with some of Jesus' opponents who asked him, "What sign do you show us, because you do these things?" (2:18), and those who said, "What sign are you doing, then, so that we may see and believe you?" (6:30).[17] The first example follows the cleansing of the temple and is a demand that Jesus should authenticate what he did that day by producing some clear evidence of divine approval. The demand was that Jesus produce some evidence to show that God was in what he did. If he did not do this, they could conclude only that he was engaging in a purely human activity and therefore need not be heeded. But if he could produce a "sign", that would be different. Then they would know that God was at work in what Jesus was doing and they would take notice. That, at least, was their claim. But doubt is thrown on their sincerity by the second passage, for that demand for a sign followed on the feeding of the 5,000, and it is not easy to see what more could be wanted as a sign than that.[18] Indeed, Jesus complains of their attitude in the address he gives on that occasion and says, among other things, "Truly, truly, I tell you,

17. It was Jewish teaching that if a prophet "gives a sign *'wt* and wonder *mwpt*, then one must listen to him; but if not, then one need not listen to him" (SBk, II, p. 480).

18. Dodd comments, "The 'signs' which the people expect from the Messiah are mere miracles; yet when they see a miracle they fail to see the 'sign' " (*The Interpretation of the Fourth Gospel*, Cambridge, 1953, p. 90).

you seek me out not because you saw signs, but because you ate of the loaves and were filled" (6:26). The physical satisfaction of the enjoyment of a meal could attract them, but they were not able to perceive the "sign" in what Jesus did on that occasion.[19] This is all the greater pity in that this sign pointed to a truth of great importance, namely that Jesus provides for our deepest spiritual need and this provision is not made apart from him.[20]

On another occasion Jesus remarked that his hearers would not believe unless they saw "signs and wonders" (4:48). They looked for spectacular, miraculous acts and would not recognize the Messiah unless they saw them.[21] They wanted, moreover, acts of their own choosing. One would have thought that the series of "signs" narrated in this Gospel would be sufficient evidence of miraculous power, but Jesus' opponents were not convinced. In time they recognized that Jesus did work miracles and even used the word "signs" to describe them ("this man is doing many signs," 11:47). But even so, they did not discern the hand of God and were all the more ready to oppose Jesus. Of course from ancient times individuals who did not belong to the people of God had done miracles (such as the magicians in Egypt in the time of Moses), and Israel was warned not to be misled by such people and their deeds (cf. Deut. 13:1-5). Evidently the Jewish leaders had some such view of Jesus' signs: they recognized them as the kind

19. Reginald H. Fuller remarks, "The Jews did not appreciate the signs as signs in the true, Johannine sense, as pointers away from themselves and symbols of the whole work of God in Christ. They saw in them only miraculous physical satisfaction, to be enjoyed for its own sake. The discourse which follows expounds the feeding as a sign in the Johannine sense" (*Interpreting the Miracles*, London, 1963, p. 102).

20. Cf. G. H. Boobyer, "In John 6, the feeding of the five thousand receives a quite definite religious interpretation: it was a revelation of the truth that Jesus feeds men with the bread of life from heaven, and is himself the bread" (SPCK Theological Collections 3: *The Miracles and the Resurrection*, London, 1964, p. 43).

21. Sometimes this point is missed. Thus A. H. McNeile points out that John has given an account of signs "that ye may believe", and goes on: "The evangelist evidently realized that many of his readers would not believe without the record of signs and wonders. And in his narratives he relates that many believed because of them. They were a valid proof, though the Christian ought not to need them" (*New Testament Teaching in the Light of St Paul's*, Cambridge, 1923, p. 286). But when John speaks of "signs", he does not regard them as the more or less normal prelude to faith. He is speaking rather about a revelation which may be accepted or rejected.

of thing that ordinary people could not do, but that did not tell them anything about Jesus' person or his relationship to the Father. They did not discern the hand of God in them.

And that is to miss the whole point. R. T. Fortna points out that "to witness a miracle, even to benefit from it and seek out its author . . . and yet not to perceive it *as a sign* is to miss its point. A sign, to be understood, or 'seen,' must be recognized as full of theological meaning."[22] There were people who saw Jesus make a small amount of bread and fish into a meal for a multitude and who shared in the feast themselves, but who still asked for a sign (6:30). They had seen the miracle. They had themselves benefited from it. But they had failed to discern its meaning; they had not understood that God was active in what Jesus had done, they had not discerned the sign.

What John is saying is that they ought to have done so. What Jesus was doing was not merely miraculous (John never uses *teras*, "wonder", of what he did); it was "sign-ificant". The signs were not meant to cause people to recognize that Jesus was a wonderful person; they were meant to teach them about God, to cause them to see that God was active in what Jesus was doing, to challenge them to respond in faith to the divine initiative.[23] The trouble with the Jewish leaders was that they could not recognize the hand of God when it was actively at work before them. They saw that there was a connection between the signs and faith: "this man does many signs; if we leave him alone in this way, all will believe in him" (11:47-48). They denied neither the reality of the signs nor their power to elicit faith. They denied that God was at work in them. What should have led them to faith they saw as no more than works of power (though they used the word "signs" of them, they did not discern their significance). And because the miracles were to them no more than works of power, the result was hardening, not faith.

In one important passage John regards this failure as a fulfilment of prophecy. He says of Jesus, "But although he had done

---

22. *JBL* 89 (1970), p. 157.

23. H. Conzelmann asks, "Can miracles be narrated in such a way that a presentation of them is not only possible but necessary, because the miracle is only understood when it is seen to be directed towards us and to determine us?" (*An Outline of the Theology of the New Testament*, London, 1969, p. 347).

11

so many signs before them, they did not believe in him, that the word of Isaiah the prophet might be fulfilled which he spoke, 'Lord, who believed our report. . . ?' " (12:37-38; John is quoting Isa. 53:1; he adds Isa. 6:10). John is sure that Jesus' signs did point to God and that people ought to recognize this and behave accordingly. But he is sure also that evil people have never been conspicuous for their obedience to divine direction, as the prophets amply document. So he finds support in Isaiah for his convictions about the reason for the slowness of so many Jews to believe Jesus. They were simply walking in the classic ways of unbelief.

The quotations from Isaiah are followed by the words, "These things Isaiah said because he saw his glory, and he spoke about him" (12:41). The idea of glory is specifically linked with some of the signs. Thus at the first of them Jesus "manifested his glory" (2:11), and when Jesus was informed of the sickness of Lazarus he said, "This sickness is not with a view to death, but on behalf of the glory of God, so that the Son of man may be glorified through it" (11:4). Later he said to Martha, "Did I not tell you that if you believe, you will see the glory of God?" (11:40). Glory in this Gospel is complex and includes the thought of the glory that we see in lowliness, so that the cross is the place where Jesus can be said to be glorified. But making full allowance for that, John is making it clear that in the signs the believer may discern the glory that properly belongs to Christ.

God does not work only through signs. This Evangelist records the words of "many" who came to Jesus in that part of the country in which John the Baptist had done his work, "John did no sign" (10:41).[24] There is no denying that the hand of God was to be discerned in the work of the Baptist as the Fourth Gospel depicts him. God can and does work in people without the appearance of the miraculous. But God worked in Jesus in a special

24. Ernst Bammel has an essay on the topic "John Did No Miracle" (C. F. D. Moule, ed., *Miracles*, London and New York, 1965, pp. 181-202). He notices that the Jews put a good deal of emphasis on miraculous attestation, and concludes that the fact that John's testimony "deviates so very much from the Jewish scheme points—that can now be said with certainty—to the trustworthiness of the tradition. Being a witness without a sign it testifies to the great miracle that, nevertheless, its message was to come true" (*ibid.*, pp. 201-202).

way; the signs showed this. And it is what the signs showed that is John's special concern.

John's use of the term "sign", then, is very important. For him it is a way of drawing attention to the hand of God in the ministry of Jesus. John makes no attempt to be comprehensive: he simply selects a group of signs that show the sort of thing God did in Jesus. For him it is important that these happenings not be regarded simply as miracles. He never describes what Jesus did as a *teras* (wonder). The fact that the deed is inexplicable is not for him the significant thing. It is true that the deed cannot be explained on purely human premises, but it is not that that matters to John. For him the important thing is that the deed bears the stamp of God. We are to bear in mind that the Baptist, godly man though he undoubtedly was, did no sign. Signs were something special. They did not belong to godly men in general but to Jesus. It was what God was doing in Jesus that was significant. He was present in Jesus in a way he was not present in other people. That for John is very important, and the signs bear witness to it.[25]

Works

The importance of "signs" for John is indisputable. But we should not overlook the fact that in this Gospel Jesus mostly refers to his "works" rather than to his "signs."[26] "Works" of course is a general term; it has no necessary connection with the miraculous

25. H. van der Loos is somewhat critical of John's use of the term "signs". "The great extent to which theological speculation derives the significance of the sign from the miracle emerges from the rendering of the fourth Evangelist. The miracle stories here lack the spontaneous nature which they possess in the Synoptic versions. . . . If the miracles are evaluated solely as signs and seals, there is the danger that the dynamics of the event itself, the emotion of Jesus, and also man, who is the recipient of salvation, are lost sight of or become secondary" (*The Miracles of Jesus*, Leiden, 1965, p. 249). But it is not easy to see the "signs" in John as any less spontaneous than the "mighty works" of the Synoptists. And how calling the miracles "signs" affects "the dynamics of the event" or the emotion of Jesus or the recipient I cannot understand. Granted that there are other valuable ways of looking at the miracles, we are not justified in minimizing the significance of this way of regarding them.

26. This point is missed by a number of writers. Thus R. Bultmann says simply, "The term used for these miracles is *sēmeia* ('signs' and, secondarily, 'miracles')" (*Theology of the New Testament*, II, p. 44). I do not wish to downgrade the use of the

(which we have seen is true also of "signs"). It may be used of the works of God (6:28) or of those of men (8:39). When it is used of what people do, it may refer to good deeds (3:21; 8:39) or to bad deeds (3:19; 7:7).

The deeds people do may be characterized with reference to someone other than the people in question. Thus in responding to a claim by certain Jews that "Abraham is our father", Jesus said, "If you were children of Abraham, you would do the works of Abraham" (8:39). To be Abraham's children is to act like Abraham, to do the kind of deeds that Abraham did. But these people did not live like Abraham. They did the deeds of their father, Jesus said (8:41), and went on to explain that the devil was their father (8:44) and that was why they acted as they did.

In the light of this it does not surprise that good deeds may be called "the work(s) of God" (6:28, 29). The people asked, "What shall we do that we may work the works of God" (6:28), a question that seeks an answer to the problem of exactly what works God looks for in people, what works will please him. But interestingly in his reply Jesus replaces the plural with a singular, "the work of God"; and this, he says, "is that you believe on him whom he sent." The Jews were looking for a list of good deeds that they might do in order to please God. Jesus answers with a statement about the necessity of faith: they are not to try to earn merit before God by their own efforts but rather to trust God, which of course involves trusting him whom God sent. We should take seriously the words "of God" in this connection, for a little later Jesus says plainly, "No one can come to me unless the Father who sent me draws him" (6:44). Jesus is saying that faith is a work of God in believers, a work which brings them to himself. Good works of any kind we should understand to originate in God. Of ourselves we are not able to do what is pleasing to God. But it is Jesus' teaching that we are not left to ourselves. God has taken the initiative in sending his Son, and God works in us so that we come to do the things that are right. The saint never congratulates himself on

---

term "signs" in John; as we have seen, it is a very important term. But it is not the only term. And Bultmann overlooks something very important when he says of "works" in this Gospel, "the 'works' which Jesus does at his Father's behest . . . are ultimately one single work" (*ibid.*, p. 52). There is more to John's use than this.

the wonderful things he does; he thanks God for enabling him to do what little he can do.

Once Jesus looks forward to works that those who follow him will do after his departure. "He who believes in me," he says, "the works that I do he will do too; and greater works than these will he do, because I go to the Father" (14:12). We should probably understand this not of miracles but of mighty works of conversion and the like.[27] When we turn to Acts we do find the early Christians doing a few very striking miracles, though not I think any that we can fairly say were greater than those of Jesus. But in the power of the Holy Spirit they certainly brought people to commitment to Christ in far greater numbers than occurred during Jesus' lifetime. In the providence of God it would seem, in Forsyth's phrase, that Jesus came, not so much to preach the gospel as that there might be a gospel to preach.

But when John uses the term "works", he mostly has in mind the works that Jesus does (18 of his 27 uses of the word have to do with the works of Jesus). Sometimes this clearly means miracles. They are the works that "nobody else did" (15:24). Again Jesus said, "I did one work, and you are all astonished" (7:21). This will probably be in mind also in the passage about the greater works his followers will do which we discussed in the previous paragraph. The "works" are the "signs" under another name.

The works are performed only in the closest connection with the Father. Indeed, they can be called his works: "the Father living in me does his works" (14:10). In this Gospel Jesus never says, "my works" (though he does say, "the works that I do," 10:25; 14:12; cf. 5:36; but on each occasion the context makes clear that the Father is involved in doing the works as well as Jesus). He is not to be thought of as acting on his own initiative and in isolation from the heavenly Father.

Because of this connection with the Father Jesus can call on his hearers to believe on him "on account of the works" (14:11). They are to believe not because the works are miraculous and arouse amazement (though this is true), but rather because the Father is in them, the Father does them. This makes them of

---

27. Cf. Eduard Schweizer, "for John the supreme miracle is when a person is brought to faith" (*The Holy Spirit*, London, 1981, p. 71).

central importance to Jesus, and he can say, "My food is to do the will of him who sent me, and to accomplish his work" (4:34). The giving of sight to the man born blind is instructive. Even the terrible affliction of blindness is "in order that the works of God may be made manifest in him" (9:3); thus, confronted with the blind man, Jesus says, "We must work the works of him who sent me while it is day" (9:4). The word "must" points to a compelling divine necessity; since Jesus had been "sent", it is imperative that he fulfil his commission. Therefore the "work" of giving sight to the blind man "must" take place without delay. What the Father sends him to do must be done. We do not understand what John is saying to us if we see Jesus as a miracle-worker, a human figure separate from God, moving among the masses and winning divine approval by what he was and what he did. For John it is desperately important that the Father is active in Jesus, so active indeed that he can be said to do the miraculous works. It is none less than God who is active in the life and work of Jesus.

The works were themselves a witness to the closeness of the Father and the Son. In this Gospel it is impossible to view the works of Jesus as either the activity of the human Jesus or of the divine Father. Both are involved, and unless we see this we do not understand an important point John is making. Because Jesus' Jewish opponents did not see it, they were so vigorously opposed to him that on one occasion they tried to stone him, which caused him to respond, "Many good works I have shown you from the Father" (they were not the works of the man from Galilee; in their essence they were "from the Father"); "on account of which work of them are you stoning me?" (10:32).

When some opponents accused him of blasphemy, Jesus said to them, "If I do not do the works of my Father, do not believe me; but if I do, even if you do not believe me, believe the works . . ." (10:37-38). Faith is a very important activity in this Gospel, and the works can bring it about; indeed, Jesus is saying here that the works may be more effective in producing faith than his teaching. From a slightly different point of view Jesus says, "The works that the Father has given me so that I should do them, the works themselves that I do, bear witness about me, that the Father has sent me" (5:36). The thought of the works bearing witness comes out again when Jesus responds to the Jews pressing round him in

Solomon's colonnade and asking him to say whether he is the Christ, "the works that I do in the name of my Father, these bear witness about me" (10:25). The works are a standing testimony to the fact that the Father is active in what Jesus is doing. They show that the Father "has sent" Jesus. If these Jews had considered what Jesus had in fact done or what the Father had in fact done in and through him, they would not have been asking such a question.

In their function as revelation the works come pretty close to the words; thus Jesus can say, "The words that I say to you I do not speak of myself, but the Father dwelling in me does his works" (14:10). So also he says, "of myself I do nothing, but as the Father taught me, these things I speak" (8:28). He moves easily from the words to the works and from the works to the words. Rudolf Bultmann is probably going too far when he says, "the *works of Jesus* (or, seen collectively as a whole: his work) *are his words.*"[28] There is no point in confusing two different things: that they are closely connected does not make them identical. But the connection should not be missed.

The works are astonishing, and Jesus on one occasion speaks of doing greater works than his hearers have seen, "so that you may marvel" (5:20). But this is a by-product, not the essential thing about the works. It is the divine, not the marvellous that should command attention, and not only attention but faith and obedience as well. We should not miss the truth that the works are central for Jesus on account of their origin with the Father.

Mostly the word is in the plural, and we have noticed a number of passages which speak of the "works." But now and then it is in the singular, referring not to one particular miracle, but to the whole life of Jesus. Thus early in his ministry Jesus spoke of how important it was for him "to do the will of him that sent me, and to accomplish his work" (4:34). And right at the end he could say in his prayer, "I have glorified you on the earth, having accomplished the work which you gave me to do" (17:4). The whole of his time here on earth could be seen as one work of God. He

---

28. *Theology of the New Testament*, II, p. 60. He further says, "*The identity of work and word* can be further seen in what is said of the effect of the word. 'The words that I have spoken to you are spirit and life' (6:68)" (*ibid.*, p. 61). But no more than the others does this saying speak of an identity; it speaks of a close connection between word and deed, but this does not make them the same thing.

came not to do this particular deed or that, but through his whole life to accomplish the saving purpose of the Father.

This directs our attention to another reason for using the word "work" for what Jesus did. It is a term that applies to the nonmiraculous as well as the miraculous, indeed to the non-miraculous more especially. It points us to the truth that while we may distinguish between Jesus' deeds, labelling some of them as miracles and some as nonmiraculous, for him the distinction was not important. They were all "works." It is perhaps significant that in this Gospel Jesus almost invariably refers to his "works" rather than to his "signs." John reports him as using the term "signs" on two occasions, once when he referred to those who would not believe without "signs and wonders" (4:48) and once when he spoke of people who came to him because they ate the loaves and not because of the signs (6:26). But on all the other occasions Jesus speaks of "works." John pictures for us a Jesus for whom "works" was a more natural term than "signs." "Works" were the things he did, easily and naturally. We may classify them into those that are natural and those that are supernatural, but that is our classification. For Jesus they were all "works."

This usage points also to the important truth that Jesus' life was an indivisible whole. We should not say that he did some things as God and some things as man. He was not a split personality, moving from deity to humanity and back. He was one person, albeit a person who quite naturally did some things that we can do and other things that we cannot do. Consistently Jesus did the work of God, whether that meant living quietly the life of a Galilean peasant or whether it meant doing some stupendous miracle. And because he was doing the work of God, the glory of God was shown in all he did; in the miracles, certainly, but also in the quiet deeds of everyday life. There was glory in it all.

For someone as steeped in the Scriptures of the Old Testament as John, there is another feature of the references to works. In the Old Testament there are many references to "the works of God", and it is impossible that they were completely out of mind when John wrote his Gospel. All the more is this so in that Jesus' gift of the living water (4:10) brings to mind passages like "the fountain of living waters" (Jer. 2:13; 17:13) and God's invitation to the thirsty to come to the waters (Isa. 55:1), the references to the manna (6:31, 49) remind us of God's gift to his people of old (Exod. 16:13-15, 33-35), and the true light that lightens everyone (1:9) evokes recollections of God's creation of light (Gen. 1:3) and of passages like "the Lord is my light" (Ps. 27:1). But the expression "the works of God" is used in the Old Testament more particularly of what God did in creation (Gen. 2:2-3; Ps. 8:6, etc.) and in the deliverance of his people (Ps. 44:1; 78:4, etc.). These correspond to two facets of the work of Christ that are of particular importance in John. This Evangelist says that all things came into existence through him (1:3), and throughout his Gospel he tells of the new life Christ brings to believers. And, of course, it is the deliverance that Christ brought about by his death on the cross that is the climax to which everything leads up. There is a continuity between the works of God done in days of old and the works of God done in his Son. It is the same God working out salvation.

CHAPTER 2

The Relation between the Signs and the Discourses

T HERE ARE SEVEN GREAT DISCOURSES IN JOHN, AND this exactly matches the number of the signs (i.e., provided that we include the walking on the water in 6:16-21; it is not expressly called a sign, but it seems to many that it has all the qualities of a Johannine sign). There seems no doubt that there is some connection between the signs and the discourses, though it is not easy to say exactly what it is. Many would follow Raymond E. Brown when he speaks of "the Johannine custom of having a miraculous work followed by an interpretative discourse."[1] He holds that John 1:19–12:50 is largely concerned with signs and "discourses which interpret the signs."[2] This makes for a very close connection between the signs and the discourses and means that we must turn to the discourses if we would understand what the signs mean. Such views are widespread, though not held universally. R. Schnackenburg is a notable dissentient. He thinks that some "clearly defined complexes of discourse" interrupt the flow and that they are where they are because of redactional work, while "The rest of the discourses are often loosely attached to their contexts".[3] With such sharp differences of opinion, the question is complex and will bear examination.

The first point to be determined is the number of the signs. There are only four happenings which John explicitly calls by this name: the two miracles at Cana (2:11; 4:54), the feeding of the multitude (6:14; i.e., if *sēmeion* is the correct reading; many MSS have the plural, but even this probably includes the feeding), and the

---

1. *The Gospel according to John (i–xii)* (New York, 1966), p. 527.
2. *Ibid.*, p. CXXXIX.
3. *The Gospel according to St John*, I (New York, 1968), p. 67.

raising of Lazarus (12:18). We should probably include the giving of sight to the blind man in John 9, for in the discussion that followed, some of the Pharisees asked, "How can a man who is a sinner do such signs?" (9:16). The term "sign" is not explicitly applied to the healing of the lame man in John 5, but most agree that it is to be regarded as a sign. There would be wide agreement on these six signs. The walking on the water is not expressly designated by this term, and the discourse that follows it is related to the feeding of the multitude that precedes it. Such considerations lead many to hold that John does not regard it as a sign. On the other hand, if Jesus walked on the water, which seems to be the meaning of the narrative, this is a miraculous happening and we should probably include it among the signs (just as we do the miracle of healing the lame man). This would lead us to a total of seven signs.

John is much more likely to speak of signs in the plural as he refers to Jesus' deeds (e.g., 2:23; 3:2; 6:2). Each of the happenings he explicitly calls a "sign" is a miracle, and there is general agreement that John means the term to denote something miraculous.[4] Some scholars, however, hold that certain nonmiraculous events are to be understood as signs, the two usually selected being the cleansing of the temple (2:14-17) and the washing of the disciples' feet (13:1-11). Some think that the passion is to be accounted another sign, and this time the miracle of the resurrection is associated with it.[5] But since John never uses the term "sign" of any of these events, it may legitimately be doubted whether he wants us to regard them as signs, at least in the sense in which he uses the term of miracles. He can use the expression "signs and wonders" (4:48), which seems to point to the miraculous element (though we should bear in mind that John never uses the word "wonder" [*teras*] by itself; the miraculous as such is of little inter-

4. But C. H. Dodd warns us that "to the evangelist a *sēmeion* is not, in essence, a miraculous act, but a significant act, one which, for the seeing eye and the understanding mind, symbolizes eternal realities" (*The Interpretation of the Fourth Gospel*, Cambridge, 1953, p. 90). While a miracle is involved, it is the meaning on which the emphasis falls.

5. Rudolf Bultmann holds that "the resurrection appearances just like the miracles of Jesus . . . are reckoned among his 'signs'" (*Theology of the New Testament*, II, London, 1955, p. 56).

est to him; what concerns him is the miraculous that points to something beyond itself).

If we understand the term "sign", then, to mean a miraculous happening that points to some spiritual truth, there are seven signs in the body of the Gospel. The miraculous catch of fish in chapter 21 would certainly qualify, except for the fact that this lies outside the public ministry of Jesus. Further, whether or not chapter 21 is from the same hand as the rest of the Gospel, it is agreed that it forms something in the nature of an appendix. If we concentrate on the public ministry of Jesus as this Gospel records it, there are seven signs.

There are also seven discourses, taking the word "discourse" in a wide sense to include meaningful conversations with individuals as well as addresses given to groups. The coincidence in number, taken with the fact that the signs and the discourses are often adjacent, raises the question of whether the two are meant to be linked in such a way that each discourse corresponds to a sign. Each sign would in this case be given a Johannine interpretation. We must be on our guard, for John never draws attention to the number of either, and in fact never explicitly uses the number "seven." But it would be hypercriticism to doubt that some of the signs are related to some of the discourses. Few would doubt, for example, that the feeding of the multitude is to be taken with the discourse on the bread of life or that the discourse on the light of the world is linked in some way with the giving of sight to the man born blind. The question is how far this kind of link extends. Are we to think that each of the signs is meant to be read in conjunction with a particular discourse? The answer is not obvious, but the question is worth looking into.

It is, of course, possible that more than one discourse may be used to bring out the meaning of one sign, and alternatively that more than one sign may be associated with a single discourse. C. H. Dodd works through the section of this Gospel that deals with the ministry of Jesus and find seven "episodes", where an episode may include more than one sign and more than one discourse. His first episode, for example, goes from 2:1 to 4:42. He summarizes it in these terms: "In ii.1-10 water is replaced by wine; in ii.14-19 a new temple is foretold; the dialogue with Nicodemus in ch. iii is about new birth; the dialogue with the Samaritan woman in ch. iv contrasts both the *phrear* of Jacob with 'living water', and the ancient cults of Jerusalem and Gerizim with the worship *en pneumati kai alētheiai* for which the time is ripe. We may therefore best treat these two chapters as forming a single complex or episode, consisting of two *sēmeia*, or significant actions, and two discourses developing their significance."[6] Dodd follows this with a second episode which includes the healing of the nobleman's son (4:46-54), the healing of the lame man by the pool of Bethesda (5:1-16), and the discourse that followed it (5:17-47).[7] This time he has two healings and one discourse. Dodd argues his case with considerable learning, and in the end we must agree that what he says may well be the way we should take what John has written.[8] But if the signs and the discourses are related in such a way that the discourses give us the meaning of the signs, it seems somewhat more likely that there ought to be a correlation such that each sign is interpreted by a discourse. At least we ought to examine the possibility before we accept such a scheme as that of Dodd.

We might set forth the lists of signs and discourses as follows:

Signs	Discourses
1. Water into wine (2:1-11)	1. The new birth (3:1-21)
2. Healing the nobleman's son (4:46-54)	2. The water of life (4:1-42)
3. Healing the lame man (5:1-18)	3. The divine Son (5:19-47)
4. Feeding the multitude (6:1-15)	4. The bread of life (6:22-65)
5. Walking on the water (6:16-21)	5. The life-giving Spirit (7:1-52)
6. Sight to the man born blind (9:1-41)	6. The light of the world (8:12-59)
7. Raising of Lazarus (11:1-57)	7. The good shepherd (10:1-42)

We proceed to test the view that each of the signs is accompanied by a discourse that brings out its meaning. If there is such a correlation, the discourse may precede or follow its sign: there is no uniformity.

6. *The Interpretation of the Fourth Gospel*, p. 297.
7. *Ibid.*, pp. 318-32.
8. R. Schnackenburg, however, gives cogent reasons why we should not follow Dodd in linking the healing of the nobleman's son in Cana with the healing of the paralytic in Jerusalem (*The Gospel according to St John*, I, pp. 476-77).

New Beginnings

There is quite a reasonable link between the first pair.[9] The changing of water into wine is surely meant to bring out the power of Jesus to bring about new beginnings. John is showing that Jesus "changes the water of Judaism into the wine of Christianity, the water of Christlessness into the wine of the richness and the fulness of eternal life in Christ, the water of the law into the wine of the gospel."[10] There is also a forward look at the way salvation will be wrought out in the reference to Jesus' "hour", the hour of the cross (2:4).[11] What this means for the individual in seen in chapter 3. If anyone in Judaism is right with God, it is surely Nicodemus, this "man of the Pharisees", this "ruler of the Jews", this "teacher of Israel" (John 3:1, 10). But he has not received the transforming power that Jesus brings, and he is told that he must be "reborn from above", "born of water and the Spirit" (3:3, 5, 7). If the miracle and the teaching were not designed to go together, at least they fit very well. It is hard to think that John's arrangement is accidental.

We should not overlook the little section that connects the sign with the discourse. After the story of the miracle we find the story of the cleansing of the temple. The Synoptists have a temple cleansing at the end of the ministry, and there has been a good deal of discussion as to which has placed it correctly or whether there may have been two cleansings. This is not the place to dis-

9. *Pace* R. T. Fortna, who holds that "As they stand in the gospel, the two Cana miracles are unique in that each (a) is *self-contained*, having no explicit connection with its respective context . . ." (*The Gospel of Signs,* Cambridge, 1970, p. 48). He does note, however, that "in subtle and profound ways John has integrated them into his *schema*" (*ibid.*, p. 48, n. 2).

10. Leon Morris, *The Gospel according to John* (Grand Rapids, 1971), p. 176.

11. Cf. R. H. Fuller, "The wine which Jesus gives is a symbol of the Messianic salvation, revealed throughout the ministry and supremely accomplished on the cross. It has often been maintained that the Christ of the fourth gospel is a revealer rather than a redeemer. But, as the marriage of Cana shows, the revelation *is* the redemptive act, the Messianic purification" (*Interpreting the Miracles,* London, 1963, p. 98). We may doubt whether the revelation is the redemption, but that the wine is the symbol of the messianic salvation is important. H. J. Richards finds other pointers to the passion and resurrection, namely the references to the third day, to glory, to the "hour", and to Jesus' mother, who is mentioned again in this Gospel only at Calvary (*The Miracles of Jesus,* London, 1975, pp. 31-32).

24

cuss these questions;[12] here we are concerned rather with the meaning John saw in what Jesus did. It is noteworthy that he follows it by saying that the Jews "answered" with a question: "What sign do you show us because you do these things?" (2:18).[13] They saw a challenge in what Jesus had done, and they called on him to justify his action. Jesus did so in enigmatic words: "Destroy this temple, and in three days I will raise it up" (2:19). The Jews took this to refer to a literal destruction and raising again of their beautiful building in Jerusalem, but John goes on to explain that "he said this about the temple of his body" (2:21). John is leading right on from the new life symbolized in the change of water into wine to a cleansing of the temple, the holy place at the center of Jewish life, and then to his death and resurrection. We should surely see the point that this whole Gospel emphasizes, namely that Jesus came to bring new life and that he brought it by his death and resurrection. Of itself the turning of the water into wine does not tell us how the new life comes about. This supplement tells us of the importance of Jesus' death and resurrection.

Living Water

There is likewise a connection in the second pair, for both call attention to life. Jesus spoke to the woman at the well about the "living water" that will be in the one who drinks it "a fountain of water leaping up into life eternal" so that he will never thirst again (4:10, 14). The woman did not take Jesus seriously at first, but her question whether he was greater than Jacob who gave the well from which she was about to draw (4:12) is interesting. Clearly in including this in his story John is once more contrasting the best that Judaism could do with the life that Jesus would bring. To the

12. I have examined them in *The Gospel according to John,* pp. 188-91.

13. That John records a request for a sign immediately after the cleansing of the temple seems to show that he did not regard that vigorous action as a "sign" even though there are scholars who hold that we should so regard it. It is true that after the sign of the multiplication of the loaves some opponents of Jesus asked him, "What sign do you do?" (6:30), so that the consideration is not complete proof. But in chapter 6 the opponents were clearly looking for something like the manna (to which they immediately refer). There is no equivalent in chapter 2.

woman it was unthinkable that Jesus could compare with Jacob; to John it was unthinkable that Jacob could compare with Jesus. Jesus had not come to bring a revised Judaism but to bring living water such that the spiritual thirst of whoever drinks it will be quenched once and for all. Nothing in Judaism could do this.

We should understand this against a background in Judaism that so often links water with the law. Thus we read in Sirach that "he who holds to the law will obtain wisdom"; the passage goes on to affirm that "she . . . will give him the water of wisdom to drink" (Sir. 15:1-3). In the Talmud we read a saying of R. Johanan speaking in the name of R. Simeon b. Yohai which explains the words "Blessed are ye that sow beside all waters . . ." (Isa. 32:20) as "Whoever is occupied with (the study of) the law" (Baba Kamma 17a); much more could be cited to the same effect.[14] John is surely making it clear that the law, on which the Jews prided themselves so greatly, was ineffective. It could not give the life that does not end, "eternal life" which John introduces in the conversation between Jesus and the disciples. Jesus tells them that "he who reaps receives a wage and gathers fruit unto life eternal . . ." (4:36). The living water that Jesus gives brings life, but the law, the Torah, does not.

At a later time Jesus would refer to "rivers of living water" and explain, "This he spoke about the Spirit, whom those who believed in him would receive" (7:38-39). This thought is not developed at this point in the narrative, but we must bear it in mind as part of what John is telling us through his Gospel.

We should not miss the further point that as the conversation goes on, the woman's sin is exposed and with it the inadequacy of the Samaritan way she has been following (4:16-18). Her attempt to bring in the rival merits of Gerizim and Jerusalem as places of worship is negated by Jesus' pointing out that "an hour is coming when neither in this mountain nor in Jerusalem will you worship the Father" (4:21), which is followed by the information that "salvation is of the Jews" and that "true worshippers will worship the Father in spirit and truth" (4:22, 23). All this adds up

---

14. See the evidence in SBk, II, pp. 433-36. They date R. Simeon c. A.D. 150. H. Odeberg cites from a variety of Jewish sources which link the symbolism of water with the law (*The Fourth Gospel,* Amsterdam, 1968, pp. 155ff.).

to a further emphasis on the truth that Jesus brings people life, life in the Spirit.

This is brought out in the "sign" of the nobleman's son. When he was told of the plight of the sufferer, Jesus said to the boy's father, "Go; your son lives" (4:50). The words of power occur twice more (vv. 51, 53), and the threefold repetition of "lives" is important.[15] Some have understood the story in the sense that Jesus simply prophesied that the boy would live. Thus, for example, RSV translates, "Your son will live" (so H. J. Schonfield; cf. E. J. Goodspeed, "Your son is going to live"). But this is surely not doing justice to the Johannine method. The repetition emphasizes the truth that Jesus gives life. Barnabas Lindars finds the expression "deliberately chosen to point to the fulfilment of the promise of life already given in the discourse with the Samaritan woman. It thus carries with it the larger sense of salvation, or eternal life, which is the point of John's insertion of this story here."[16] This seems the right way to understand what John has written. The miracle and the discourse complement one another.

The Father and the Son

The third sign is the healing of a man who had been lame for 38 years. He was lying by the pool of Bethesda in the hope that he might receive a cure from the healing waters. Again we see the water motif, with its associations of the law, the way so beloved of the Jews. And again we see that this way is ineffective, but that what the water could not do for the man Jesus did with a word.

An unusual feature of this miracle is Jesus' introductory question, "Do you *will* to be made well?" (5:6), which is taken up in the discourse when Jesus says, "you do not *will* to come to me to have life" (5:40; there are other references to the will in vv. 21 and 35).[17] Possibly the use of *egeirō* in both sections is significant (vv.

15. John Marsh finds in this "already a reference to eternal life", and he says, "The fact that the phrase is repeated . . . adds significance to it as a key theological word in the narrative" (*The Gospel of St John*, Harmondsworth, 1968, p. 240).

16. *The Gospel of John* (London, 1972), p. 204.

17. Cf. C. H. Dodd, who says that the man's reply "is a feeble excuse. The man has not the will. The law might show the way of life; it was powerless to create the will to live" (*The Interpretation of the Fourth Gospel*, p. 320).

8, 21), though the one refers to the man's rising up to walk and the other to God's raising of the dead. John's arrangement brings out significant connections. The discourse makes clear what is implied in the act.

The incident took place on a Sabbath.[18] Jesus questioned the lame man about his will to be well (5:6), and commanded him to take up his bed and walk. This provoked a dispute with the Pharisees, and Jesus went on to speak of his place as the divine Son, stressing his relationship to the Father and the witness borne to him by a variety of witnesses such as John the Baptist, Jesus' own works, and, most importantly, the heavenly Father. There may be a link between the sign and the discourse in the emphasis on power. To have spent 38 years unable to walk was to have endured unutterable hardship in a condition beyond all normal human modes of help. The discourse that stresses the power of the Son to raise the dead and to be the Judge of the entire human race (5:25-29) is accordingly very relevant.

But more important is the Sabbath motif. That the miracle was performed on the Sabbath stamped Jesus as an evildoer in the eyes of Pharisaic officialdom. The sign is Jesus' assertion that he could do on the Sabbath things that the Pharisees could not do. His relationship to God differs from theirs. Apart from God Jesus is helpless (vv. 19, 30), so that the healing of the man must not be seen as simply a magnificent human achievement. As John relates it, it is a deed in which God set his seal on the work of his Son.[19] The Jews were very interested in the Sabbath and engaged in discussions of the intent of God's activity on that day. Obviously the whole fabric of the world would perish if God did not sustain his creation, and there were some ingenious ways of combining the thoughts that God respected the Sabbath that he had ordained and that he yet continued with his work of upholding all things. Thus Philo

18. R. Bultmann and others regard the Sabbath motif as a secondary addition (see *Das Evangelium des Johannes*, Göttingen, 1956, p. 178, n. 4). Brown, however, rejects such views, holding that the Sabbath reference is original (*John*, I, p. 210).

19. Fuller sees 5:17, 18b as an addition of the Evangelist which "introduces the theme of the relationship between Jesus and the Father, to be developed in the discourse which he appends in 5.19-47" (*Miracles*, p. 100). That is to say, as this Gospel stands, the miracle leads to the discourse, the connection being the relationship between the Father and the Son. Fuller also stresses the importance of judgment.

says, "God never leaves off making, but even as it is the property of fire to burn and of snow to chill, so it is the property of God to make: nay more so by far inasmuch as He is to all besides the source of action." He makes a distinction between what "is apparently making" and God's actual making; the former ceases, the latter does not.[20] Another way of looking at it emerges from the *Midrash Rabbah*. We are told of four Rabbis challenged to explain why God commands Israel to abstain from work on the Sabbath while he himself does not do so. They asked, "Is not a man permitted to carry on the Sabbath in his own courtyard?" and pointed out that both "the higher and lower regions are the courtyard of God", so that in his own way God is keeping the Sabbath.[21] Only it is not the way earthlings keep it. Jesus is saying that he observes the Sabbath in the same way the Father does. The Jews recognized that his claim meant that he was asserting that God was his own Father, his Father in a special sense, for he was "making himself equal to God" (5:18). But Jesus did not mean this in the sense that he was a second god, a being quite separate from the Father. He says that he is quite unable to do anything apart from himself, and that what the Father does the Son does (5:19). He does not say that he does similar things, but that he does the same things.

The close relationship between the Father and the Son is fur ther brought out in the Son's appointment to raise the dead (C. H. Dodd finds the "dominant theme" in the discourse in the words *ho huios hous thelei zōopoiei*,[22] with which, of course, is linked his work of judgment (5:21-22). The purpose (*hina*) of this is that all should honor the Son as they do the Father (5:23). The discourse goes on to the theme of witness. Jesus has made some far-reaching claims, and he goes on to point out that there is adequate witness to the truth of what he has been saying.

The Bread of Life

It is scarcely necessary to labor the connection beween the feeding of the multitude and the teaching about the bread of life. The

---

20. *Legum Allegoriae* I.5-6 (Loeb translation).
21. *Exodus Rabbah* 30.9 (Soncino translation).
22. *The Interpretation of the Fourth Gospel*, p. 318.

feeding of the 5,000 is the one miracle found in all four Gospels, so clearly did it make a special appeal to those in the early church. John has a few details peculiar to himself, such as Philip's calculation to show the impossibility of feeding the people and Andrew's action in bringing forward the boy with the loaves and fish. He alone tells us that the loaves were barley loaves. But such information is minor. Essentially John tells the same story as the other Evangelists.

We should bear in mind that bread occupied a much larger place in the diet of first-century Palestinians than it does in developed twentieth-century countries. Bread could be used to sum up food in general, as when Adam was told as he was expelled from Eden, "In the sweat of your face you shall eat bread" (Gen. 3:19). So we read that bread sustains the heart of man (Ps. 104:15), even though we are also told to remember that "man does not live by bread alone" (Deut. 8:3). In line with this, eating and drinking can be taken to indicate prosperity. "Man has no good thing under the sun but to eat, and drink, and enjoy himself" (Eccl. 8:15). Disaster can be described in these terms: "Thou hast fed them with the bread of tears" (Ps. 80:5), or with interesting imagery there may be a reference to breaking "every staff of bread" (Ps. 105:16), which NIV translates, "destroyed all their supplies of food."

We have seen that water can be used metaphorically for the law, and the same is true of bread. It is said, for example, that the proselyte Akilas visited R. Eliezer with a question about Deuteronomy 10:18 and was referred to Genesis 28:20, Jacob's prayer for "bread to eat" (among other things). Apparently somewhat dissatisfied, he went on to R. Joshua, who "began to comfort him with words: *'Bread'* refers to the Torah".[23] This imagery seems to have been widespread and must be borne in mind throughout this chapter. It seems that from another point of view John is bringing out the superiority of what Jesus has done to the pursuit of the law so characteristic of Judaism.

Very important also as background to this section of John's Gospel is the gift of the manna in Old Testament days (Exod.

---

23. The passage is in *Genesis Rabbah* 70.5. R. Eliezer is dated *c.* 90, so the incident is dated close to New Testament times. See further the passages listed in SBk, II, pp. 483-84.

16:13-36). Quite ignoring the sign that had been given them in the multiplication of a few loaves and fish to enable them to feed more than 5,000 people, the people asked Jesus, "What therefore do you do as a sign...?" and went on to say, "Our fathers ate the manna in the wilderness, even as it is written, 'Bread from heaven he gave them to eat'" (6:30-31). It is curious that they make this demand, for surely the miracle of the loaves is much the same kind of miracle. But, of course, they could point out that Moses fed a whole nation (not a mere 5,000), and did it for 40 years (not for just one meal); Moses gave them "bread from heaven", whereas Jesus gave no more than the kind of bread people ate every day. In any case there was a Jewish expectation that when the Messiah came the miracle of the manna would be renewed (2 Bar. 29:8; Sib. Or., Frag. 3:49), and it was evidently this for which the people looked. It was the manna that would accredit the Messiah: unless Jesus could bring the manna as of old, he would not be accepted by these people.[24] But Jesus did not go along with this view, and he proceeds to explain that "the bread of God is he who (or that which) comes down from heaven and gives life to the world" (6:33). They were looking in the wrong place for the bread from heaven. It was not a novel kind of manna; it was the one who came from heaven to give life, not to Israel only but "to the world". This leads Jesus to say, "I am the bread of life; he who comes to me will certainly not hunger, and he who believes in me will certainly not thirst, ever" (6:35).

That makes it clear that it was Jesus who was the source of life, and in one way or another the claim is repeated (6:40, 48, 50, 51). That this is not always recognized arises from the fact that it is necessary for the Father to draw people before they will come (6:37, 40, 44). There is a strongly predestinarian strain in this Gospel, and it comes through in this discourse. Jesus brings life,

24. Cf. G. H. C. MacGregor, "There is evidence to show that Jewish theology regarded the giving of *the* manna as the miracle *par excellence,* the *non plus ultra* even for the Messiah. In fact, the Rabbis taught that Messiah would prove his authority by repeating just this miracle by which, they held, Moses had proved his. 'As was the first Redeemer,' so ran the Midrash, 'so shall be the final Redeemer; as the first Redeemer caused the manna to fall from heaven, even so shall the second Redeemer cause the manna to fall" (*The Gospel of John,* London, 1928, pp. 142-43). The passage to which MacGregor refers is *Ecclesiastes Rabbah* 1.9.

but it is necessary for a divine work to be done in people before they will understand this. It is not a natural achievement to discern the divine in what he does. But that does not stop him from making the facts plain.

The idea of heavenly nourishment leads on to the thought that it is the flesh of Christ and his blood that forms food and drink "for the life of the world" (6:51, 53-57). Jesus indeed brings life, but the bringing of life means that he must die.[25] The great saving act is seen on the cross and at the empty tomb. Jesus will bring life, indeed, but at the cost of his own death.

The miracle, then, is eloquent of Jesus' power to supply the bread people need, and the discourse underlines Jesus' power to supply their spiritual needs with the references to his gift of bread from heaven (vv. 31, 32), to the bread of God as coming down from heaven (vv. 33, 41, 50, 58), to Jesus as the living bread (vv. 35, 48, 51), and to Jesus' flesh as the bread that he will give (vv. 51, 56-58). The bread symbolism is complex, but clearly Jesus is the supplier of our deepest needs. The Old Testament has many references to bread of a metaphorical character, so that Jesus is building on a rich symbolism well known to his hearers.[26] But here he is going well beyond anything the Old Testament says about bread, especially when he refers to his own sacrificial death.

Jesus' Presence

There is more of a problem with our fifth pair, and some deny outright that there is a connection beween the walking on the water and any discourse in this Gospel.[27] But the matter is not simple. The sign is introduced with the information that some of the

25. Walter Lüthi comments on the unusual character of Jesus' kingship: he is "the King who reigns by the grace of Heaven alone. And in case anyone is still not quite sure that this is the only true King, Jesus puts it even more clearly. He Himself, who has come from the Father, will die according to the will of the Father. His death will provide the meat and drink that gives eternal life to all those who believe" (*St John's Gospel*, Edinburgh and London, 1960, p. 90).

26. See the passages listed in my *The Gospel according to John*, p. 340.

27. Cf. Fortna, "the Johannine dialogue which follows this story has no relation to it whatever" (*Gospel of Signs*, p. 64). So also Fuller (*Miracles*, p. 102), Richards (*Miracles*, p. 66), C. K. Barrett (*The Gospel according to St. John*[2], London, 1978, p. 279), and others.

crowd who had been miraculously fed wanted to make a king out of Jesus, a complete misunderstanding of what the miraculous feeding signified. It showed that they did not know what Messiah meant. They thought that they were close to Jesus and that they were advancing his messianic purpose, whereas in all that matters they could scarcely have been farther away from him. It was different with the disciples. The miracle took place against a background of disciples toiling hard against a contrary wind and with their lives evidently in some jeopardy. It was dark, and Jesus had not come to them (6:17). Jesus seemed absent at a time of hardship and danger. But in a striking demonstration of his sovereignty over nature, Jesus came to them where they were. He had not deserted them. They had been in darkness and had not recognized what he was doing nor when his presence woud be manifested. They were like the king-makers in misunderstanding, but unlike them in that they did not see Jesus in essentially worldly terms. With all their hesitations and misunderstandings and fears they were committed men. And Jesus meets the needs of such.

This is surely the point of the fifth discourse. The motif of failure to recognize Jesus[28] comes through right at the beginning with the challenge of his brothers, "show yourself to the world" (7:4), a challenge which John makes clear arose from men who "did not believe in him" (7:5). The failure to recognize Jesus is emphasized throughout chapter 7 to a greater degree than we have encountered earlier in this Gospel. John is making it clear that hostility to Jesus was mounting and that there was a good deal of uncertainty about him. In Jerusalem there was uncertainty, with people "whispering" about Jesus (7:12); plainly his messiahship was not clear to people at large, and equally plainly there was danger. So people spoke softly. And when in due course Jesus appeared in the city there was astonishment at his teaching, which led him to say that his teaching was not his own

---

28. Daniel Lamont sees part of this failure in that some of the disciples were probably involved in the attempt to make Jesus king (6:15; cf. Matt. 14:22). This sign, he thinks, brought home to them that "Jesus, though He declined an earthly crown, was yet King of nature and of life" (*Studies in the Johannine Writings*, London, 1956, p. 94).

but came from God (7:16). His further claim that his hearers did not keep Moses' law because they were trying to kill him led to the accusation, "You have a demon" (7:20); again there is the thought of the hiddenness of Christ. Who and what he was, was not apparent.

At this point there is apparently a digression. Jesus refers to "one work" that he had done which had caused astonishment, and proceeds to speak about the Sabbath (7:21-23). This makes it clear that he is referring to his healing of the lame man (5:1-9), an incident in which it is important that his position on the Sabbath be understood. He does not criticize the Jews for being too strict in their Sabbath observance and suggest that they relax a little. He says that they have completely misunderstood the Sabbath. They might have learned something important if they had reflected on their ritual practice. They were in the habit of circumcising a boy on the eighth day of his life even if that fell on a Sabbath.[29] This shows that some good deeds (such as circumcision) must be done on the Sabbath and opens up the way for deeds of mercy such as the one Jesus had done. He is making the point that his work of healing was done not by way of concession but of fulfilling the purpose of the Sabbath. Whereas circumcision concerns one member of the body only, Jesus had made a whole man healthy.[30] The Jews did not understand the real meaning of the law that they valued so highly.

Since misconceptions about the Christ abounded, it is clear that the people in Jerusalem were not a little confused. Some wondered whether the rulers really recognized that Jesus was the Christ (7:26), but found a problem in that they knew where Jesus came from, whereas no one, they said, would know where the

29. The command is given in Leviticus 12:3, a passage which does not say what is to be done if the eighth day falls on a Sabbath. But Jewish writings are clear that the eighth day must be scrupulously observed; the command about the day overrode the command about the Sabbath (see Mishnah, *Shab.* 18:3; 19:1, 2; *Ned.* 3:11).

30. The Rabbis could recognize something of this: "If circumcision, which attaches to one only of the two hundred and forty-eight members of the human body, suspends the Sabbath, how much more shall (the saving of) the whole body suspend the Sabbath" (Talmud *Yoma* 85b). They used this to justify healing on the Sabbath when the patient was in danger of dying, but they refused to allow healing when death was not imminent.

Christ comes from (7:27).[31] There is irony here, for if they had really known where Jesus came from they would have known that he was indeed the Messiah. But they did not know, and this is part of the way John is working out Christ's hiddenness. He goes on to say, "You will look for me, and you will not find me, and where I am, you (emphatic) cannot come" (7:34).

Then at the climax Jesus cries, "If anyone thirsts, let him come to me and drink. He who believes in me, as the Scripture said, rivers of living water will flow from his inner being." John explains, "This he spoke about the Spirit, whom those who believed on him would receive" (7:37-39). Jesus would in one sense be absent. But in the person of the Spirit he would be present to meet the needs of his own.[32]

This fifth discourse is separated from the fifth sign; quite obviously the connection between the sign and the discourse is not as plain as in the other cases. In the end the right conclusion may be that they are not meant to be linked. But it is not the only possible conclusion. It is possible to reason that John saw a connection, for what the sign signifies is much the same as what the discourse teaches. There is a unifying thread in that Jesus' absence is no more than apparent.

The Light of the World

Our sixth pair are obviously connected. Jesus is twice said to be the light of the world (8:12; 9:5), where the first reference introduces the discourse in which Jesus explains how people are in the darkness of sin and of bondage to the evil one, while the second initiates the story of the miracle in which Jesus sets a man free from his prison of darkness and brings light into his life.[33] For

31. There seem to have been different opinions. The view put forth here is supported by the dictum of R. Zera: "Three come unawares: Messiah, a found article and a scorpion" (Talmud, *Sanh.* 97a). But the scribes Herod consulted were able to name Bethlehem (Matt. 2:4-6), and this view is found later in this same chapter (v. 42).

32. J. T. Forestell thinks that in the miracle of the walking on the waters "the evangelist understands Jesus' appearance as a divine presence out of the darkness of the world" (*The Word of the Cross*, Rome, 1974, p. 70).

33. Cf. Brown, "Just as the OT prophets accompanied their spoken word by symbolic actions which dramatized their message, so also Jesus acts out here the truth he

John the coming of light necessarily means judgment on darkness, and the note of judgment is found in both (8:16, 26, 50; the thought of judgment, though not the word, is found also in vv. 21 and 24; so, too, in the miracle there is the reminder that Jesus came into the world "for judgment", 9:39).[34]

The discourse is introduced with the majestic words, "I am the light of the world" (8:12). Since the Rabbis on occasion used "Light" as a designation of the Messiah,[35] this may not be out of mind. Perhaps more important for what John is telling us is the fact that "I am" is in the emphatic style of deity, a form of expression that recurs, though without a predicate, in the expression "Before Abraham was, I am" (8:58). That had such an effect on Jesus' hearers that they tried to stone him; clearly they recognized the magnitude of his claim. With respect to his being the light, we should bear in mind that elsewhere God himself can be said to be light (1 John 1:5). And Jesus claims to be light in no small parochial measure, but "the light of the world." This is a stupendous claim. We should be in no doubt but that John is speaking in terms that make Jesus superior to all on earth. John is classing him with God, not created beings.

These words are immediately followed by a statement about what this means for the people Jesus meets: "He who follows me will certainly not walk in darkness, but will have the light of life" (8:12). "Follows me" refers to meaningful discipleship, not some superficial approval of Jesus' teaching.[36] The present participle

proclaimed in viii 12, 'I am the light of the world' " (*The Gospel according to John*, I, p. 379). Similarly, E. C. Hoskyns views chapter 9 as "a commentary in action" on the words "I am the light of the world" (*The Fourth Gospel*, London, 1947, p. 331).

34. Dodd stresses the note of judgment in chapter 9: "It appears then that the dominant theme of this episode is not the coming of light as such, but its effect in judgment. The fact that the coming of Christ brings light into the world is stated symbolically with the utmost brevity, and the weight is laid upon the elaborate dialogue which dramatically exhibits judgment in action" (*The Interpretation of the Fourth Gospel*, p. 358).

35. John Lightfoot cites R. Biba Sangorius for the statement "Light is the name of the Messiah", a statement the Rabbi supports from Daniel 2:22. He finds the same ascription in R. Abba Serongianus (*A Commentary on the New Testament from the Talmud and Hebraica*, III, Grand Rapids, 1979 reprint of 1859 edition, pp. 330-31).

36. W. Hendriksen finds an analogy with those in the wilderness who followed the pillar of light: "Those who had followed it and had not rebelled against its guidance had reached Canaan. The others had died in the desert. So it is here:

signifies a continuing adherence. And this has consequences. The committed disciple is taken clean out of the ways of darkness; henceforth his characteristic is to enjoy "the light of life."

Jesus divides people. There are those who prefer the comfort of their familiar darkness, and there are those who welcome the light that God gives. Those who walk in Jesus' way are delivered from all that darkness means and are introduced into life of a very different character. But those who reject it are confirmed in their darkness. John immediately gives an example, with the Pharisees objecting to what Jesus has said on the grounds that his testimony is "not true" (8:13). It was a rabbinic axiom that "none may be believed when he testifies of himself. . . . None may testify of himself" (Mishnah, *Ket.* 2:9). So the Pharisees gave no attention to the substance of the claim. They preferred to live on the basis of an adherence to correct technicality. This enabled them to live in their comfortable darkness. They did not really want the light.

Jesus tells his opponents that they know neither him nor his Father (8:19), that they will die in their sin (8:21, 24), that they are from below, of this world (8:23). They do not have God as their Father as they claim, but the devil (8:42-44). They cannot show that Jesus has committed any sin, but they still do not believe him (8:46). They are not God's people (8:47). This is a thoroughgoing indictment, and it is not surprising that they regard Jesus as possessed by a devil (8:48) and that in the discussion about Abraham they continue to oppose Jesus (8:52-59). But mixed in with this is the fact that many believed in him (8:30).[37] Divided opinions are also found among the Pharisees after Jesus had given sight to the blind man, some saying that Jesus was a sinner and others asking how a sinner could do such signs (9:16). There is also the motif of the uncommitted in the persons of the man's parents (9:20-23), and the interesting argument between the formerly blind man and the Pharisees.

---

the true followers not only will not walk in the darkness of moral and spiritual ignorance . . . but will reach the land of light" (*Exposition of the Gospel according to John,* II, Grand Rapids, 1954, p. 42).

37. Their faith may not have been very deep (cf. F. L. Godet, "Instead of treating these new believers as converts, He puts them immediately to the test" (*Commentary on the Gospel of John,* II, Grand Rapids, reprint of 1893 edition, p. 105). But at least for the time they aligned themselves with Jesus.

What it all adds up to is that throughout these two chapters Jesus is thought of as the light of the world, both in his teaching and in his giving of sight to the blind. This is not universally accepted. The teaching of Jesus may be rejected, and people may refuse to receive the blind man. There are those who welcome the light and those who reject it.

Death—and Life!

The final discourse and the final sign have no obvious link. The raising of a man from the dead seems quite different from teaching about shepherds.[38] But there are links, even if not those we might expect. The point of the miracle in John 11 is that Jesus is Lord of life. John narrates the story as the climax of Jesus' public ministry. He is showing us that Jesus is stronger than death and well able to care for his people. As far as men were concerned, the position of Lazarus, who had been in the grave for four days, was hopeless. He had left the land of the living and now belonged to the domain of the dead. But when Jesus spoke the word of power, death was defeated. This corresponds to the teaching in the discourse that the good shepherd is sovereign over death. He lays down his life, it is true (10:11, 15, 17), but it is also significant that he takes it again (10:17-18). The point is emphasized, for Jesus says, "No one takes (my life) from me, but I lay it down of myself. I have authority to lay it down, and I have authority to take it again"—a statement he reinforces by adding, "This command I received from my Father" (10:18). The word "authority" comes first in each clause, which gives it emphasis ("Authority I have to lay it down, and authority I have to take it again"). Thus in both the discourse and the sign the truth is set forth emphatically that Christ has supreme authority over death, a claim that no mere man could make.

A feature of the discourse, of course, is the way it brings out the care of the good shepherd for his sheep. A paid helper will not display the same care, for his interest is in his pay, not in the sheep (10:12-13). This forms another link with the sign, for the miracle shows care for Lazarus, as do express statements (11:3, 5, 36). There

38. Thus Brown and Dodd both place chapter 11 in a different division of the Gospel, effectively separating the two.

is care also for Martha and Mary, though no particular emphasis is put on it. The thought of care is involved also in the truth that the shepherd "must" bring his sheep to the fold (10:16) and in the repeated statement that he gives his life for the sheep (10:11, 15, 17).

The teaching about the good shepherd emphasizes the "Lord of life" motif. Jesus is not the victim of death.[39] He does not say that men will kill the good shepherd, but that he will lay down his life. He will also take it up again (10:17, 18). He says, "I have authority (or power, *exousia*) to lay it down, and I have authority to take it up again" (v. 18). In both the narrative and the discourse the thought is that Jesus is superior to death. He shows this in the way he calls his friend back from the realm of the dead, and also in the way he goes to his own death and rises from it.

Some of the discourses are so obviously connected with particular signs that there is no need to argue the point. But this examination has shown, I think, that even where there is no obvious connection there is nevertheless always some link. It is a question whether we should take these links as the clue to the whole, for some of them seem rather tenuous. We should not overlook them even though it is right to bear other considerations in mind.

Other Possibilities

One such consideration is that it is quite possible to see this Gospel as put together on a quite different plan. For example, J. N. Sanders holds that John has six signs, not seven, and that the number is important. Being one less than the perfect number, they lead up to the great sign of the resurrection.[40] He sees the six as arranged in two groups of three, each comprising a nature miracle followed by two healings.[41] He also sees chapters 7–10 together

---

39. Cf. Alf Corell, "For just as Christ the King wins his people and gathers them together through his death on the Cross, so also does Christ the good shepherd gather together his sheep by offering his life for them. This sacrifice is not an expression of weakness on the part of the shepherd, but rather of his power over life—over his own life as well as over that of his flock" (*Consummatum Est*, London, 1958, p. 25).

40. *A Commentary on the Gospel according to St John*, edited and completed by B. A. Mastin (London, 1968), p. 5.

41. *Ibid.*, p. 156.

with much of chapter 12 as "a complex mosaic", and he finds chapters 5 and 11 linked.[42]

Or consider R. H. Strachan. He connects the changing of the water into wine and the cleansing of the temple as "Two symbolic signs", but he does not link a discourse with either. Then he proceeds to notice "The universal appeal of the gospel", which he finds illustrated by variety in Christian converts, "Nicodemus the Jew, the Samaritan Woman, the Gentile Nobleman."[43] It cannot be denied that this is a possible way to link these sections. Other interesting ways of approaching the Gospel are Dodd's seven "episodes"[44] and John Marsh's five sections of "Deed and Word" and four of "Rite and Reality".[45]

I have looked at the possibility of linking a sign with a discourse. But it is also possible to link a sign with a sign. The two miracles at Cana form an excellent example. The turning of the water into wine shows that Jesus can transform and give new life, as does the healing of the nobleman's son. Indeed, the giving of life might be linked in one way or another with all the miracles. The man lame for 38 years did not really live in any full sense until Jesus healed him, the feeding of the multitude points to "the bread of life", walking on the water leads to the thought that Jesus' people are never alone in life's difficulties but that he always comes to sustain them, the "light of life" is indicated by the giving of sight to the blind, while the raising of Lazarus is obviously a gift of life.

Clearly the question of John's method is a complicated one. The link between signs and discourses is a real one. But it is not the only one, and scholars discern a wide variety of links, as may be seen from the diverse classifications in the "Outlines" given in commentaries. What I think emerges from all this is that the Gospel must be seen as a unity with a number of threads running right through and making their appearance at a variety of points. D. Moody Smith considers this sort of thing very important: "Despite the division between the public ministry and the minis-

42. *Ibid.*, pp. 246, 262.
43. *The Fourth Gospel* (London, 1955), p. 97. He goes on to see chapters 5–12 as "The conflict between the church and the world", so his view of the connections differs from that of most.
44. *The Interpretation of the Fourth Gospel*, p. x.
45. *The Gospel of St John*, pp. 86-87.

try to his disciples which occurs at the end of chapter 12, the Gospel of John manifests an overall unity of style, theme, and content that distinguishes it among NT Gospels. It portrays Jesus Christ as the only Son of God, who knows where he has come from and where he is going, i.e., that he has come from God, and through his acceptance of the cross goes to God."[46] This overall unity of theme makes it hazardous to differentiate too sharply between the parts. Thus it may be preferable to see all the parts as making their contribution to the one great theme than to try to discern too close ties between sections.[47] This seems to be what John is saying when he tells us why he has written his book (20:30-31).

The Prologue introduces many of the Gospel's themes. Whether it was an original composition of the Evangelist or not, it was what was intended to be read first in the Gospel as we have it and it sets forth themes that will be developed throughout the writing. It begins with a reference to the Logos, and though the term is not used in this Gospel outside the Prologue, the idea that in Jesus we see the divine Logos pervades everything. Very little of this Gospel is not concerned in one way or another with the truth that "the Word became flesh and lived among us, and we saw his glory" (1:14). So with life. This theme is found in the conversation with Nicodemus (or its sequel, 3:16), in that with the woman at the well (4:10-11), the healing of the nobleman's son (4:50, 51, 53), the discourse on the divine Son (5:24, 26, etc.), that on the living bread (6:27, 33, 51, 57, etc.), that on the life-giving Spirit (7:38), on the light of the world (8:12), on the good shepherd (10:10, 28), and in the raising of Lazarus (11:25).

Similarly, we find the idea of light widespread (3:19-21; 5:35; 8:12; 9:5; 11:9-10), as is that of mission, of being sent (3:17; 4:34; 5:23-24; 6:29, 38-39; 7:16, 18; 8:16, 18; 9:4; 10:36; 11:42). The concept of witness is found not infrequently (3:11; 4:39; 5:31; 7:7; 8:13; 10:25). The importance of believing is seen in the fact that there is a reference to it in every chapter in our part of the Gospel, while God is seen as Father in every chapter except chapters 7 and 9. That God

---

46. *John* (Philadelphia, 1976), p. 17.

47. R. Kysar notes a tendency to see the signs as christological and as pointing to Jesus' messiahship (*The Fourth Evangelist and His Gospel,* Minneapolis, 1975, pp. 226-27).

is Father is, of course, taught throughout the New Testament, but it is especially prominent in John, where *patēr* occurs 137 times, more than twice as often as in the book where it is used next most frequently (Matthew with 64), and where 122 of them refer to God. The word "world" recurs in 3:16-17; 4:42; 6:14, 33; 7:4, 7; 8:23; 9:5, 39; 10:36; 11:9, 27. So also glory is a theme in the Prologue, but we find it again in 2:11; 5:41; 7:18; 8:50; 9:24; 11:4, 40.

We should take seriously John's declared aim of writing so that his readers may believe that Jesus is the Christ, God's Son, and believing have life in his name (20:31). John is a master at hammering away at his point from a number of angles. That Jesus is the Word made flesh underlines all he writes. His great themes center on Christ; the oneness of Christ with the Father, his dependence, his functions as light of the world, as life, as truth, as the way. These and other themes may be woven into a discourse or begun in one discourse and taken up in another. They may be set forth symbolically in a sign and explained in a discourse. The sign brings out the truth that the very power of God is at work in Jesus, and the discourse makes it clear that the wisdom of God is on his lips. Any of John's great themes may be found in several discourses and illustrated by several signs. Every sign can be linked in some way with a discourse, and such links are part of the way John carried out his plan. In John the words and the works go together.[48] But basically such links stem from the fact that John is working out one consistent purpose throughout his entire Gospel. He is writing to show that Jesus is the Christ, the Son of God, so that people may believe and have life. Everything he writes bears on this overriding purpose. The Gospel is a unity and must be understood as such.[49]

48. Cf. K. H. Rengstorf, "If the *logos* interprets the *sēmeion*, the *sēmeion* authenticates the *logos*" (*TDNT*, VII, p. 252). Bultmann comments that Jesus "gives the light and at the same time he is it. He gives it in that he is it, and he is it in that he gives it. The interrelation of these two ideas is decisive for the concept of revelation" (*Johannes*, p. 261).

49. Cf. Kysar, "Recent investigations have decisively demonstrated that each religious theme in the gospel is tied with many, if not all, of the other themes" (*The Fourth Evangelist and His Gospel*, p. 260). He also points to the significant fact that monographs purporting to deal with a single theme in this Gospel often end up discussing almost all the other themes (*ibid.*, p. 273).

CHAPTER 3

Jesus, the Man

JOHN TELLS US THAT THE "SIGNS" WE HAVE BEEN looking at were done by "Jesus", and that human name is important. In this Gospel we are reading about a man, an unusual man indeed and one who did all sorts of things that other men have not been able to do. But unless we see that John is writing about a real man, one who knows our human limitations because he has experienced them all himself, we miss an important part of what he is saying. John's concern for the "signs" Jesus did and for his all-important connection with the heavenly Father, together with some unusual features of his manner of living, leads many writers these days to hold the view that John does not really write about a human Jesus. His concern, it is said, is with a heavenly being in much the same way as quite a few authors of antiquity who told anecdotes about celestial visitants to this earthly scene. John was so concerned with the heavenly Jesus, they argue, that he found little or no place for an earthly Jesus.

Perhaps no one in recent times has denied the real humanity of the Johannine Jesus more forcefully and more cogently than Ernst Käsemann. I do not consider his case compelling, but it is certainly an interesting one. In this chapter I plan to concentrate on it, for if we look at the case Käsemann makes out and the objections that are brought against it, we will, I think, cover most of the ground. A few years back I wrote an appraisal of Käsemann's view for the *Festschrift* presented to George E. Ladd, and for the most part I reproduce that article (though with some updating).

"From the historical viewpoint, the Church committed an error when it declared the Gospel to be orthodox", Käsemann says forthrightly about the Fourth Gospel.[1] He, of course, sees a

---

1. *The Testament of Jesus* (London, 1968), p. 76. He thinks that this Gospel's

wide diversity in the teachings of the various parts of the New Testament. Probably no one in recent years has done more to emphasize the variety of teaching in the New Testament than he. He has argued that "early Catholicism" is to be found in writings like the Gospel of Luke and the Pastoral Epistles, and that this must be set in opposition to the teaching of Paul. He is quite ready to accept the concept of a canon within the canon, accepting Pauline teaching as essential Christianity and rejecting the early Catholicism that he sees as in opposition to it. In Johannine studies he has argued forcefully that John cannot be thought of as in essential agreement with other early Christians, and in the sentence I have quoted he gives it as his opinion that John's Gospel is not "orthodox". Such views are, of course, not uncontested. G. E. Ladd, for example, stresses the unity in the New Testament, though he recognizes that there is diversity there too: "Our thesis is that the unity of New Testament theology is found in the fact that the several strata share a common view of God, who visits man in history to effect the salvation of both man, the world, and history; and that diversity exists in the several interpretations of this one redemptive event."[2]

Käsemann's position opens up many issues, but the one with which we are concerned here is his view that John has a docetic Christology and that this is central to his Gospel. Käsemann says things like "John changes the Galilean teacher into the God who goes about on earth."[3] More than once he refers to John's "naive docetism",[4] and he can speak of "my key word, unreflected docetism".[5] Several times he repeats the statement that this Chris-

---

"acceptance into the Church's canon took place through man's error and God's providence" (*ibid.*, p. 75).

2. *The Pattern of New Testament Truth* (Grand Rapids, 1968), p. 41; see also pp. 108-11. Stephen S. Smalley argues similarly with regard to this Gospel, "Diversity and Development in John", *NTS* 17 (1970-71), pp. 276-92.

3. *Testament*, p. 27.

4. *Ibid.*, pp. 26, 45, 70.

5. *Ibid.*, p. 66. There are some who object to the use of such designations as "docetism". For example, George T. Montague says, "to apply to Jn the later categories which developed as a result of isolating and emphasizing certain Johannine tendencies seems to err by reading back into the Gospel a historical situation that is post-Johannine, as one might accuse Mt of Ebionitism or Paul of Marcionism" (*CBQ* 31, 1969, p. 438).

tology is of central importance.[6] Obviously, this
the Jesus of Saint John is a real man, living under
tions that we know so well, that is one thing. If he i
figure, who is not genuinely human but only appears to c
to human limitations, that is quite another. It is worth looking
the evidence.

Käsemann has argued his case convincingly, and we may take
his statement as the normative case for regarding the Johannine
Christ as a docetic figure. He gives us an excellent summary of
the kind of thing that impresses him and leads to his verdict of
docetism when he says we must ask,

> In what sense is he flesh, who walks on the water and through
> closed doors, who cannot be captured by his enemies, who at
> the well of Samaria is tired and desires a drink, yet has no need
> of drink and has food different from that which his disciples
> seek? He cannot be deceived by men, because he knows their
> innermost thoughts even before they speak. He debates with
> them from the vantage point of the infinite difference between
> heaven and earth. He has need neither of the witness of Moses
> nor of the Baptist. He dissociates himself from the Jews, as if
> they were not his own people, and he meets his mother as the
> one who is her Lord. He permits Lazarus to lie in the grave for
> four days in order that the miracle of his resurrection may be
> more impressive. And in the end the Johannine Christ goes vic-
> toriously to his death of his own accord. Almost superfluously
> the Evangelist notes that this Jesus at all times lies on the bosom
> of the Father and that to him who is one with the Father the an-
> gels descend and from him they again ascend. He who has eyes
> to see and ears to hear can see and hear his glory. Not merely

6. Käsemann, *Testament,* pp. 42, 50, 58, etc. Perhaps we should notice that
some see the emphasis otherwise. Thus F. V. Filson holds that the author of this
Gospel makes "the theme of life so central that the Gospel is rightly called the
Gospel of Life" ("The Gospel of Life, A Study of the Gospel of John", in *Current
Issues in New Testament Interpretation: Essays in Honor of Otto Piper,* eds. W. Klas-
sen and G. Snyder, New York, 1962, p. 123). We should not miss either
R. Schnackenburg's point that John's Christology "is completely orientated
towards soteriology" (*The Gospel according to St. John,* I, New York, 1968, p. 548).
But others support Käsemann. Thus W. Nicol writes, "This intense concentration
on Jesus alone is the primary characteristic of the Fourth Gospel. The Synoptic
Gospels place Jesus in the frame of the Kingdom and Paul of the eschatology, but
the fourth Evangelist brings Jesus alone on the stage with all lights on Him"
(*Neotestamentica* 6, 1972, p. 17).

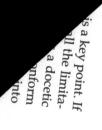

ι the mouth of Thomas, but from the
s the confession, "My Lord and my
agree with the understanding of a

s last question must be, "It does not
go on to ask whether the evidence is
ann says it is. When we look at the en-
h Gospel, this does seem a lop-sided
ʒemann himself concedes that there are
some other ᵣₑ...

> I am not interested in completely denying features of the lowli-
> ness of the earthly Jesus in the Fourth Gospel. But do they
> characterize John's christology in such a manner that through
> them the "true man" of later incarnational theology becomes
> believable? Or do not those features of his lowliness rather rep-
> resent the absolute minimum of the costume designed for the
> one who dwelt for a little while among men, appearing to be
> one of them, yet without himself being subjected to earthly
> conditions?[8]

This time we must answer his question with a resounding
"No!" We must take a hard look at questions like "Are these other
features as unimportant as Käsemann says they are?" and "Is the
evidence for docetism as weighty as he says it is?" He argues as
though the evidence is clear and straightforward and that only
the reluctance of Christians to face its implications has kept them
from seeing that John does depict a docetic Christ. Yet every item
on his list is contestable, and some are certainly erroneous. Since
his position is complex, we should be on our guard against attempts at oversimplification. Let us look first at the evidence
Käsemann adduces for docetism.

Evidence for Docetism

He begins by telling us that Jesus "walks on the water". This
gives impression that in the Fourth Gospel Jesus habitually en-
gages in the practice. Yet there is only one possible instance in

7. *Testament,* p. 9.
8. *Ibid.,* p. 10.

John, and even here there is nothing to match the plain statements of the Synoptists (who, Käsemann agrees, picture Jesus as a man). The question concerns the right understanding of the statement that the disciples saw Jesus walking *epi tēs thalassēs* (6:19). In my opinion Käsemann is right in seeing a reference to walking on the water, but he might have noticed that this is not beyond all doubt and that in any case there is what Raymond E. Brown calls John's "lack of emphasis on the miraculous."[9] The identical expression is found in John 21:1, where the meaning is "by the sea" and not "on the sea". Indeed, some exegetes think that in the present passage John means no more than that the disciples saw Jesus walking on the shore.[10] They point to the statement in the next verse, "immediately the boat was at the land to which they were going." If John's Christ was docetic, would he have left any doubt?

It is a strange assertion that Jesus walks "through closed doors". There is no example of this at all during his entire earthly life. Presumably Käsemann is referring to the post-resurrection appearances, but the Synoptists are just as definite as John that Jesus' resurrection body was not subject to the limitations that characterized the pre-resurrection body. We cannot argue from the one body to the other. Jesus did not walk through closed doors on earth. There is not one example during the whole period of the incarnation.

Käsemann's next point is that Jesus "cannot be captured by his enemies". Why then does John say that he "walked in Galilee, for he would not walk in Judea, because the Jews were trying to

---

9. *The Gospel according to John*, I (New York, 1966), p. 254.

10. J. H. Bernard, for example, thinks that if we had only John's account "we should have no reason to suppose that he intended to record any 'miracle.' . . . It is probable that he means here that when the boat got into the shallow water near the western shore, the disciples saw Jesus in the uncertain light walking by the lake, and were frightened, not being sure what they saw" (*A Critical and Exegetical Commentary on the Gospel according to St. John*, Edinburgh, 1928, p. 185). W. Barclay is another who sees no miracle, and A. M. Hunter holds that "it is far from certain that John 6:16-21 implies a miracle: the crucial phrase *peripatounta epi tēs thalassēs* would naturally mean 'walking by the sea'" (*According to John*, London, 1968, p. 66). Later he says that in this narrative John "appears to 'demiraculize' the miraculous" (*ibid.*, p. 71). R. Bultmann cites B. Weiss as another who sees no miracle here.

kill him" (7:1;[11] cf. 11:53-54)? In using these words John is clearly saying that Jesus' enemies could have captured him, and that it was to avoid this that he went to Galilee. It is true that on one occasion John says that a band of men failed to arrest Jesus, but there is no indication in the narrative that this was because Jesus was immune to capture. As John tells it, the arresting posse gave as their reason that they were impressed by Jesus' teaching (7:45-46) and the Pharisees that these officers were "deceived" (7:47). In John's account there is no hint of anything docetic. On other occasions the Evangelist tells us that no one laid hands on Jesus "because his hour was not yet come" (7:30; 8:20). But these passages surely do not mean that Jesus was immune from arrest. They simply affirm the operation of divine providence. Jesus would not die before his time. Indeed, John Calvin sees here an illustration of "a general doctrine . . . though we live unto the day, the hour of every man's death has nevertheless been fixed by God . . . we are safe from all dangers until God wishes to call us away."[12] Is John really saying anything more than this?

Jesus "desires a drink, yet has no need of drink". Is there any evidence of this at all? Käsemann cites none. In the context of his request for a drink made to the woman at the well it is explicitly said that Jesus was "wearied (*kekopiakōs*) from his journey" (4:6), which does not read as though it referred to someone who had no physical needs and no physical problems. When he hung on the cross Jesus said in set terms, "I am thirsty" (19:28), and he drank some wine when it was brought to his lips (an incident, by the way, which the Synoptists do not record). Where does Käsemann get his idea that Jesus "had no need of drink"? Certainly not from the evidence.

Again, Käsemann tells us that Jesus' food is "different from that which his disciples seek." The reference is surely to 4:32, where Jesus was sustained during his counselling of the Samaritan woman. But is this really so strange? Everett F. Harrison sees the words as meaning that "Christ had lost for the time

---

11. C. K. Barrett comments, "the Jewish opposition had been fierce. The step taken in v. 10 was therefore both dangerous and decisive" (*The Gospel according to St. John*,[2] Philadelphia, 1978, p. 310).

12. *The Gospel according to St. John 1–10* (Grand Rapids, 1959), p. 193.

the desire for food in the consuming joy of pointing a needy soul to the place of forgiveness and rest."[13] Do John's words mean more? And cannot many of us testify to something of the same experience? When we have been actively engaged in doing the Lord's work we have known what it is not to feel hunger. There is no docetism here. Moreover, it should not be overlooked that the disciples lived with Jesus, and there is nothing in the record to show that his food was different from theirs. On this occasion they could think only that someone had given Jesus something to eat (v. 33). This was a misunderstanding, but we should not miss the point that, as John sees it, those who were closest to Jesus took it for granted that the food Jesus would eat would be the ordinary food that sustained them. If there was a docetic Christ they knew nothing about him.

"He cannot be deceived by men, because he knows their innermost thoughts even before they speak." I do not know whether this is true of the Johannine Christ or not, but I suspect it is not.[14] It is a pity that Käsemann cites no evidence, and accordingly we do not know precisely what passage he has in mind. He may be referring to 2:24-25, but this simply means that Jesus was not deceived by facile protestations of belief. He knew people better than that. There is no reference to people's thoughts. It is, of course, the case that John does ascribe unusual knowledge to Jesus. As I have written elsewhere, "John clearly regards Jesus as possessed of a knowledge that is more than human, but just as clearly he does not regard this as vitiating His real humanity. Jesus' knowledge is derived from His close communion with the Father (8:28, 38; 14:10)."[15] John makes it plain that Jesus had all the knowledge he needed to fulfil his mission, and that this knowledge came from God. But this is not the knowledge of omniscience. It is the outworking of the Father's commission when he sent Jesus.

13. *John: The Gospel of Faith* (Chicago, 1962), p. 34.

14. J. H. Bernard agrees that knowledge like this is possessed by God and that the Old Testament makes this clear. "But it is also, in its measure, a prerogative of human genius; and (with the possible exception of 1[48]) it is not clear that Jn. means us to understand that the insight of Jesus into other men's motives and characters was different in kind from that exhibited by other great masters of mankind" (*John*, p. 99).

15. *The Gospel according to John* (Grand Rapids, 1971), p. 207, n. 99.

And is there any evidence that Jesus knew people's thoughts before they spoke? I know of none. But there is certainly evidence that John saw Jesus as subject to human limitation. For example, he had to "find" the man he had cured of blindness (9:35) after he had heard that he had been put out of the synagogue (he also "found" the man he cured of lameness, 5:14). After the feeding of the multitude, Jesus "came to know" (*gnous*) that the mob wanted to make a king out of him—apparently he did not know it intuitively. To avoid this he withdrew to the mountain: he did not perform some miracle. He did not know where the tomb of Lazarus was and asked a question to find out (11:34). Indeed, in this Gospel Jesus constantly asks questions (see 1:50; 3:10, 12; 5:6, 47; 6:5, 67; 7:19, 23; 8:43, 46; 11:34; 16:31; 18:4, 7, 21, 23, 34). Some of these prove nothing, being the kind of questions asked when one knows the answer and is not seeking information. For example, Jesus asked his audience, "Why do you not understand my language?" and answered, "Because you cannot comprehend my thought" (8:43; Rieu's translation). The rhetorical question simply drives the point home. But other questions are different, such as that seeking the whereabouts of the tomb of Lazarus, or the one that Jesus put to Pilate, "Do you say this of yourself, or did others tell you about me?" (18:34). It is plain that in some matters Jesus was ignorant just as in others he had unusual knowledge.[16]

As to Jesus' debating "from the vantage point of the infinite difference between heaven and earth," this appears to be a private opinion of Käsemann's. F. C. Burkitt had a very different estimate with his well-known objection to the authenticity of the teaching John ascribes to Jesus: "It is quite inconceivable that the historical Jesus of the Synoptic Gospels could have argued and quibbled with his opponents, as He is represented to have done in the Fourth Gospel."[17] We do not have to agree with Burkitt to understand that he is drawing attention to aspects of Jesus' teaching that have apparently escaped Käsemann's notice. The measure of truth in what Käsemann says is that John sees Jesus as living

16. The questions asked by the risen Christ (20:15; 21:5, 15, 16, 17, 22) are not relevant to our subject, since on any showing the risen Lord was in some respects significantly different from the earthly Jesus.

17. *The Gospel History and its Transmission* (Edinburgh, 1907), p. 228.

closer to the Father than other men do, and as speaking out of the enlightenment that that gave him. But in some measure it is true of every great saint that he speaks "from the vantage point of the infinite difference between heaven and earth." That is what distinguishes him from the worldly-minded. John sees this as true in especial measure of Jesus, but he does not depict it as a nonhuman trait.

"He has need neither of the witness of Moses nor of the Baptist." But what does this mean? Surely that Jesus had the deep-seated conviction that the Father was bearing witness to him in the works he was doing (5:36-37) and that therefore he needed nothing more.[18] Is not this a perfectly human trait? Is it not true of all of us that in the last resort we rely on the conviction that what we are doing is right in the sight of God, not necessarily that it is attested by Moses or the Baptist or Luther or Calvin or whoever? And if Jesus did not rely on Moses or the Baptist, he was clear that both did bear witness that agreed with what he was doing (5:33, 46).

"He dissociates himself from the Jews, as if they were not his own people." What then are we to make of the words, "You worship you know not what; we know what we worship, for salvation is of the Jews" (4:22)? Quite early John assures us that the Baptist saw the manifesting of Jesus "to Israel" as the purpose of his baptizing (1:31). And we should not forget that Jesus' greeting to Nathanael was, "Look, truly an Israelite" (1:47), nor that he was not denigrating Nicodemus when he called him "the teacher of Israel" (3:10). He insisted that Moses, the great lawgiver of the Jews, wrote about him (5:46) and that Abraham, the progenitor of the Jewish nation, rejoiced to see his day (8:56; cf. 8:39-40). He constantly appealed to the Jewish scriptures. John twice records the use of the title "King of Israel" (1:49; 12:13), and he puts some emphasis on the fact that Jesus was crucified as "King of the Jews" (19:19-22).

There is anger against "the Jews" in this Gospel, and there is upbraiding of those who profess to be God's people and are not. But that does not mean that Jesus dissociates himself from the na-

18. Cf. C. K. Barrett, "Jesus, who knows the witness of the 'Other', is independent of human witness" (*John*, pp. 264-65).

tion. On the contrary. To the very end he remains a faithful Jew, worshipping in the temple and observing the Jewish feasts. Käsemann does not notice that in this Gospel the expression "the Jews" often refers to a part of the nation only, as when the parents of the man born blind, who were clearly Jews themselves, are differentiated from "the Jews" (9:22). Nor that Jesus' sheep are of the "fold" of the Jews in the first place, even though there will be others "not of this fold" (10:16). Nils Dahl points out that "the Jews who do not believe because they are 'of the world' have never been true children of Abraham."[19] True Jews belong to Jesus, and this is an important part of the Fourth Gospel. Dahl also sees significance in the early disciples' reference to Jesus as "him of whom Moses and the prophets wrote" and their "we have found the Messiah."[20] Such sayings affirm a continuity with Israel, not a separation from it. It should not be overlooked that other ways of understanding "the Jews" have been accepted. Thus some have understood the expression to mean "Judaeans as opposed to Galileans."[21] O. Cullmann holds that "the way in which the Gospel speaks in so many places of 'the Jews' as a collective enemy could derive from the terminology which heterodox communities applied to official Judaism."[22] And there are other possibilities.

That "he meets his mother as the one who is her Lord" does not address the real question, namely, "Was he her Lord?" If he was, there is no problem. If he was not, then not only John but all the other New Testament writers as well have been led astray and John has no special position.

Jesus and Death

"He permits Lazarus to lie in the grave for four days in order that the miracle of his resurrection may be more impressive." This is obviously wrong. Neither Jesus nor John says that the delay was

---

19. "The Johannine Church and History", in *Current Issues*, p. 138.
20. *Ibid.*, p. 136.
21. G. J. Cuming, *ET* 60 (1948-49), p. 292. He thinks that the way John uses the term "strongly suggests that the Evangelist was a Galilean" *(ibid.)*.
22. *The Johannine Circle* (London, 1976), p. 38.

to make the miracle more impressive. This has to be read into the narrative. As John tells it, Jesus could not possibly have reached Bethany in time to save Lazarus from death. It was a day's journey from that village to the place where he was in trans-Jordan. The four days John mentions will be taken up with one day for the journey of the messengers, the two days Jesus remained where he was, and one more day for Jesus' journey. Putting all this together, John is saying that Lazarus must have died shortly after the messengers left Bethany. He must have been dead well before the messengers reached Jesus. Jesus could not possibly have gotten there in less than two days after the death, and we can only conjecture as to why he waited two more days. The journey undoubtedly involved danger (11:8, 16), and Jesus may have taken time to be sure that it was the right thing to do.[23] If so, the delay was certainly due to a very human reason. Or the delay may have been connected with John's picture of Jesus as moving in his own time and not as he is advised by others.[24] Or there may have been some other reason. It is better to admit our ignorance than to assert dogmatically that John depicts Jesus as allowing his friends to suffer the grief of bereavement for four days simply to enhance a miracle. That would be quite out of character.

"And in the end the Johannine Christ goes victoriously to his death of his own accord." I am more in agreement with this than with what Käsemann has said previously. John does depict Jesus as sovereign in the way he went to his death, but this is no more than a matter of emphasis. The Synoptists are just as definite that Jesus knew what lay ahead of him, but went forward to meet it. They tell of Gethsemane, which means that Jesus knew what was coming and had time to flee but did not. In the Synoptists, too, he went to death of his own accord. Moreover, it is quite possible for one who is no more than a man to approach death in the manner

---

23. Cf. A. Henderson, "It was not that he made up his mind not to go to Bethany for two days; but that for those two days he waited for light, which he was sure would come, as to his Father's will. When it came he set out, doubting and fearing nothing" (quoted by T. E. Pollard, *SE*, VI, p. 438).

24. Barrett rejects the view that Jesus waited for Lazarus to die "in order that a more glorious miracle might be effected", and thinks it more probable "that John wished to underline the fact that Jesus' movement towards Jerusalem, and so to his death, was entirely self-determined" (*John*, p. 391).

of a conqueror. Ignatius is an early example that springs to mind, and he is all the more important in that he owed his attitude to what Jesus had done for him. If the follower could choose a death he saw as victorious, why could not the leader?

In his conviction that the death of the Johannine Christ is victorious Käsemann does not stop to notice that death is not a docetic feature. When the docetists in due time made their appearance they held that Jesus did not really die, but that he "seemed" to die or that the divine Christ left Jesus before the moment of death. John has no such teaching. Like the other Gospels, John's Gospel comes to its climax with the passion narrative. And John is not making a conventional gesture to the Savior's death, for he includes a number of items like the spear thrust and the coming out of water and blood that are certainly not docetic. The harsh reality of the death of Jesus must always be taken into account when we are facing the question of a docetic Christ.[25]

The Father and the Angels

"Almost superfluously the Evangelist notes that this Jesus at all times lies on the bosom of the Father and that to him who is one with the Father the angels descend and from him they again ascend." Two sentences later Käsemann says that the Godhead is seen "Not merely from the prologue and from the mouth of Thomas." But where is there a reference to the Father's bosom other than in the Prologue? And Käsemann has heightened even this reference by inserting an "at all times" of his own, and making it "lies on" instead of the simple "is in" (1:18). In his Prologue John is saying that Jesus, from his close communion with the Father, has been able to declare him to all people. But it is a far cry from this to the assertion that, in this Gospel, Jesus is "at all times" lying on the Father's bosom. In fact, there are some who deny that the words as used in this Gospel have any reference to the earthly life

25. C. K. Barrett speaks of "the alleged docetism of the Gospel", and holds that there is "artificiality" in some of John's references to Jesus' humanity. He goes on, "though it must also be recognized that there is no artificiality about death, and that the Johannine Jesus shares with mankind the human property of dying" (*Essays on John*, London, 1982, p. 11).

of Jesus. Thus T. C. De Kruijf writes, "this must mean the present situation, the situation of the glorified Christ after the resurrection. It is not a metaphorical statement."[26] It is not necessary to agree with this to realize that Käsemann's is not the only possible interpretation of the words.

Again, Käsemann scarcely seems to be dealing fairly with the reference to the angels. He makes it sound as though the heavenly train was constantly waiting on the heavenly visitant to earth in order to serve him and to manifest his glory. But the Jesus of John's Gospel does not say that "to him who is one with the Father the angels descend. . . ." He says to Nathanael, "You (plural) will see heaven opened, and God's angels going up and going down on the Son of man" (1:51). The words are not an abstract statement about the nature of Jesus. They are words of encouragement to a new believer and an assurance that Jesus will bring him (and others) into further knowledge of heavenly realities. "The wide open heaven, and the ascending and descending angels symbolize the whole power and love of God, now available for man, in the Son of man."[27] At the very least, these words of R. H. Strachan are a possible understanding of the words, so that Käsemann's assumption that his is the only view must be rejected. And in my judgment Strachan's view is not only different, it is better. That is surely what Jesus is saying. We should also notice that nothing in the text corresponds to Käsemann's "to him who is one with the Father", and that the reference to angels does not necessarily point to deity, as is evident from the fact that there is a strand of rabbinic interpretation of Genesis 28:12 which sees angels as ascending and descending on Jacob.[28] I do not believe that this is the right understanding of the Genesis passage, nor do I think that John is saying that Jesus was no more than Jacob. But the existence of that exegesis is a fact, and it shows that Käsemann's claim about the angels is exaggerated.

26. "The Glory of the Only Son", in *Studies in John Presented to Prof. Dr. J. N. Sevenster on the Occasion of his Seventieth Birthday* (Leiden, 1970), p. 121. Bernard sees the words as expressing "the intimate relationship of love between the Son and the Father" (*John*, p. 32).

27. R. H. Strachan, *The Fourth Gospel* (London, 1955), p. 11.

28. The relevant passage is quoted in H. Odeberg, *The Fourth Gospel* (Amsterdam, 1968), pp. 33-34. See also the notes in the commentaries of Bernard and Barrett.

Glory

It is one of Käsemann's contentions that John 1:14 has been misunderstood. People have put their emphasis on "the Word was made flesh", whereas they should have seen that John is emphasizing "we beheld his glory". He finds the rest of the Gospel full of the thought that the glory of God is revealed. But it may be doubted whether Käsemann is doing justice to either half of the statement.

Let us look at the "glory" that matters so much to him. And let me say immediately that I agree that there is glory throughout this Gospel. But there is a paradox which Käsemann does not mention, the paradox that real glory is to be seen in lowliness rather than in a display of majesty. There is what Origen long ago called "humble glory".[29] The Johannine Christ does not seek glory for himself but for the Father (7:18; 8:50). The glory he has is not self-derived but given him (8:54). We see something of the complexity of the idea of glory in this Gospel when we look at the raising of Lazarus. That man's sickness was "not with a view to death but for the glory of God, that the Son of God might be glorified through it" (11:4). There is to be no doubt about the glory. The glories of both the Father and the Son are involved, and these two glories are intimately connected. What makes for the glory of the One makes for the glory of the Other. The outcome of the miracle in which the glory is manifested is twofold. First, as a result of the raising of the dead man, many believed (11:45). This is what we immediately recognize as glory. Jesus is seen as the wonderful being he is, and people believe. But John puts little stress on this. He goes on to point out that another result of the miracle was that events were set in train that would lead to the cross (11:50). There is glory there, too. We should overlook neither aspect if we are to understand John's view of glory.

As we have seen, the glory of the Father is closely linked with that of the Son. This is shown in a number of places, but we might profitably notice the prayer Jesus offered with the cross in immediate prospect: "Father, the hour has come; glorify your Son, so that the Son may glorify you" (17:1). There can be no question

29. Cited in M. F. Wiles, *The Spiritual Gospel* (Cambridge, 1960), p. 82.

but that he has the cross in mind. That is "the hour" to which everything in this Gospel leads up. And in the cross will be seen, not only the glory of the Son but that of the Father too. The two are not to be separated.

Throughout the Fourth Gospel Jesus takes a lowly place, and it is one of John's great paradoxes that the true glory is to be seen in this lowly service and especially in Jesus' death on the cross (12:23-24; 13:31). Käsemann finds references to glory, but incredibly he does not notice the paradox.[30] Even when the paradox is not stressed, as for example when Jesus' glory is shown in miracles, the glory may be perceived only by a restricted circle. Thus, at the wedding in Cana of Galilee the disciples saw Jesus' glory and believed (2:11). But John says nothing of any effect on the ruler of the feast or the guests, or even on the servants who knew that what had been taken to the ruler of the feast was water (v. 9). It is quite a different picture in Acts 14:8-18, where the people of Lystra thought themselves the recipients of a divine visitation. They saw glory in the healing of the lame man and immediately hailed Barnabas and Paul as gods. They brought bulls and garlands in order to offer sacrifice to them. That is the kind of thing that may be expected when the gods come to earth. There is no equivalent in John. He is writing about something quite different.

There is an interesting note about glory in 12:39-43. Here the Evangelist quotes a prophecy of Isaiah which explains why many people did not believe in Jesus: their eyes were blinded, their hearts were hardened, and so forth. Then John adds, "Isaiah said these things because he saw his glory." We might have expected "because he saw his rejection" or the like. But for John there was glory in Jesus' acceptance of the way of rejection and suffering, and it is glory that he links with the prophecy of rejection.

---

30. As C. K. Barrett, for example, does: "the story of Jesus can be told in terms of glory—he has laid aside but will resume the glory he had with the Father before creation; he seeks not his own glory but the glory of the Father, yet in his voluntary humiliation and obedience, and pre-eminently in the disgrace of the cross, he is glorified, and manifests his glory.... There is a characteristic Johannine paradox here" ("The Theological Vocabulary of the Fourth Gospel and of the Gospel of Truth", *Current Issues*, pp. 211-12). Vincent Taylor could write, "There could be no vainer controversy than the dispute whether in these passages (i.e. 3:14; 8:28; 12:32) the crucifixion or the exaltation is meant. The death *is* the exaltation" (*The Atonement in New Testament Teaching*, London, 1946, p. 147).

And if Käsemann does not do justice to John's paradoxical view of glory, neither does he give sufficient weight to the Evangelist's declaration that "the Word was made flesh".[31] Even if Käsemann were right in seeing the emphasis on the reference to glory (and we have just seen that this is debatable), these other words must be given their due meaning, and it must be recognized that *sarx* is a strong term that puts emphasis on the physical reality of the incarnate Jesus. John does not say, "the Word became man", or even, "the Word took a body". He uses the forceful, almost crude, word "flesh". There should be no denying the physical reality of one of whom this can be said. The word "expresses that which is earth-bound (3:6), transient and perishable (6:63), the typically human mode of being, as it were, in contrast to all that is divine and spiritual."[32] Schnackenburg notes that there was a widespread idea at the time that divine beings might appear on earth.

> But after the affirmation of the Incarnation in 1:14 the Christian teaching on the Son of God made man cannot be reduced to one variety among others: it can only be understood as a protest against all other religions of redemption in Hellenism and Gnosticism. It is a new and profoundly original way of confessing the Saviour who has come "palpably" (1 Jn 1:1) in history as a unique, personal human being, who has manifested himself in the reality of the "flesh".[33]

---

31. S. Smalley holds that "It is possible to expound" this expression "in the manner of either Bultmann or Käsemann only if violence is done to the balance between humanity and divinity, humiliation and glory, that are an inescapable part of the Johannine perspective" (*SE*, VI, p. 498).

32. R. Schnackenburg, *John*, I, p. 267. He goes on to notice that what Bultmann calls "the language of mythology" "takes the utmost pains to avoid the term *sarx* and it never speaks of 'becoming flesh'" (*ibid.*, p. 268). A. B. du Toit thinks *sarx* points to "the typical human mode of existence in all its frailty, brokenness and defectiveness in contrast to the heavenly, divine mode of existence" (*Neotestamentica* 2, 1968, p. 15). R. Bultmann sees *sarx* as referring in John "to the sphere of the human and the worldly as opposed to the divine, i.e. the sphere of the *pneuma*, 3.6; 6.63 . . . but whereas *skotos* refers to the worldly sphere in its enmity towards God, *sarx* stresses its transitoriness, helplessness and vanity (3.6; 6.63)." He holds that "the Revealer is nothing but a man" and that "the *offence* of the gospel is brought out as strongly as possible by *ho logos sarx egeneto*" (*The Gospel of John: A Commentary*, Oxford, 1971, pp. 62, 63).

33. *John*, I, p. 268.

The verb *egeneto* is also significant. It indicates a change (whether we translate "was made" or "became"), and it seems impossible to reconcile the use of this verb with the view that the divine Christ remained as he was, in all his glory. Du Toit maintains that the verb "bridges the enormous distance between the divine Logos and the *sarx*", that it "states the solid, the 'crude' fact of the incarnation", and that it "entirely cuts off the possibility of any docetic misinterpretation."

> The incarnation means, according to verse 14, that the divine Logos substituted his heavenly way of existence for the frail, broken, earthly, human way of existence. This human existence of the Word is not to be understood in a docetic way, a mere being "in the flesh," but as a "becoming flesh," and yet without sacrificing his essential being as Logos.[34]

The combination of the verb *egeneto* and the noun *sarx* points irresistibly to a genuine incarnation, with all that that means. It conveys the thought that Jesus did not play at becoming man; he really became man and accepted all the limitations and suffering and so on that that involves.

Jesus, the Man

The reality of Jesus' manhood might be deduced also from the repeated references to him as a man; see 4:29; 5:12; 7:46, 51; 8:40; 9:11, 16 *(bis);* 10:33; 11:47, 50; 18:14, 17, 29; 19:5. Of these we might notice particularly 8:40, where Jesus himself says, "you are trying to kill me, a man who has spoken the truth to you", and 10:33, where the Jews say, "We are not stoning you for a good work but for blasphemy, and because you, being a man, make yourself God." The former gives Jesus' own claim as John sees it, and in the latter the Jews call Jesus a man at the very same time as they recognize that he claims to be something more. The claim carries no conviction to them because, whatever else he was, he was certainly a man, and that for them had implications. John's repeated use of "man" in reference to Jesus gives food for thought. If he

34. *Neotestamentica* 15-16, pp. 16-18.

was trying to depict a docetic Christ, why this repeated stress on his real humanity? It makes no sense.[35]

Käsemann seems to undervalue the passion narrative. Convinced as he is that John portrays a docetic Christ, he can make nothing of the narrative of Jesus' death other than a reluctant acceptance of a tradition too firmly held to be dismissed. He regards it as "a mere postscript which had to be included."[36] We are tempted to retort, "Some postscript!" This is a full and absorbing narrative. It cannot be said that John has skimped on this part of his story; his inclusion of details found nowhere else indicates an interest in the subject.

R. T. Fortna has another objection when he says that "all the themes pervading the gospel and coming to a climax in the crucifixion — most notably, Jesus' 'hour', his 'glorification', and the completion *(telein)* of his work—are plainly Johannine insertions into the older narrative material."[37] I am not persuaded that these are "insertions", but they are certainly there, and they tell us something of what John is about. In any case, Fortna's view ought to be considered and Käsemann does not consider it. Fortna makes another (and in my judgment a better) point when he says, "in the present gospel it is no longer the resurrection as such that carries the greater weight but Jesus' glorification on the cross, by which he draws all men to himself (xii.32)."[38] The whole Gospel emphasizes the cross. "Even before Jesus appears his mission is summarized as tragic (i.10f.)."[39] When he comes to the story of the actual death of Jesus, John seems to go out of his way to emphasize its physical aspects. He tells us of Jesus' thirst

35. Cf. the essay by G. Sevenster, "Remarks on the Humanity of Jesus in the Gospel and Letters of John", in *Studies in John*, pp. 185-93. He gives particular attention to John 19:5.

36. *Testament*, p. 7.

37. "Christology in the Fourth Gospel: Redaction-Critical Perspectives" (*NTS* 21, 1974-75, p. 497). Barnabas Lindars holds that Käsemann "relies almost exclusively on the later strands of the gospel from the point of view of literary criticism (the Prologue, the Supper Discourses, the Prayer), which represent the mature reflection of the evangelist rather than his original impetus; and that the exegesis is so heavily worked into the categories of contemporary German thought that it constitutes a creative theology rather than an exposition" (*Theology* 72, 1969, p. 157).

38. "Christology", p. 497.

39. *Ibid.*, p. 502.

(19:28). He alone tells of the spear thrust and the water and the blood (19:34-35). There seems to be an opposition to anything docetic in his insistence that there is a witness who can bear testimony to the fact that water and blood flowed from the side of the crucified Jesus. There are mysteries here, but at the very least there is emphatic testimony to a dead body. One does not write thus about a docetic being.

As we saw earlier, Käsemann says that he is "not interested in completely denying features of the lowliness of the earthly Jesus in the Fourth Gospel" but holds that these do not picture Jesus as "true man". He asks, "do not those features of his lowliness rather represent the absolute minimum of the costume designed for the one who dwelt for a little while among men, appearing to be one of them, yet without himself being subject to earthly conditions?"[40] This immediately raises the question of whether Käsemann has done justice to Jesus' dependence on God. The Johannine Jesus says plainly, "the Father is greater than I" (14:28),[41] and the Gospel is filled with the thought that he cannot act by himself. "The Son can do nothing of himself," Jesus says, "but only what he sees the Father doing" (5:19).

Dependence on God

This aspect of Johannine teaching is emphasized by J. Ernest Davey, who devotes 67 pages (far and away the longest chapter in his book) to "The Dependence of Christ as presented in *John*".[42] He speaks of Jesus as dependent on the Father for power ("I can do

---

40. *Testament,* p. 10.

41. C. K. Barrett has a thought-provoking article in the Schnackenburg *Festschrift* entitled " 'The Father is greater than I' (Jo 14,28): Subordinationist Christology in the New Testament." He argues that John has an important strand of teaching in which he depicts the Christ as subordinate to the Father. There is an element of paradox here: "It is natural, and not in the end wrong, to describe the result in the language of paradox: one speaks of majesty veiled in humility" (*Neues Testament und Kirche,* ed. J. Gnilka, Freiburg-Basel-Wien, 1974, p. 158; Barrett refers to Hoskyns and Davey). There is a problem, and Barrett does not claim to have solved it, but we do not get rid of it by denying one element in the paradox, which is what Käsemann seems to do. John has something more in mind than God walking on earth.

42. *The Jesus of St. John* (London, 1958), pp. 90-157. Similarly Leonard Hodgson draws attention to passages such as Jesus' declaration that he has com-

nothing by myself", 5:30), for knowledge ("my judgment is true, because I am not alone, but I and he that sent me", 8:16), for his mission and message ("My food is to do the will of him who sent me and accomplish his work", 4:34), for his being, nature, and destiny (the Father "has given to the Son to have life in himself", 5:26; "I live through the Father", 6:57; "the cup which the Father has given me", 18:11), for authority and office ("as thou hast given him authority", 17:2; the Father gave him authority to judge, 5:22, 27, and to lay down his life, 10:18), for love (3:16; 17:24-26), and for glory and honor (God "will immediately glorify him", 13:32; "my glory, which thou hast given me", 17:24; the Father has given all judgment to the Son "so that all may honor the Son", 5:23). Christ is pictured as obedient to the Father (his food is to do the Father's will, 4:34), as dependent on him for his disciples ("all that the Father gives me will come to me", 6:37, and negatively, "no one can come to me unless the Father who sent me draws him", 6:44; "the men whom thou gavest me out of the world", 17:6). He depends on the Father for testimony ("If I bear witness about myself, my witness is not true; there is another who bears witness about me"; "the Father who sent me has borne witness about me", 5:31, 37), for the Spirit (who descends on him at baptism, 1:33, and whom the Father gives him without measure, 3:34), for guidance (Davey sees this as the meaning of passages like "if anyone walks in the day he does not stumble because he sees the light of this world [i.e., God]", 11:9; "Here mystical guidance is clearly expressed"). Jesus' dependence is seen in his relationships with God ("he who sent me is with me, he has not left me alone", 8:29) and men ("you will know that I am in the Father and you in me and I in you", 14:20), and is illustrated by his prayers (chap. 17) and by his titles (there are 22 in the Gospel and 1 John, and most imply dependence, e.g., "Son" depends on "Father", "Lamb of God" probably points to "the victim offered by and sent from God", etc.).

---

pleted the work the Father gave him to do and proceeds: "The more one studies the Fourth Gospel on these lines the more curious it appears that the portrayal of our Lord in it should be thought to be one in which His humanity is minimised and emphasis laid on His own personal claims to divinity. Of all the Gospels it is the one in which the keynote of our Lord's thought is *dependence*, dependence on the Father" (*And Was Made Man*, London, 1933, p. 198).

Davey agrees that there are aspects of the Johannine presentation which might be taken in a docetic sense.[43] He denies, however, that these give us the typical Johannine view. That is rather dependence. "Few persons who have not studied the Fourth Gospel with care in this regard can have any conception of the extent to which this idea of dependence is emphasized in it as the chief constituent in Christ's experience of God the Father; one might indeed call this dependence the ruling element in John's portrait of Christ."[44]

There is then in John a strong and important stress on Jesus' dependence. But there is more: the whole of Jesus' life is human. We might start with the name itself, for John uses the human name "Jesus" 237 times (Matthew has this name 150 times, Mark 81 times, and Luke 89 times), more than a quarter of the total in the entire New Testament (905 times). "Jesus Christ" is found twice only, while the title "Christ" occurs 19 times (in accordance with John's declared aim of showing Jesus to be the Christ, 20:31). This human Jesus seems to have enjoyed normal family relations (2:12). He went to a wedding with his mother (2:1). He had brothers who told him what he ought to do in a manner which anyone who has grown up with brothers will immediately recognize (7:3-5). He was concerned for his mother, even as he hung on the cross (19:26-27). He loved his friends, Martha, Mary, and Lazarus (11:5).

Jesus was troubled at the prospect of his death and wondered whether he should pray to be delivered from it (12:27). He could be tired and thirsty (4:6, 7); he could be ignorant and ask questions. He could shed tears (11:35) and be troubled in spirit (11:33). John twice uses of Jesus the unusual verb *embrimaomai* (11:33, 38), which is properly applied to the snorting of horses.[45] It is a very

43. *Ibid.*, pp. 18, 85, 133, 186.
44. *Ibid.*, p. 77. He goes on to refer to the view that John portrays a Christ "who is omniscient, omnipotent, self-determining and independent" as "a myth". He thinks that theologically the Synoptists emphasize the deity of Christ and the Fourth Gospel the humanity, though, of course, both elements are found in all four Gospels (*ibid.*, p. 170). A. M. Hunter accepts Davey's argument (*According to John*, p. 115).
45. Cf. the definition in G. Abbott-Smith, *A Manual Greek Lexicon of the New Testament* (Edinburgh, 1954), s.v.: "*to snort in* (of horses, Aesch.), hence, to speak or act with deep feeling" (here he sees the meaning, "to be moved with anger").

down-to-earth word. There is dispute among commentators as to whether we should take it in John 11 to refer to anger or some other deep feeling, but none about the very human quality of the emotion it denotes. Jesus could not prevent some of his followers from falling away from him (6:66), and one of them from betraying him. On one occasion he said, "Now my soul is troubled (*hē psychē mou tetaraktai*)" (12:27), and John tells us that in the upper room Jesus "was troubled in spirit (*etarachthē tōi pneumati*)" as he contemplated the betrayal (13:21). All this is part of the evidence and points to a real humanity.[46]

There are also a few passages in which the view that Jesus is simply God on earth appears to be denied. Thus in the Prologue we read that "no one has ever seen God" but that Jesus has set him forth (1:18), which distinguishes between Jesus and the God he set forth. This is reinforced when Jesus later says of God, "you have neither heard his voice nor seen his form" (5:37), and again, "Not that anyone has seen the Father" (6:46). In each case the position is somewhat complex. In the Prologue Jesus appears to be called *monogenēs theos*; in chapter 5 he claims that he has intimate knowledge of the Father; and in 6:46 he goes on to differentiate himself from those who have not seen the Father by claiming that he has done just this. I am not arguing that any of these passages is simple, but rather that Käsemann is oversimplifying by not considering the implications of such words. If, as he claims, Jesus was simply "the God who walks on the face of the earth",[47] then many people had seen God and heard his voice. But that is not what John is saying. His emphatic words to the contrary should not be overlooked.

Again, we should bear in mind that the Gospel of John does not stand alone. It is one of five writings which together make up the Johannine literature. Whether any one author wrote more than one of these books is hotly disputed, but it is undeniable that the Gospel and 1 John, if not from the same pen (though many do hold to unity of authorship), are clearly from the same circle and

46. Franz Mussner points out that in this Gospel "The believer in the act of knowing sees, of course, just as 'the world' does, Jesus in his sheer humanity", and goes on to maintain that this "sheer humanity" does not become "transfigured even for the believer and knower but is radically maintained" (*The Historical Jesus in the Gospel of St. John*, New York, 1967, p. 28).

47. *Testament*, p. 66.

the same basic situation. There is no doubt that 1 John opposes teachings of a docetic kind with its stress on handling as well as seeing and hearing the word of life (1 John 1:1), its insistence on confessing that Jesus Christ has come "in the flesh" with its counterpart that to deny this is to manifest the spirit of the antichrist (1 John 4:2-3; cf. 2:22), its stress on seeing Jesus as the Son of God (1 John 4:15) and as the Christ (1 John 5:1), and its emphasis on the importance of Jesus' coming "not in the water only, but in the water and in the blood" (1 John 5:6). It is not easy to see how and why the Gospel should be setting forth a teaching which the Letter combats so vigorously.[48]

Oversimplifying

From all this it is clear that Käsemann is oversimplifying. That is my quarrel with his whole book. I have spent many years in the study of the Fourth Gospel and have reached the highly unoriginal conclusion that it is a complex and difficult book. I am at a loss to understand why Käsemann makes it all sound so simple. On his view we have nothing more complicated than a picture of "one who dwelt for a little while among men, appearing to be one of them, yet without himself being subjected to earthly conditions."[49] This seems to me to be nothing less than a refusal to face the problems of the Fourth Gospel (incidentally, a favorite accusation of Käsemann's against the generality of Johannine scholars). It results from a selective reading of the evidence, ignoring or minimizing the force of all that does not fit into the desired picture. For the fact is that the Jesus of the Fourth Gospel is at one and the same time both supremely great and very lowly. He is fully God, certainly. Käsemann sees this with crystal clarity. But he is also fully man, and that should not be overlooked.

48. C. F. D. Moule criticizes Käsemann for "detaching the Gospel from the First Epistle in an unjustifiable way" (*Studies in John,* p. 158). Elsewhere he refers to "a motive which runs right through the Gospel and the Johannine Epistles — that of affirming the reality of the incarnation as against 'docetist' theories" (*Worship in the New Testament,* London, 1961, p. 34, n. 2). Hoskyns paid a good deal of attention to 1 John in setting forth his view that the Fourth Gospel opposes docetism (E. Hoskyns, *The Fourth Gospel,* London, 1950, pp. 48-57).

49. *Testament,* p. 10.

Others do recognize the complexity of the problem. For example, G. E. Ladd writes, "We may conclude that John portrays Jesus in a twofold light without reflection or speculation. He is equal to God; he is indeed God in the flesh; yet he is fully human."[50] That is the conclusion to which the evidence points us. Raymond E. Brown has also looked at the problem and is unimpressed by the view that this Gospel was written to refute docetists of some kind. He finds features that are anti-docetic, but they are not prominent enough to give us the main motive for composing the book. He sums up with, "An honest judgment would be that an anti-docetic motif is possible and even probable in the Gospel, but it has no great prominence."[51] Brown wrote before Käsemann's book appeared, so he is not directly dealing with his contentions, but his judgment has relevance all the same. A survey of the evidence convinces him that not a docetic thrust but an anti-docetic thrust is probable.

Nils Dahl is another who finds John opposed to docetism. He thinks that a docetic Christology "may have been supported by allegorical interpretations of the Old Testament. Over against such tendencies, John bears witness to the true humanity of Jesus and to the reality of his death (6:41-42, 61; 19:35)."[52]

Herman Ridderbos has given attention to the Prologue and surveys a number of views of its composition and significance.[53] From his study he concludes,

> The Gospel, therefore, is not in the first place a witness of the faith, but of that which has been seen and heard and handled with the hands. And, therefore, whoever asserts that the back-

50. *A Theology of the New Testament* (Grand Rapids, 1974), p. 252.
51. *John*, I, pp. lxxvi-lxxvii.
52. "The Johannine Church," *Current Issues*, p. 142. In the same volume Markus Barth, writing on Hebrews, says, "No other book of the New Testament (except the Fourth Gospel) puts the real deity and true humanity of Jesus Christ so clearly side by side" ("The Old Testament in Hebrews, An Essay in Biblical Hermeneutics", p. 58). O. Cullmann more than once says that in this Gospel there is at least an implicit opposition to docetism (*The Johannine Circle*, pp. 17, 58, 61). See also R. H. Strachan, *John*, pp. 44-45; T. W. Manson, *On Paul and John* (London, 1963), pp. 156-57, etc.; R. Kysar, *The Fourth Evangelist and His Gospel* (Minneapolis, 1975), pp. 157-59.
53. "The Structure and Scope of the Prologue to the Gospel of John" (*NovT* 8, 1966, pp. 180-201).

ground of the faith of the evangelist is another than that of the
events which he narrates, attacks not only the narrative, but also
the Kerygma of the evangelist at its very heart.[54]

The genuine humanity of Jesus in this Gospel, his becoming *flesh*,
is at the heart of the matter as Ridderbos sees it.

From the evidence, then, it seems that Käsemann is oversimplifying. No one who studies John's Gospel will want to deny
that Jesus is there depicted as divine. He is the very Son of God
sent to earth to bring about our salvation. But to say that therefore he is not also very man is to overlook a great proportion of
the evidence. There seems no doubt whatever that those scholars
are right who discover a balance in John between the deity and
the humanity. For all its brilliance, nothing in Käsemann's study
disturbs this conclusion.

54. *Ibid.*, p. 200.

CHAPTER 4

The Christ of God

WITH US "CHRIST" HAS BECOME A PROPER NAME. We often refer to our Savior simply as "Christ", and even if we use the fuller name "Jesus Christ" we still employ the term as no more than a name and we do not see the meaning as "Jesus the Christ". This way of using the term is, of course, derived from the early Christians, and there is no difficulty in finding places in the New Testament where it is used in this way. But it is not the only way and it is not the original way. We could perhaps put it this way: Jesus was called "Christ" because he fulfilled all that the title signifies and in due course his title was employed so often that it came to be used as a name with no particular emphasis on its meaning. But when John tells us that he wrote "that you may believe that Jesus is the Christ" (20:31), he is using the title with all the meaning it can convey. If we are to understand what John is saying throughout his Gospel, we must be clear on what "Christ" meant to first-century Christians.

The term is, of course, basically a Hebrew term. We start with the Hebrew word *māšîaḥ*, the participle of the verb meaning "to anoint". Thus the word basically means "anointed". If we transliterate this into English we get "Messiah", and if we translate it into Greek it becomes *Christos*, which we transliterate as "Christ". Thus we get the equation "Christ" = "Messiah" = "anointed". The basic question accordingly concerns the meaning of anointing.

It turns out that more than one answer could be given to this. The Hebrew verb signifies either a smearing or a pouring. We see the former meaning when it is used of putting oil on a shield (Isa. 21:5) or paint on a house (Jer. 22:14). Most agree that when it is used of persons it means pouring over them, as when oil is poured on a priest (Exod. 28:41) or a king (1 Sam. 16:13) or a prophet

(1 Kings 19:16). Anointing was part of ordinary life, and more than one verb was used for it. Ruth was instructed to anoint herself before going to Boaz's threshing floor (Ruth 3:3), and Amos complains of people who "anoint themselves with the finest oils" (Amos 6:6). This was clearly a use more or less like that of perfume in modern times. Anointing might be used in times of festivity and be a sign of joy (Ps. 45:7); therefore it does not surprise us that it was not used in a time of mourning (2 Sam. 14:2; Dan. 10:2-3), and apparently not when fasting (2 Sam. 12:20; Matt. 6:17). Guests might expect to be anointed by their host, and Jesus pointed out the discourtesy when this was not done (Luke 7:46). Plainly anointing was widely carried out in Bible times and people then were much more familiar with the practice than we are. But these anointings in everyday life are not the significant ones for our purpose; our concern is with specifically religious anointings.

Interestingly "Messiah", "anointed one", in the sense of God's chosen one, turns out to be an infrequent Old Testament term. It does occur (Dan. 9:25, 26),[1] but not often. In the Old Testament it is not the precise term but the concept of anointing that is important. The first example of the practice in our Old Testament is at the consecration of Aaron and his sons. God tells Moses that he is to "anoint them and ordain them and consecrate them" (Exod. 28:41), which makes it plain that the anointing was a solemn religious ceremony with far-reaching significance. It was part of the process by which a priest was set apart for his office. When he was ordained to his ministry he was consecrated to the service of God, and his anointing symbolized this. Precise directions were given as to the composition of the oil that was to be used on such occasions (Exod. 30:22-25), and it was expressly laid down that this "holy anointing oil" was not to be used at any other time. Anyone who offended by a profane use of this oil was to be cut off from his people (Exod. 30:32-33). So significant was the act of anointing that the priest

---

1. Since there is no article, most translations agree with RSV, "an anointed one". Eric Heaton reminds us that "the title *the* Messiah never occurs in the OT", and he sees here a reference to the high priest (*The Book of Daniel*, London, 1964, p. 214).

could be called "the anointed priest" (Lev. 4:3). Anointing was extended to the altar (Exod. 29:36) and to a variety of objects used in worship (Exod. 30:26-28).

In Old Testament usage, while the anointing of priests was clearly very important, it was the anointing of leaders, and especially of kings, that was most often mentioned. Thus Saul was to be anointed "to be prince over my people Israel" (1 Sam. 9:16), as was David (1 Sam. 16:12-13). Israel's king is frequently called "the Lord's anointed" (e.g., 1 Sam. 26:16; 2 Sam. 1:14, 16; cf. Ps. 2:2, etc.).[2] Indeed, sometimes Yahweh is said to do the anointing, though of course he does it through an agent (2 Kings 9:3, 6; cf. 2 Sam. 12:7). Apparently anointing was the decisive act in making someone king, for we read such things as "they had anointed him king in place of his father" (1 Kings 5:1); "I anoint you king over Israel" (2 Kings 9:3).[3]

These are the two figures who are most spoken of in connection with anointing, the priest and the king. Occasionally there is an anointing of a prophet (1 Kings 19:16), and this, of course, may have taken place on unrecorded occasions. But as far as our records go, this was not frequent.[4] The concept may be used metaphorically, and other servants of God are sometimes described as anointed. Thus the heathen king Cyrus is spoken of in this way (Isa. 45:1), and the prophet speaks of being anointed "to bring good tidings to the afflicted" (Isa. 61:1). Ezekiel speaks of "an anointed cherub" (Ezek. 28:14), a mysterious figure, but clearly one who is specially chosen by God to render significant service.[5] Zechariah

2. F. Hesse finds this use 30 (29) times. He adds that the high priest is given the title six times (*TDNT*, IX, p. 502).

3. The Old Testament never says why anointing was used in the making of kings, but S. Szikszai may be right when he says, "it was of decisive importance, for it conveyed the power for the exercise of royal authority" (*IDB*, I, p. 139).

4. Ps. 105:15 records God as saying: "Touch not my anointed ones, do my prophets no harm!" on which A. F. Kirkpatrick comments, "The patriarchs were not actually anointed, but the term is applied to them as bearing the seal of a Divine consecration in virtue of which their persons were sacred and inviolable. Abraham is called a prophet in Gen. xx.7 as an intercessor, and the term is applied to the patriarchs generally as the recipients of Divine revelation" (*The Book of Psalms*, Cambridge, 1910, p. 618).

5. Assuming that RSV is correct, John W. Wevers holds that "The word 'anointed' is a later commentary on the word, but an incorrect one" (*Ezekiel*, Grand Rapids, 1982, p. 157). Herbert G. May says that "anointed guardian cherub" is "as

speaks of "the two anointed who stand by the LORD of the whole earth" (Zech. 4:14).

That the king is the Lord's anointed gives him a special place in the Israelite understanding of things. It meant among other things that it is Yahweh who is supreme; the earthly sovereign over the people of God rules in the name of God and is answerable to God. As they looked into the future, the prophets of Israel saw a time when Yahweh would rule over all the earth. It was the rule of Yahweh that mattered, but sometimes it was held that there would be a special place for a "son of David", the king who would reign in the last days. This figure could be understood as the Messiah, and there were times when many looked for his coming. He would not be important in himself, but Yahweh would work in him to accomplish his will and it was this that gave him importance.[6] Some sections of Judaism found little or no place for the Messiah (e.g., the apocrypha, the Mishnah, Philo), though others emphasized his place. The men of Qumran thought that there would be two Messiahs, one kingly and the other priestly, and they held that the priestly Messiah would take the first rank.

Sometimes messiahship was understood in terms of the Davidic king, but there was also the Son of man in Daniel 7 to serve as the model. It cannot be said that there was anything approaching a uniform expectation, but there was enough messianic speculation and sufficient variety in the way it was understood to make this an important category for the New Testament writers. For John in particular it was highly significant, and he has a good deal to say about the Messiah and his relationship to the heavenly Father.

It is a teasing question whether John is making an allusion to messiahship in his story of Mary's anointing of Jesus (12:1-8). Nobody says anything about messiahship, but there is no doubt that John is describing an anointing. It is also a fact that Jesus in-

---

difficult to understand as to translate", but he raises no question of its originality (*IB*, VI, p. 221).

6. Cf. E. Jenni, "we must understand clearly that in OT expectations of the future the Messiah plays only a subordinate role"; the Messiah is not an independent figure but "the representative and instrument of Yahweh" (*IDB*, III, p. 362).

terprets the anointing in terms of his death (12:7), the heart of his messianic activity. Probably we should take the incident as no more than a social happening of an unusually interesting kind. But at least we can say that the Messiah received an unusual anointing.

Messianic Titles

In his opening chapter John makes use of a considerable number of titles with which to refer to Jesus. Some of them are recognized messianic titles, such as "Messiah" itself, which is then explained as "Christ" (1:41). John also writes of "the Son of God" (1:34, 49), "the King of Israel" (1:49),[7] and "the Son of man" (1:51). To them we must add a number of other titles which are not strictly messianic, but coming as they do so freely in this first part of this Gospel, they reinforce the point John is making, that they refer to one who is certainly the Messiah but who is much more than the Messiah of traditional expectation. The Messiah of whom John writes is called "the Word" (1:1), "God" (1:1), "the light of men" (1:4), "the true light" (1:9), "the only-begotten from the Father" (1:14), a greater than John the Baptist (1:15, 26-27, 30), "only-begotten God" (1:18), "the Lord" (1:23), "the Lamb of God" (1:29, 36), "he who baptizes in Holy Spirit" (1:33), probably "God's chosen one" (1:34), "Rabbi" (1:38, 49), "he of whom Moses and the prophets wrote" (1:45).[8]

As the Gospel unfolds, other titles make their appearance, such

7. R. Schnackenburg points out that Nathanael did not recognize all that "Son of God" (which precedes "King of Israel") implies; otherwise Jesus would not have promised a fuller revelation (1:50-51). He goes on, "The titles used by Nathanael are meant as Messianic, but provide the reader with the possibility of a deeper understanding" (*The Gospel according to St John*, I, New York, 1968, p. 319).

8. R. H. Lightfoot comments on the titles in this opening chapter: "In the course of this gospel we shall learn that some of these titles, although they played an important, even an essential, part in enlightening those who came to know the Lord at first through them, soon proved inadequate to describe His Person. It seems as though, in these introductory verses, St. John enumerates these titles at the outset, in order that, while not allowing them to be forgotten . . . he may pass beyond them and impart to his readers, in the chapters which describe the ministry, the deeper and fuller understanding, which he wishes them to have of the Lord and of His work" (*St. John's Gospel*, London, 1956, pp. 99-100).

as "the Holy One of God" (6:69)[9] and "he who comes in the name of the Lord" (12:13; perhaps we should take the title here as simply "the Coming One").[10] It is plain that with his mass of titles John is drawing attention to Jesus' uniqueness. The person who could fulfil all that all these titles mean was no ordinary person. He was not even an ordinary Messiah, if I may put it that way. John is not speaking of the kind of Messiah that the ordinary person in first-century Palestine might have expected or even the kind of Messiah that pious and devout servants of God might look for. He is the Messiah indeed, but the Christians gave the term a new content. We cannot look at Jewish expectation and say, "That is what John thought Jesus to be." Jesus fulfilled all that to which Jewish expectation pointed, but more, much more. And sometimes John corrects Jewish misapprehensions about the Messiah. Many of the Jewish people had profound misunderstandings of who the Messiah would be and what the Messiah would do. It was part of John's aim to correct such misunderstandings so that his readers would understand what messiahship means and how it was manifested in Jesus.

Some commentators reject the idea that Jesus was in fact recognized as the Christ as early as in Andrew's words to Peter (1:41). They point out that the Synoptic Gospels make clear that it was a long time before the followers of Jesus came to anything like an adequate understanding of his Person. But this is probably not a valid objection. It is not so much the use of the term "Messiah" as the content put into it that counts. It was one thing to say that Jesus was the Messiah and quite another to comprehend what Jesus understood the term to mean. Andrew would not have understood this so early, but that does not mean that he did not use the term. There must have been some reason for people like Andrew to associate themselves with Jesus, and a conviction that he was the Messiah, however that term was understood, would account for it.

Nathanael's greeting of Jesus as "the King of Israel" (1:49) is

9. Vincent Taylor says of "the Holy One of God" that "It describes a man set apart and consecrated to the service of God. In some early Christian communities it may have been used for a time as a Messianic name", though he does not consider it "an accepted Messianic title" (*The Names of Jesus*, London, 1953, p. 80).

10. Taylor says that this title "had only a brief and restricted currency in certain circles. It has a marked eschatological tone, and its origin is probably to be found in the proclamation of John the Baptist" (*ibid.*, p. 79).

noteworthy. Outside this Gospel the term is used twice only in the New Testament. It is used in mockery when scoffers invite Jesus to come down from the cross (Matt. 27:42), and again in Mark where the corresponding invitation is to "the Christ, the King of Israel" (Mark 15:32). While those who used the term were not serious, it is perhaps worth noting that they use the correct term for the ruler over the people of God, whereas "the King of the Jews" used by the Magi (Matt. 2:2), Pilate, and the Roman soldiers (Mark 15:2, 18, etc.) is natural enough for Gentiles, but not the term informed Jews would use. It does not bring out the people of God idea, and this was important for Nathanael (and for John). William Temple brings out another point with his comment, "Note the strongly Hebraic mentality for which it is in the order of climax to pass from *Son of God* to *King of Israel*."[11] In recording this encounter thus early in his Gospel John is making it clear from the beginning that Jesus did indeed fulfil all that is implied in the term "Christ".

The point is made in another way in some words of John the Baptist. When the delegation came from Jerusalem to look into his teaching, they asked him, "Who are you?" to which he replied, "*I* am not the Christ" (1:19-20). Now nobody had said that he was, or even raised the Christ question at all. But his *I* is emphatic; it is as though the Baptist is saying, "It is not I who am the Christ." That this is seen as important is clear from a dispute at a later time between the followers of John and a Jew about purification (3:25). For some reason the fact that Jesus was having greater success than John was brought into the discussion. John expressed satisfaction with this, and among other things he called his followers to witness that he had said, "*I* am not the Christ" (3:28). Again there is the emphatic pronoun and the implication that there was a Christ, though it was not the Baptist.[12]

The Samaritans and the Christ

The fact that Jesus is the Christ is brought out in the story of the Samaritan woman to whom Jesus talked by Jacob's well. The

11. *Readings in St. John's Gospel* (London, 1947), p. 31.
12. Marcus Dods gives the meaning of John's words as " '*I* am not the Christ,' but another is" (*The Expositor's Greek Testament*, I, Grand Rapids, 1979 reprint, p. 693).

woman tried a number of ways to avoid the challenge with which Jesus was confronting her, the last being her statement: "I know that Messiah is coming, he who is called 'Christ'; when *that one* comes, he will declare everything to us" (4:25). This leads Jesus to say, "*I AM* he, I who am talking to you" (4:26). A little later the woman puts it more tentatively when she speaks to the men of her town, asking "Can this be the Christ?" (4:29).

Unfortunately there is little information about Samaritan ideas in New Testament times. Since the Samaritans accepted the Pentateuch as sacred Scripture they recognized that the Messiah would come in due course, but their rejection of the rest of the Old Testament meant that they had little information about him. It is generally agreed that they used the term Taheb rather than Messiah and that they saw him primarily as a teacher.[13] He would restore their worship and be a priest. This meant that their concept of messiahship lacked the nationalistic features that mattered so much to the Jews, and this may be the reason why Jesus accepted the term in talking with a Samaritan lady of no influence. It is clear from all four Gospels that he did not make use of the term among the Jews in general. The Jewish expectation was so frequently identified with armies and empire, with combat and conquest, that it would be misleading for Jesus to speak of himself as Messiah before the Jewish public. But among these rural Samaritans it was quite another matter.

For John it was another opportunity to bring out one of his central tenets. He is not concerned to say in what way the Samaritan concept of messiahship agreed with and differed from the Jewish view. He is concerned with the fact that all that is meant in messiahship found its fulfilment in Jesus. Let his readers know that on one occasion Jesus had been confronted with what the Messiah would do and he had made the claim that he was that Messiah.

In doing this he reports that Jesus used the emphatic "*I AM*", speech in the very style of deity. In Greek it is, of course, not necessary to use the personal pronoun as the subject of a verb, because the form of the verb shows what the subject is (e.g., "am" can have as its subject only "I", so the Greeks saw no need to say "I"; the

13. Cf. T. H. Gaster, "The *Taheb* is not a messiah in the Jewish sense of an anointed prince. Rather is he the prophet foretold in Deut. 18:18" (*IDB*, IV, p. 194).

verb was sufficient). But if the subject is to be emphasized ("*I* am" rather than "I am"), the pronoun is used. When, however, the Old Testament was translated into Greek, the translators evidently reasoned that a specially emphatic style was appropriate to deity and they habitually put in the pronouns. It is this kind of speech that we have here. It is too much to say that Jesus is claiming to be God by speaking in this way, but it is plain enough that he is employing unusual and solemn language.[14] Ethelbert Stauffer puts a good deal of emphasis on this formula. He thinks that the woman would not have understood the full significance of what Jesus was saying but that "Jesus chooses intentionally the veiled formula of self-revelation from Isa. 52.6, without taking account of the messianist terminology of the Samaritans. His saying of self-revelation is a mystery. . . ."[15] But he goes on to affirm that John records the expression "to imply that Jesus pronounced the first significant, but as yet half-veiled, words concerning the secret of his person not in Judea or Galilee, but on that occasion in Samaria."[16] Clearly John regarded what Jesus said as highly significant for an understanding of who and what he was. And equally clearly he was linking Jesus in his essential being with God rather than with created beings.

The woman was the means of getting the men of her town to come and listen to Jesus. In the end they were led to say that they believed in Jesus, not because of anything she had said but because they had heard him for themselves and they had come to know him as "truly the Savior of the world" (4:42). This unusual expression is found again in the New Testament only in 1 John 4:14. The word "Savior" points to the truth that people cannot save themselves. We are all sinners and we need help. John is telling his readers that that help is available.[17] Jesus came as Savior.

14. Sir Edmund Hoskyns commented, "Jesus is more than either Jew or Samaritan had comprehended in the word 'Christ'. He is the answer of God to the sin of the world" (*The Fourth Gospel*, London, 1947, p. 238).

15. *Jesus and His Story* (London, 1960), p. 152.

16. *Ibid.*, p. 153. Stauffer puts these words in italics.

17. Cf. Alan Richardson, "Man is not saved by wisdom or right knowledge (Gnosticism), nor by merit or right actions (Judaism), nor yet by mystical absorption into deity (Hellenistic mysticism), but by the act of God in the birth, life, death, resurrection, and ascension of Jesus Christ" (*IDB*, IV, p. 179).

He was a teacher and a leader as well, but importantly John sees him as one who saves, a note that he strikes several times (3:17; 5:34; 10:9; 12:47). "Savior" is a general word and does not tell us in itself from what we are saved or by what means. For that we must look at the rest of the Gospel. But that Jesus is our Savior is what receives the emphasis at this point.

And the salvation he brings about is no parochial affair. He is the Savior "of the world" (so also in 3:17; 12:47).[18] Thus far John has told us a little about Jesus' ministry among the Jews, but his addition of this narrative about what happened among the Samaritans extends the horizon beyond Judaism. The Samaritans appear to recognize something of this with their reference to "the world", and certainly John will expect his readers to understand that this beginning points to the universality of the salvation Jesus would bring.

Jewish Misconceptions

Sometimes John sets forth his purpose by drawing attention to the way the Jews or some of them had misunderstood messiahship. We see this, for example, at the end of his story of the healing of the lame man by the pool Bethesda. The healing was followed by a discourse in which among other things Jesus upbraided his hearers for their lack of faith. He went on to say that they should not think that he will accuse them to the Father. Rather it is Moses in whom they trusted who will be their accuser, "for if you believed Moses, you would have believed me, for he wrote of me" (5:46). The word "Christ" is not used at this point, but clearly that is what is meant, for it is the coming of the Messiah that is at stake. The Jews rejected Jesus because they revered Moses above all else, and they could not reconcile what Jesus was saying with what Moses had written. They accepted Moses' words as the law that was above all other laws. Jesus is saying that for all their nominal adherence to the teaching of the great

18. H. Sasse points out that this gives a new meaning to "world": "The *kosmos* is now understood as the theatre of salvation history, as the *locus* of revelation in Christ, and in consequence it appears in a wholly new light. . . . The understanding of the *kosmos* depends always on what is known of the *sōtēr tou kosmou*" (*TDNT,* III, p. 892).

lawgiver they had gone astray. They had misunderstood Moses, as their rejection of him shows. Really to follow Moses means that one will follow Jesus. There is no opposition between them.[19]

Another misunderstanding follows soon afterwards. John goes on to tell the story of the feeding of the 5,000, a miracle that made a great impression on some in the crowd. They spoke of him as "truly the prophet", and as "he who comes into the world (6:14). "The" prophet is probably the prophet prophesied by Moses as being one like himself (Deut. 18:15),[20] and it is perhaps curious that they refer to this prophet rather than the Messiah. The delegation from the authorities in Jerusalem to John the Baptist certainly differentiated the prophet from the Messiah (1:19-21). But from early days the Christians held that Christ was both this prophet and the Messiah (see Acts 3:22), as apparently the Samaritans did also. A possible explanation of the present passage is that the Galileans who saw the miracle viewed the prophet and the Messiah as identical; they did not share the opinion of the Jews at Jerusalem.

This will be the explanation also of the fact that some of them wanted to make a king out of Jesus (6:15). This accords with the widespread expectation that the Messiah would defeat the Romans and drive them out of the country. But Jesus was not a military Messiah. He had no intention of killing people. On the contrary, he would give himself up to death for them. John is telling us that Jesus was indeed King, but not the kind of king the Galileans wanted.[21] There is irony in this situation. These zealots tried to make Jesus into the kind of king they wanted, one who

19. Cf. F. L. Godet, "Every true disciple of Moses is on the way to becoming a Christian; every bad Jew is on that towards rejecting the Gospel" (*Commentary on the Gospel of John*, I, Grand Rapids reprint of 1893 edn., n.d., p. 490).

20. This prophet seems to have been of interest to John, for he refers to him in 1:21, 25; 7:40 as well as here, which is more than we might have expected for a figure who does not loom large in messianic discussions generally.

21. Cf. C. J. Wright, "They wish to make Jesus to be other than Himself. The enthusiasm of the crowd is as blind as was the antagonism of the rulers in Jerusalem. . . . The rulers misunderstood the claims of one who knew the Father in unique filial trust and obedience. The crowd misunderstood the nature of His Mission. His spiritual consciousness antagonised the traditional orthodoxy of the first; His spiritual Mission was hidden to the materialistic aims of the second" (*Jesus the Revelation of God*, London, 1950, p. 170).

would lead warriors and give them victory over the Romans, and in doing so they blinded themselves to the reality that Jesus was already indeed a king and they forfeited a place in the kingdom that he was offering them.

"He who comes into the world" (cf. 11:27; 12:13) appears to be another way of referring to the Messiah. He is one whose origin is not of this earth (cf. 3:31), one who is sent by God to accomplish God's purpose. This title was not one apparently that had a wide circulation, but it does point to the fact that the Messiah would come to this earth to do God's will. There may well have been a marked eschatological emphasis, though it is hard to know how much of this would have been appreciated by the Galileans. What is clear is that they were hailing Jesus as the one prophesied long before, one who would come into the world to do God's will in a special way.

It is impossible to hold that the Galileans had a correct understanding of any of the three terms as they applied to Jesus. But John records what the Galileans said, for their words had fuller meanings than they knew. John evidently saw it as important that his readers should come to understand what those fuller meanings tell us about Jesus. His messiahship had many facets, and here John is making the point that Jesus was God's prophet, God's king, and the one that God had planned to send from of old.

In the middle of all these misconceptions, now and then the truth peeped through. John speaks of some of the Jerusalem crowd who believed in Jesus and said, "The Christ, when he comes, won't do more signs than those that this man has done, will he?" (7:31). It cannot be said that these people were profound theologians, but at least they had discerned that the miracles were more than works of power. They saw that the miracles were "signs" that pointed to Christ. And they responded to the pointers they saw as best they knew.[22]

---

22. Floyd V. Filson may perhaps be a little hard on them when he says that they believed "with a limited and querulous faith. They recognized that Jesus' miracles were signs that God approved him, but they did not confess him to be their Christ; in fact, they spoke as if the coming of the Christ were still future. They still did not have the full faith which this Gospel was written to promote" (*Saint John*, London, 1963, p. 72). Granted that their faith was not yet as full as we would wish, at least John does not criticise them for having it.

Where Does the Messiah Come from?

John records a visit of Jesus to Jerusalem at the Feast of Tabernacles and tells us that some of the Jerusalemites were very impressed by his teaching. These people were aware of a plot to kill Jesus and were astonished accordingly that he was teaching openly and unhindered. "Surely the rulers do not know truly that this man is the Christ?" they asked (7:26). The form of their question shows that they expected the answer "No", but the interesting thing is that they felt constrained to ask it. If there was a plot to kill Jesus and if he was teaching openly, then it was to be expected that the rulers would arrest him. But they were taking no action. Why not? The Jerusalemites were puzzled, and their tentative explanation was that the rulers knew in reality (*alēthōs*) that Jesus was the Messiah. That would explain their failure to take action against him, but, of course, it did not explain the plot to kill him. It was all very puzzling.

Could Jesus really be the Messiah? They look at the question and bring forward an objection. "This man we know," they say, and go on that they know where he comes from, but as for the Messiah, "when he comes, no one knows where he is from" (7:27).[23] As we saw earlier, many ideas about the Messiah were in circulation and there was disagreement about his origin. Some found no great mystery. For example, when King Herod asked the scribes where the Christ would be born, they were able to point to a prophecy of Micah and tell him that Bethlehem was the place (Matt. 2:4-6). Later in this chapter John tells of people who could cite Scripture to show that the Messiah would be born in Bethlehem of David's line (7:41-42). But it is beyond doubt that some among the Jews held that the origin of the Messiah was quite unknown.

One way of expressing this was to say that he would suddenly "come up out of the heart of the sea" (4 Ezra 13:3). Another way

23. Lesslie Newbigin puts their attitude this way: "Is he really the Messiah? No—that is impossible. It is universally accepted that the coming of the Messiah will be a mystery. His origin will be unknown. 'The Lord whom you seek will come suddenly to his temple' (Mal. 3:1). But there is no mystery about this man: he is Jesus the carpenter from Nazareth in Galilee" (*The Light Has Come*, Grand Rapids, 1982, p. 97).

was to say that he would be "revealed", the implication being that he was existent, but not known to people as the Messiah until the revelation took place (4 Ezra 7:28; 13:32; 2 Bar. 29:3). This idea is found among the Rabbis, as when we read a saying of R. Zera: "Three come unawares: Messiah, a found article and a scorpion" (*Sanh.* 97a). The idea persisted, and in the second century Justin gives expression to it in some words of Trypho: "But Christ—if He has indeed been born, and exists anywhere—is unknown, and does not even know Himself, and has no power until Elias come to anoint Him, and make Him manifest to all."[24] The Jewish passages cited do not say expressly that Messiah's origin is unknown, but they presume that he will exist as a man in this world, quite unknown as Messiah until the time comes when God would have him commence his work. This idea may well have been derived from some Old Testament passages. Thus we read: "Behold, I send my messenger to prepare the way before me, and the Lord whom you seek will suddenly come to his temple; the messenger of the covenant in whom you delight, behold, he is coming, says the LORD of hosts. But who can endure the day of his coming, and who can stand when he appears?" (Mal. 3:1-2; cf. Dan. 9:25).

The idea that the origin of the Messiah is quite unknown was clearly the concept of messiahship that this section of the crowd had grasped. They say that they know where Jesus comes from (7:27), and therefore he is disqualified from being the Messiah. It is another piece of Johannine irony that if they really had known where Jesus came from, they would have known that he was indeed the Messiah. But their confident knowledge of his earthly family blinds them to the reality of his relationship to the heavenly Father.

Jesus uses this statement of the Jerusalemites to introduce some teaching about his origin. He starts from their claim: "So you know me, and you know where I am from!" (7:28). He does not dispute their claim, which in one sense was true: they knew that he came from Nazareth. But more important was the fact that they did not know that he came from God, they did not know that he was not on some self-chosen mission but had been sent by the

---

24. *Dialogus contra Tryphonem* 8; ANF, I, p. 199. I am not aware of any other passage that speaks of Elijah as anointing the Messiah.

heavenly Father. An important point throughout this Gospel is that Jesus had been sent,[25] and sent, as Jesus now says, by him who is true, "whom you do not know" (7:28). Being Messiah means (among other things) being sent by God.

A little later this question of origin comes up again. Some of the people were impressed by Jesus' teaching and thought he must be "the prophet" (i.e., the prophet of Deut. 18:15), which provoked others to say that he was the Christ (7:40-41). This was immediately rejected on the grounds that Jesus came from Galilee, whereas the Christ comes "of the seed of David and from Bethlehem, the town where David was" (7:42). They say, "the Scripture said", which usually denotes a definite passage in Scripture, but there is none that records the words they actually use. It seems that they are trying to give the general tenor of scriptural teaching. And since their Bible located the Messiah in Bethlehem, they held that it ruled out any possibility of a Galilean Christ.

Once again we have an example of John's irony. Had they but known it, their very objection was an attestation of Jesus' messiahship, for he was in fact born in Bethlehem. The irony may in fact go deeper, for the place of birth of God's Messiah here on earth is not nearly as important as the fact that his origin is in heaven and that it is the heavenly Father who has sent him on his mission.[26]

Opposition

In the discussions among the crowds in Jerusalem at which we have just been looking, it becomes clear that there were differing opinions about the Messiah. Some people felt that Jesus was indeed the Messiah, and some held that there were insuperable dif-

25. John uses *apostellō* 28 times and *pempō* 32 times, in both cases the most in any New Testament book. He uses both verbs for a variety of sendings. Thus the view that he uses one of them to denote sending on a mission and the other sending generally seems without foundation. More important is the fact that with both verbs in the majority of cases the sending by the Father is in mind (*apostellō* 17 times out of 28; *pempō* 24 times out of 32). That God has "sent" Jesus is one of the key thoughts of this Gospel. See further pp. 102-104 below.

26. Cf. Barrett, "all disputes about the birth place of the Messiah, the heavenly Man, are far wide of the point" (*The Gospel according to St. John*,[2] Philadelphia, 1978, p. 331).

ficulties in the way of holding such an opinion. It seems that among the rulers opinion was hardening since they declined to give credence to what Jesus was teaching. This comes out clearly in the story of the man blind from birth to whom Jesus gave sight. The miracle provoked spirited discussion, and the cured man put up a surprisingly strong argument when he was confronted by the Pharisees who wanted to condemn Jesus. At one point in the discussion "the Jews" (evidently the Jewish authorities) summoned the man's parents to ask how he had received his sight. They testified to the fact that the healed man was their son and that he had been born blind, but they would say nothing about how he had received his sight. John explains that they were afraid of the Jews, for the Jews had agreed "that if anyone confessed him to be Christ, he should be put out of the synagogue" (9:22).

The term I have translated "put out of the synagogue" (*aposynagōgos*) is not explained, but it is generally agreed that it means something like excommunication. The problem is that, while excommunication in some form is certainly ancient (cf. Ezra 10:8), there is very little information about what it involved and how it was carried out in New Testament times. The Mishnah says that Simeon b. Shetah spoke of pronouncing a ban against Onias the Circle-maker (*Taan.* 3:8), and since that Rabbi is dated *c.* 80 B.C. it is clear that the practice antedates New Testament times. At a later time there were two kinds of excommunication, *nidduy,* which lasted for 30 days, and *ḥērem,* a lifetime ban. Both cut the banned off from all normal dealings with the Jewish community, though apparently they could still join in worship (*Midd.* 2:2). The ban could be lifted if the elders thought it proper to do so.

All this makes it very curious that so many scholars assume that John is making an anachronistic statement here and reading back the practice of his own time into the time of Jesus.[27] The fact is that we have no more real knowledge of the way excommunication was practised at the time this Gospel was written (and for that matter, no real knowledge of the date of the Gospel)

27. Cf. Barnabas Lindars, "commentators generally see here, not a reference to punishments for normal offences, but the actual situation which obtained after the expulsion of the Minim in the late eighties of the first century" (*The Gospel of John,* London, 1972, p. 347).

than of what was done in Jesus' day. Specifically, while a general curse on heretics was included in the prayers towards the end of the first century and Christians may well have been included in this, we have no information about any formal excommunication of Christians until after any feasible date for this Gospel. There was certainly no automatic exclusion of Christians from the synagogue during the New Testament period, for in Acts we see them constantly at worship in the synagogues, and Paul, for example, seems to have made a practice of going to the synagogue first when he came to a new centre. But excommunication did exist, and opposition to Jesus did exist. We have no real reason for denying what John says;[28] our best understanding is that the Jerusalem authorities imposed some form of ban arising out of their hostility to Jesus, but that this was not yet a formal and lasting policy.

What John is telling us, then, is that some people were saying that Jesus was the Christ and that the Jerusalem authorities were imposing some form of punishment on anyone who did this. Again he is emphasizing the centrality of Jesus' messiahship and suggesting that it was important to hold to it even though it might mean suffering.

Perplexity about the Christ

What has been clear in the references to Jesus' messiahship we have looked at so far is that Jesus understood the term in a way very different from that held by most of his contemporaries. He did not often use the term, and it would seem that to a large extent this was because it would have given his hearers a wrong impression. They would have thought of him in terms of armies and battles and the overthrow of oppressors like the Romans. He was concerned with alienation from God, with the salvation of people from their sinful and self-centred lives, with the importance of love and lowly service rather than the selfish pursuit of one's own ends.

28. "It is questionable whether there is any inherent reason for declaring this to be unhistorical" (C. F. D. Moule, *The Birth of the New Testament*, London, 1962, p. 107).

This was bound to bring him into conflict with some of his hearers. John tells us of an incident at the time of the Feast of the Dedication when Jesus was walking in Solomon's colonnade. Some Jews crowded round him and asked a question whose meaning is not completely clear. Most translations agree with RSV, "How long will you keep us in suspense?" (10:24).[29] If this is the way the words are to be taken, the Jews are accusing Jesus of obscurity; he had not made his claims plain and they did not know whether he was saying that he was the Messiah or not. It is somewhat surprising that so many translations give this rendering since the Greek does not usually have this kind of meaning elsewhere.

An alternative is to understand the words as signifying something like, "Why do you take away our life?" This can be supported by the fact that no farther away than verse 18 we have an example of this verb with the meaning "No one takes it (i.e., my life) from me". If this is the way it is to be understood, then the Jews are discerning that the general thrust of Jesus' teaching meant the end of Judaism as they knew it (cf. the chief priests and the Pharisees in 11:48). He has told them that they will die in their sins unless they put their trust in him (8:21, 24), and the sheep not of this fold (10:16) seems to mean that he will have followers outside the fold of Judaism. The kind of Judaism with which they were familiar with all its exclusiveness and its contempt for the Gentiles is not compatible with such a program.

They realize that at the heart of it all is the question of Jesus' messiahship. If he really is the Messiah, that is one thing; if he is a false claimant, then it is quite another. As we have seen in our study of earlier passages, there is quite a bit in Jesus' teaching that makes it clear that he is indeed the Messiah, but his concept of messiahship is very different from that of the Jews in general. He will never be recognized as Messiah by people who are set in the old ways and cannot conceive of the Messiah as anything other than a conquering general. He can be recognized only by those who are really his sheep (10:26).

---

29. The Greek is *heōs pote tēn psychēn hēmōn aireis*; BAGD cite one passage where the expression has a meaning like RSV, but mostly in LXX *tēn psychēn airō* refers to lifting up the soul to God and the like (Ps. 25:1; 86:4, etc.).

So when they say to him, "If you are you the Christ, tell us plainly" (10:24), they are asking for something impossible. They did not understand what the Messiah would be like, so how could he give a plain reply to their demand? To answer either "Yes, I am" or "No, I am not" would be misleading. What Jesus does accordingly is to say, "I told you and you do not believe", and then to go on, "the works that I do in the name of my Father, these bear witness about me" (10:25). This can scarcely mean that Jesus has said anything like "I am the Messiah", for he has not done this (other than exceptionally to the woman of Samaria, 4:26, and the man born blind, 9:35-38). He is saying that "the works" are important. If his questioners had paid attention to what Jesus actually did instead of looking for him to tell them whether he fitted their specifications of the Messiah or not, they would have had the answer to their question. His deeds showed plainly enough that he had come from God to do God's will. His whole manner of life shows who he is.

"But", Jesus says, using the strong adversative, "*you* (emphatic) do not believe, because you are not of my sheep" (10:26). In recording these words John is making it clear that Jesus' messiahship is such that it is not visible to unbelievers. Those who set their face against the witness God provides will never see Jesus as Messiah. That does not mean that he is not the Messiah. He is. But being Messiah means doing the works that God has given him to do, and Jesus has done that.

Lifting Up the Messiah

In the chapter in which he concludes his account of the public ministry of Jesus, John tells us that the Master said to the people, "And I, if I be lifted up from the earth, will draw all people to myself", to which he adds this explanation, "This he spoke signifying by what death he would die" (12:32-33). This elicits a surprising response. The crowd sets itself in opposition to Jesus with some emphatic pronouns: "*We* have heard . . . how do *you* say. . . ?" (12:34). They are not going along with what he has said but recognizing opposing points of view. They say that they have heard from the law "that the Christ abides for ever"—which leads us to wonder where they got this from. While the sentiment is unobjectionable, it is not easy to see this teaching in the law and they cite no reference. They go on to ask, "How do *you* say that the Son of man must be lifted up? Who is this Son of man?" Apparently they recognize that being "lifted up" means dying, and they cannot reconcile this with their understanding of Scripture.

It is surely this that John has in mind. For the Jews the "lifting up" of Jesus on the cross, the sign of the curse of God (Deut. 21:22-23), showed that he could not possibly be the Messiah. For John, being lifted up on the cross was the heart of messiahship. Once again this Evangelist is making it clear that Jesus is the Messiah but that the character of his messiahship is all too readily misunderstood by many of his hearers. Being Messiah, as John was conveying the thought to his readers, was not a matter of a victorious military campaign followed by a reign in splendid earthly magnificence. It was a death on a cross.

The truth about messiahship could be recognized, and John has given an example in the case of Martha. When her brother died and Jesus came to the sisters, he said that the person who lives and believes in him will never die, and asked Martha, "Do you believe this?" She replied, "Yes, Lord. I believe that you are the Christ, the Son of God, he who comes into the world" (11:26-27). The words match up with those John uses when he writes of the purpose of his Gospel (20:30-31). They show that there were people who could understand something of his messiahship and enter into life by believing in him.[30]

That true messiahship meant something very different from messiahship as it was currently understood among the Jews is made clear by some words in the great prayer recorded in chapter 17, where we read, "And this is life eternal, that they may know you, the only true God, and him whom you sent, Jesus Christ" (17:3). Here messiahship is linked with eternal life, and this life is understood as the knowledge of God and of Jesus the Messiah. We are a long way from armies and battles and politics and all the paraphernalia of Jewish messianism. This is the case also when

30. Cf. J. C. Ryle, "Dark and dim as her views were, it was a great thing for a solitary Jewish woman to have got hold of so much truth, when within two miles, in Jerusalem, all who held such a creed as hers were excommunicated and persecuted" (*Expository Thoughts on the Gospels, St. John,* II, London, 1957, p. 300).

John tells us that the reason for writing his book is "that you may believe that Jesus is the Christ, the Son of God", and adds, "and that believing you may have life in his name" (20:31). It is important that the readers of this book understand what "Messiah" means because it is only by seeing what "Messiah" really means and seeing also that Jesus was that Messiah that they will believe in him and so will enter into life. Small wonder that throughout his book John has given such close attention to the importance of understanding what Messiah signifies. He has sometimes done this by drawing attention to things that Jesus said and did, and sometimes he has preferred to bring out the true meaning of Messiah by citing the erroneous views of the Jews of the day and letting his readers appreciate the falsity of such views. But throughout he has made it clear that Jesus was indeed the Messiah of Jewish expectation and that in him all the messianic hopes and promises find their fulfilment.

CHAPTER 5

The Son of God

THE NORMAL USE OF THE TERM "SON", IN SCRIPTURE as everywhere else, is to denote a male child. There are hundreds of examples in the Old Testament, and it would be superfluous to cite passages. Less usual and more interesting for our present inquiry is the fact that the term may be used metaphorically. Thus the aged Eli called to Samuel, "Samuel, my son" (1 Sam. 3:16), and King Saul more than once referred to "my son David" (1 Sam. 26:17, 21, 25). A related usage is that which we see so often in Proverbs wherein the teacher addresses his pupil in this way: "My son, keep my words and treasure up my commandments with you" (Prov. 7:1). The general proposition may be laid down: "A son honors his father, and a servant his master" (Mal. 1:6). Perhaps from this kind of reasoning we are to understand the use when a man describes himself as the son of someone to whom he is not related, presumably to indicate submission and perhaps affection. King Ahaz did this when he tried to enlist the help of Tiglath-pileser; he sent a message beginning, "I am your servant and your son" (2 Kings 16:7). Or it may figure in a claim to superiority, as in the words attributed to Pharaoh: "I am a son of the wise, a son of ancient kings" (Isa. 19:11).

Since the Hebrew language is not as strong in adjectives as some languages, a frequent substitute is "the son of —."[1] Thus "brave men" may be called "sons of valor" (Deut. 3:18), while "an evil man" is "a son of wickedness" (Ps. 89:22). People in trouble are "sons of affliction" (Prov. 31:5). "Son" may be called in to help in indications of time, as when we find that Noah was a "son of five hundred years" (Gen. 5:32) or in the regulation that "a son of

---

1. For this construction see A. E. Cowley's revision of E. Kautzsch, *Gesenius' Hebrew Grammar* (Oxford, 1910), p. 418.

eight days" is to be circumcised (Gen. 17:12). People worthy of death may be called "sons of death" (1 Sam. 26:16). It is perhaps in this area that we should understand the reference to the "Day Star, son of Dawn" (Isa. 14:12).[2] It is the star we see in the early morning.

All this prepares us for some element of metaphor when "son" is used in the Old Testament in relation to God. Occasionally the term is used of the angels (Job 1:6; 38:7), presumably because of their closeness to God and the way they do the will of God. A second way of using the concept is seen when the nation is regarded as a unit, for example when God says, "Israel is my firstborn son" (Exod. 4:22; this is followed by "Let my son go . . ."). This is a way of bringing out God's love and care for his people. The first-born son was regarded with special affection in a typical family, and that is the way Yahweh sees Israel. In this strain also Jeremiah tells us that the Lord asked, "Is Ephraim my dear son? Is he my darling child?" (Jer. 31:20).[3] Such passages bring out the truth that God has a deep love for his people, a love that may be expressed in terms of family connection. It also implies that those loved in this way will respond with affection and obedience. Thus "Let my son go" is followed by "that he may serve me" (Exod. 4:23), and not long after "Is Ephraim my dear son?" we find, "Set up waymarks for yourself, make yourself guideposts. . . . Return, O virgin Israel" (Jer. 31:21-22).

A third use is when God's love is exercised towards an individual. Thus the word of the LORD came to David, saying with respect to Solomon, "He shall be my son, and I will be his father" (1 Chron. 22:10).[4] There can be no doubting that these words indicate both a depth of love for Solomon and the thought that the

2. John Mauchline comments, "the term, from a verbal root meaning 'to shine brightly', means the morning star, which is particularly bright throughout the Near East; it fades out before the rising sun" (*Isaiah 1–39*, London, 1962, p. 140).

3. J. A. Thompson comments, "Yahweh's reply to a cry of repentance is to assure Ephraim of his deep longing that Ephraim should return to him. The thought of this verse is strongly reminiscent of Hos. 11:1-4, 8-9. The terms of endearment are different but the love is the same, *my dear son, a child in whom I delight* or 'my darling child' " (*The Book of Jeremiah*, Grand Rapids, 1980, p. 575).

4. James D. Newsome, Jr., says, "one cannot escape the conclusion that the Chronicler's view of history included the declaration not only that God stood in a close supervisory relationship to Israel's history in the past, but also that he would

young man was commissioned to do an important work for God, the building of the temple. Both love and service are involved. The Israelites did not think their king was a demigod as was the case with a number of nations in antiquity, but this passage shows that in the case of Solomon at any rate there was a specially close relationship to Yahweh. There is no reason for doubting that later kings applied the same kind of thinking to their own situations and that they thought they were God's sons.

Another reference to a king as God's son comes in Psalm 2: "I will tell of the decree of the LORD: He said to me, 'You are my son, today I have begotten you'" (Ps. 2:7). This psalm clearly refers to the accession of an Israelite king, and "today" indicates that the time of his enthronement is in mind. The New Testament writers paid a good deal of attention to this psalm and saw it as pointing forward to Christ, and indeed as finding its fulfilment only in him (cf. Acts 4:25-26; 13:33; Heb. 1:5; 5:5).[5] It certainly makes use of language that is not easy to apply to any Israelite king of whom we have knowledge and that we see reaching its fulfilment in Jesus Christ.

There is thus some Old Testament preparation for the New Testament use of the expression "the Son of God", although in the nature of the case there can be no exact parallel. But these Old Testament passages point us to the truth that "son" may be used to bring out something of the love and esteem God has for his people. There is also the thought that that love should be returned and that the loved one should respond with obedience and service. From another point of view Psalm 2 in particular uses language that the church has always seen as applying in its fulness only to Christ.

The Only Son

When we turn to John's Gospel, we should first notice a little peculiarity of John's usage. He employs the word *huios* in the

---

do so in the future" (*JBL* 94, 1975, p. 210). H. G. M. Williamson, however, holds that "although this verse may have contributed to messianic formulations, it should not itself be so interpreted" (*1 and 2 Chronicles,* London and Grand Rapids, 1982, p. 155).

5. Cf. Derek Kidner, "A greater, however, than David or Solomon was needed to justify the full fury of these threats and the glory of these promises" (*Psalms 1–71,* London, 1973, p. 50).

normal way for a son in an ordinary family (e.g., 4:46), and he uses it also of Christ as the Son in the heavenly family. But although he uses the word "Father" for the Father of us all (cf. "your Father", 20:17, and the claim of the Jews in 8:41), he never uses "son" for the other members of the heavenly family. This is not so elsewhere in the New Testament. Paul, for example, uses *huios* quite freely for the human "sons" of the heavenly Father. But whenever John uses "son" with respect to the heavenly Father, he always means Christ. For the human members of the family he prefers to use *tekna*, "children" (e.g., 1:12). In this unobtrusive way he makes a distinction between believers and the Christ. We may certainly claim membership in the heavenly family; John insists on that. But we must bear in mind that our sonship is not the same as that of Christ. His relationship to the Father is special.

John brings out the uniqueness of that relationship by referring to Christ as God's "only" Son, for example when he says, "God so loved the world that he gave his only (*monogenē*) Son" (3:16). The adjective *monogenēs* has sometimes been understood in the sense "only-begotten", but we should bear in mind the fact that it derives from *gen–*, the stem of *ginomai*, not *gennaō* (one *n*, not two); it is "only-being" rather than "only-begotten". But it certainly points to uniqueness. It may be used of an only child (Luke 7:12; 8:42; 9:38), but perhaps we see more of its distinctiveness when we notice that it is used of Isaac as Abraham's "unique" son (Heb. 11:17). Isaac was not Abraham's only son, for he had many sons (Ishmael, Gen. 16:11; the sons of Keturah and of his concubines, Gen. 25:1-6). But Isaac was unique: he was the son given to Abraham and Sarah as the result of the promise of God. The people of God were to be descended from him and not from any of the other sons of Abraham.

That Jesus Christ is God's *monogenēs* then means that he is "Son of God" in a unique way. Others may be called "sons of God", but they are not "sons" in the same sense. They are sons in some such sense as Solomon was, but when he uses the term of Jesus John is not saying the same thing as was the writer of 1 Chronicles when he used the term of Solomon. He is saying that no one else stands in the same relationship to God the Father as does Jesus Christ. Christ is the Son of God not only in the sense that he is the object of God's love, but also in the sense that his being is bound up with the being of the Father.

This is seen also in the fact that John tells us that the gift of the Son shows, not simply the love of Jesus, but the love of God. If the Father and the Son were two completely separate beings, then the death of Jesus might show us the love of the Son, but it would scarcely show us the love of the Father. That it shows us the love of the Father means that in some sense the Father and the Son are one; the act of the one is the act of the other.

We might perhaps deduce this also from the further statement about the fate of unbelievers. The person who does not believe in Christ, John tells us, "has already been condemned, because he has not believed in the name of the only Son of God" (3:18). The condemnation that stands over against eternal life must be viewed as the most serious of all condemnations, and that it comes about because of a wrong attitude to the Son shows clearly that the Son is possessed of a superior dignity. His position is that of deity.

Believing "in the name" means, of course, believing in all that the name stands for. In biblical times "the name" stood for the whole person and somehow summed up the whole person. To believe in Jesus' "name" thus means to believe in him as the one who came from God, taught the things of God, died in the service of God, and rose in the power of God. In the Prologue we find that those who are members of the heavenly family are those who "believe in his name" (1:12), and when John first speaks of Jesus in Jerusalem he says that many believed in his name because they saw the signs he was doing (2:23). And at the end we learn that this whole Gospel was written so that people might believe, and "believing have life in his name" (20:31).

The most frequent use of Jesus' "name" comes in passages dealing with prayer. Jesus tells his followers that he will grant "whatever you ask" in his name (14:13); it is important that here it is Jesus, not the Father, who will answer the prayer and, further, that this answering means that "the Father will be glorified in the Son" (*ibid.*). Jesus repeats the promise immediately (14:14); it is clearly important. But prayer may also be to the Father in the name of the Son (15:16); thus it is interesting that Jesus urges his followers to live fruitful lives in order that they may have this kind of prevailing prayer. We generally think of the importance of praying in order that we may live fruitfully. This way of putting it makes it clear that prayer is very important in itself. Prayer to the Father in the name of the Son will surely result in our receiving what we ask (16:23). Throughout the Son's life on earth the disciples had not prayed in this way, but now this is the way they should pray so that their joy may be filled full (16:24). Jesus looks forward to the day when they will pray like this (16:26).

Sometimes "the name" is used in connection with the service Jesus' followers will render. People will persecute them "on account of (his) name" (15:21). From another point of view Jesus speaks of the sheep hearing the voice of their own shepherd (10:3), which surely refers to more than animal husbandry. His own followers know his voice, whereas the world does not. And it is important for their service that in due course the Father will send the Holy Spirit, and he will send him "in the name" of Jesus (14:26).

Already in his Prologue John has a striking statement about the Word in which he makes use of this adjective. "The Word became flesh and dwelt among us," he writes, "and we saw his glory, glory as of an only one with the Father, full of grace and truth" (1:14). The glory that is proper to one with a unique relationship to the Father must be supreme glory indeed. We have had occasion to notice that John often uses the concept of glory in the sense of "humble glory", the glory of someone who is entitled to a high place but who leaves that in order to render lowly service. We need not doubt that this is the meaning here, but we should notice further that the glory in question is described as that of one uniquely related to the Father.

That it is full of grace and truth underlines this. It is curious that John uses the term "grace" four times only (all in the Prologue), for the concept of grace runs through his whole Gospel. One who is "full of grace" is thus one who is supremely important. We must add the same when "truth" is added to "grace", for truth is another of the important ideas in this Gospel.

John has one further use of *monogenēs*, namely when he says that no one has ever seen God and adds either that "only God"

94

or "the only Son" has declared him (1:18).[6] The textual problem is interesting, but most recent scholars, it would seem correctly, hold that "God" is likely to have stood in the original text.[7] Whichever we read, John is ascribing a unique place to the Word. It is he and he only who has brought people to know God as he really is. The Word is said here to be "in the bosom of the Father", and however this be understood it points to the closest possible relationship to the Father.

From all this it is clear that when John uses *monogenēs* of Christ he is ascribing to him a unique relationship to the Father, a relationship shared by no one else. In the passages we are about to consider, John uses the term "Son" to indicate that relationship, and this is the term theologians generally use to bring out Christ's uniqueness. Others may be "sons of God", but in the full sense there is only one "Son of God". It is this unique Son of whom John writes and in whose hands is the final destiny of us all.

The Son of God

John does not have the expression "the Son of God" very often.[8] We find it in many manuscripts early in the Gospel when the Baptist says, "I have seen and have borne witness that this is the Son of God" (1:34). Some significant manuscripts, however, have "God's Chosen One" (so NEB, JB), and since scribes would be more likely to alter this reading into "the Son of God" than the reverse procedure, it is not unlikely that it is original. Whichever reading we adopt, these words come as the climax of a passage in which the Baptist explains that Jesus is the one who came after him but was really before him, a way of explaining that Jesus was greater by far than he. He goes on to say that, although he did not know him, he had come baptizing people in water in order that in due course this great one should be made manifest to Israel. He

6. BAGD give the meaning *"an only-begotten one, God* (acc. to his real being), or *a God begotten of the Only One."*

7. See the note in Bruce M. Metzger, *A Textual Commentary on the Greek New Testament* (London and New York, 1971), p. 198.

8. But S. E. Johnson can say, " 'Son of God' is the title of Jesus most characteristic of the Gospel of John" (*IDB*, IV, p. 412). He probably includes passages referring to "the Son".

goes on to say that he saw the Holy Spirit coming down on him in the form of a dove and staying on him. He says again that he did not know him but that he who sent him to baptize in water had told him that the one on whom he saw the Spirit descending and remaining was the one who would baptize in Holy Spirit. It is after this explanation that the Baptist concludes: "And I have seen, and have borne witness that this is the Son of God (or, God's Chosen One)" (1:30-34).[9] Clearly the lengthy buildup to the saying is a way of underlining the importance of the one to whom the title is applied. The Baptist is making it clear that Jesus is someone very special: he is giving the title all the meaning he can put into it.[10]

There is another "Son of God" passage in this first chapter, namely when the guileless Nathanael, having found that Jesus knew of his experience under the fig tree (whatever that was), immediately responds with, "Rabbi, *You* are the Son of God, *You* are the King of Israel" (1:49). No more than the Baptist does Nathanael explain what he means by "the Son of God", but the circumstances call for a full content for the expression. Jesus has just astonished an initially sceptical man (1:46) with a display of knowledge both of Nathanael's character ("truly an Israelite in whom there is no guile", 1:47) and of some important experience the man had had (1:48). So when he hails him as "the Son of God", he is saying something significant. We see this also in the fact that he joins with it "the King of Israel". If we are inclined to play this down a little

9. Dom John Howton argues that both the Baptist and Nathanael used the expression "the Son of God" and that in reporting this "St John was not . . . disturbing the order of events, that he reports fact and not his own interpretation of the fact in thus reproducing the words of the Baptist to whom the title already meant something; and that the remainder of the Gospel then helps to bring out and underline the implications inherent in the early confession. On the one hand St John wanted to show the comprehensiveness of the title as used by these early followers, and, on the other hand, at the same time to underline its inadequacy, in the sense understood by John and Nathanael, and to give its meaning a content far fuller than they could have imagined" (*NTS* 10, 1963-64, p. 227).

10. Raymond E. Brown accepts the view that the meaning is "God's chosen one", and finds in the expression an echo of Isa. 42:1. Of the passage 1:19-34 he says, "When we look back on the wealth and depth of the material contained in the intervening verses, we appreciate John's genius at incorporating a whole christology into one brief scene" (*The Gospel according to John (i–xii)*, New York, 1966, pp. 66-67).

after "the Son of God", we should bear in mind that for Nathanael it was probably something of a climax.[11] For him no title could be higher than "the King of the Jews".

But at the time this Gospel was written its believing readers would undoubtedly regard "the Son of God" as the more significant, and they would do so in the full light of Nathanael's experience. What Jesus had done on the occasion when he met this man was more than any mere earthling could possibly do, be he King of Israel or of any other kingdom. It showed that he stood in a relationship to God such that no created being could possibly share in it, and thus put a profound meaning into "the Son of God". It is perhaps worth noting that John's account of Jesus' encounter with those who were to become his followers ends on the same note as the account of his baptism in the Synoptic Gospels —he is hailed as God's Son (Matt. 3:17; Mark 1:11; Luke 3:22). Early in all four Gospels the point is made firmly.

We have already noticed a further use of the title when John tells us that those who believe have life, while anyone who does not believe "is condemned already, because he has not believed in the name of the only Son of God" (3:18). With this we may take Jesus' words, "an hour is coming and now is, when the dead will hear the voice of the Son of God, and those who hear will live" (5:25). The addition of "and now is" to "an hour is coming" seems to show that Jesus is referring to the present and is speaking of the life that he gives here and now to the spiritually dead. But he goes on say that all who are in the tombs will hear his voice; they will come out for the resurrection of life or of condemnation (5:28-29). That he gives life now and that at the end of the age he will call people from the grave into their final state show plainly that his divinity is to be taken seriously.

The term comes up again in a dispute Jesus has with the Jews in which they attempt to stone him (10:31) because, they say, he is making himself God (10:33; later they will repeat the accusa-

11. Cf. Raymond E. Brown, "His kingdom does not belong to this world (xviii 36); and his subjects are not Jews but believers. It is Nathanael, the genuine Israelite, who hails him; and therefore 'the King of Israel' must be understood as the king of those like Nathanael who believe. In this sense, this title is climactic in the series of titles that we have seen" (*The Gospel according to John (i–xii)*, p. 87).

tion before Pilate, 19:7). Jesus quotes Psalm 82:6 to point out that the term "gods" may sometimes be used of men, and goes on, "of him whom the Father sanctified and sent into the world do you say, 'You are blaspheming', because I said, 'I am the Son of God'?" (10:36).[12] We should not take this passage to mean that Jesus is simply classing himself with other men. He specifically says that the Father sanctified him and sent him into the world. And if there is no other passage recorded in which Jesus specifically said, "I am the Son of God", yet this was clear from his general claims and the way he had spoken of his relationship to the Father. He does not think he should be stoned for what he said, but he certainly claims to stand in a unique relationship to the Father.

A little later we find Jesus saying that the sickness of Lazarus was not with a view to death but "for the glory of God, so that the Son of God should be glorified through it" (11:4). In the narrative leading up to the raising of the dead man John records Martha's matchless confession, "Lord, I have believed that *you* are the Christ, the Son of God, he who comes into the world" (11:27), a confession that matches pretty well John's declared aim in writing his book (20:31). When this confession is taken also in the light of the fact that the words are recorded in the context of calling back Lazarus from the dead, we should see yet once more that John is giving expression to the full deity of the Christ.

The Son

As our discussion has shown, John uses the expression "the Son of God" a number of times. But he prefers to say simply "the Son", and the way he uses this expression shows that he means much the same as when he uses the fuller "the Son of God". The shorter

12. Oscar Cullmann remarks, "The fourth evangelist certainly appeals to an old tradition here when he sees the 'blasphemy' not in the messianic claim but in Jesus' claim (veiled though it may be) to sonship. His messianic claim was really offensive only to the Romans. To the Jews, on the other hand, the claim to sonship in the particular form represented by Jesus' self-consciousness gave the most offence, for they correctly interpret Jesus' claim to be 'Son' as identification with God: '... you, being a man, make yourself God' (John 10.33)" (*The Christology of the New Testament,* London, 1959, p. 302).

expression points us to the closeness of the tie that binds Christ to the Father, just as the longer one does.

John may record sayings that stress the closeness of the two.[13] Thus we read, "the Father loves the Son, and has given all things into his hand" (3:35), where both the love and the giving of "all things" are important. The Father's love is spoken of again in 5:20, this time linked with knowledge, for the Father has shown him all the things that he himself does. It would be possible to speak of the Father's love for created beings (we have his love for "the world" in 3:16), but the gift of all things and the conveying of the knowledge of all that the Father does lift these passages out of those that may apply to people such as we are. They show us that the Son is to be understood on a higher plane.

It follows from this that the life of the Son is closely bound up with that of the Father. Indeed, Jesus says, "I and the Father are one" (10:30). We should not read too much into "one", for the word is neuter, not masculine; it means "one thing", not "one person". It is worth bearing in mind that Paul can say in similar fashion, "he who plants and he who waters are one" (1 Cor. 3:8). For that matter John records the prayer in which Jesus asks that his followers "may be one as we are" (17:11). In both these passages we have the same neuter "one" as in 10:30. But if we must not push the expression too far, we must not minimize it either. It certainly does speak of a close unity, and it is significant that Jesus begins with "I and the Father"; who else could link himself with God in this way? Moreover, we must bear in mind that the Jews would not have regarded a statement that Jesus was conforming his will to that of the Father as blasphemy, but they did regard these words as blasphemous,[14] as the immediately following words show (vv. 31-33). He is claiming a unity with the Father closer than any unity that others can claim.

Elsewhere that unity is clear when Jesus says that he can do

13. Martin Hengel comments, "The danger of ditheism was also averted, for the Son was involved in a complete union of action and love with the Father (John 3.35; 8.19, 28, 40; cf. 1.18; 10.30; 17.11, 21-26)" (*The Son of God*, London, 1976, pp. 91-92).

14. Cf. E. C. Hoskyns, "the Jews would not presumably have treated as blasphemy the idea that a man could regulate his words and actions according to the will of God" (*The Fourth Gospel*, London, 1947, p. 389).

nothing of himself, only what he sees the Father doing, and adds that whatever the Father does, the Son does likewise (5:19). This leads us on to the thought that the Son gives life to whom he wills, just as the Father raises the dead and gives them life (5:21). This is not unlike the later statement that the Son gives freedom (8:36). People are naturally caught up in slavery to sin, which is their handicap through life and the cause of condemnation when they die. But the Son came to deliver people from this predicament: he gives freedom now, and he gives life in the world to come. We get the same thought from another angle when we read, "He who believes on the Son has life eternal; but he who disobeys[15] the Son will not see life, but the wrath of God remains on him" (3:36). It is our attitude to the Son that is finally decisive: if we believe in him we have life, whereas if we do not, we can look forward only to the wrath of God.

This truth may be expressed in another way. The Father, we read, "has given all judgment to the Son" (5:22); he "has given him authority to execute judgment because he is the Son of man" (5:27).[16] Jewish writings do not ascribe the function of final judgment to the Messiah; this is a teaching we find for the first time in the New Testament.[17] John is thus not enunciating a commonplace; he is giving new and distinctive teaching. It is teaching, moreover,

---

15. There is discussion about the meaning of *apeithōn*. The structure of the sentence is such that we would expect "he who does not believe" (cf. JB, "refuses to believe"). BAGD sum up the position: "since, in the view of the early Christians, the supreme disobedience was a refusal to believe their gospel, ἀ may be restricted in some passages to the mng. *disbelieve, be an unbeliever*. This sense, though greatly disputed (it is not found outside our lit.), seems most probable in J 3:36. . . ." Probably our discussion of the exact meaning is somewhat academic, for the rejection of the gospel surely involves both unbelief and disobedience.

16. Some hold that we should understand this in the sense "a son of man" and take the meaning to be that Jesus can execute judgment because his humanity is real; he knows human life and is qualified to be our judge. But this seems a slender qualification for such an important function; after all, this could be said of every member of the human race. It is much more likely that we should see here an example of Colwell's rule (*JBL* 52, 1933, pp. 12-21), that when the predicate precedes the verb (as it does here) it should be taken as definite unless the context positively excludes this. It is "the" Son of man, not "a" son of man, that is meant.

17. Cf. SBk, "According to the Rabbinic view it is exclusively God who will judge the world. . . . In Rabbinic literature there is no passage which unam-

that makes it clear that the Son has a high dignity. To be the one who determines the eternal destiny of all the race is to have a very high position indeed.

This high dignity is to be seen also in the honor accorded the Son. Indeed, Jesus says that judgment is given into his hands "in order that all may honor the Son even as they honor the Father." To this is added the rider, "He that does not honor the Son does not honor the Father who sent him" (5:23).[18] This is typical Johannine doctrine. The Father and the Son are to be considered together: the honor given the one must be given to the other, and anyone who fails in his duty to the one fails also in his duty to the other. The Jews were ready to give honor to the Father, but their failure to recognize what the Father was doing in the Son meant that they were failing in their rendering of honor to the Father. They did not see him as the one who in the person of his Son came to earth to live in lowliness and to bring salvation to all who believe. That God was in Christ is very important for our understanding of the nature of the Father as well as that of the Son.[19] If in fact God was not incarnate in Christ, then in the last resort when people had gone astray in sin God in effect said, "I'll send someone to bring them back." If God was incarnate in Christ, he said in effect, "I'll go myself." There is all the difference in a God who saves sinners himself and a God who asks someone else to do this. That surely is what is in mind when we read, "God is love" (1 John 4:8, 16). We cannot put full meaning into the love of God if in the end God leaves the task of salvation to someone else. We must see this behind the words of John 5. When people refuse to give the Son the honor they give the Father, they are not only coming short in the honor they ought to be giving the Son but they are also coming short in the honor they ought to be giving the Father.

We have had occasion to notice that the concept of glory in the Fourth Gospel is complex and that there is an unexpected emphasis on lowliness associated with it. But for our present pur-

biguously places the judgment of the world in the hand of the Messiah" (II, p. 465).

18. Ernst Haenchen stresses the connection with judgment: "if the son is the almighty world judge, then Christians will take care not to withhold appropriate honor to this powerful figure" (*John*, I, Philadelphia, 1984, p. 251).

19. Cf. D. Moody Smith, in Christ, the Word, "the God who creates the world

pose we should notice that the Father and the Son are associated in glory as in honor. Thus Jesus tells the disciples that they may pray with confidence, for "whatever you ask in my name, this will I do, in order that the Father may be glorified in the Son" (14:13). It is striking that he says that he himself will answer their prayers, and it is important to realize that the purpose of this is not that the Son should be glorified, but that the Father should be glorified. He will be glorified in the Son, it is true, but it is the Father who will be glorified in what the Son does. The glory of the two is inseparable.

This comes out again in Jesus' prayer on the eve of the passion when he says, "Father, the hour has come; glorify your Son, in order that the Son may glorify you" (17:1). With the cross in immediate view there is something of the humble glory concept here, the idea that true glory is to be seen in taking the lowly place.[20] But the important thing for our present purpose is the linking of the Father and the Son, and that in terms of glory. Jesus looks to the Father to glorify him in order that he may glorify the Father: in some sense the two glories are one; they are bound up with one another.

The Sending of the Son

"God did not send the Son into the world to condemn the world, but so that the world might be saved through him" (3:17). The thought that the Son has been "sent" into the world is a very important one for John. He does not very often explicitly connect the sending and the title "Son", but the idea that Jesus has been sent is very frequent and "the Father who sent me" is an expression that recurs (5:37; 6:44; 8:16, etc.). We also read often of "him who sent me" (6:38; 7:16; 12:44, etc.). John uses both *pempō* and *apostel-*

---

now saves it from its evil and folly. . . . The God who creates through his Word also reveals himself and saves through the same Word" (*John*, Philadelphia, 1976, p. 25).

20. Walter Lüthi emphasizes this: "He has shown the splendour of His Father's glory in the blind and lame, in lepers, in the rich and the poor, and even in the dead. The world is corrupt, groping in darkness and ignorance, and choked with indifference or hatred towards God and His cause, and the name of God is abused daily. . . . He glorifies God by establishing the commandments of His Father in Heaven, wherever He passes in this sordid world, and by respecting the

lō in such expressions, and seems to put little difference between them. Some have argued that one of these verbs means "send with a special commission" while the other refers to the general idea of sending, but unfortunately there is no agreement as to which does which.[21] We should take this as another example of John's habit of using synonyms without any great difference of meaning. It is the thought that God has "sent" the Son that matters, not any precise differentiation between various words for sending.

And as we noticed at the beginning of this section, the sending of the Son has to do with salvation. John is clear that there are those who do not believe and whose ultimate fate is loss, but he makes it clear that in sending the Son it was not God's purpose to bring condemnation. He sent the Son so that people might be saved. John applies the concept of sending to others than the Son, such as the Baptist (1:6, 33) or the disciples (4:38; 13:20), but in the overwhelming majority of cases "sending" means that the Father has sent the Son. And John is much more interested in this concept of mission than is any other writer: he uses both verbs for sending more often than in any other book in the New Testament.[22]

For our present purpose it is important to notice the references to Jesus as having been sent "into the world" (3:17; 10:36; 17:18). The clear implication in each case is that he has been sent from heaven,[23] and thus that heaven is his proper abode. John does not explicitly say "sent from heaven", but he does say "sent" and he does say that Jesus came from heaven (3:13, 31; 6:33, etc.).

---

will of God even to the point of dying on the Cross" (*St John's Gospel*, Edinburgh and London, 1960, p. 236).

21. Thus B. F. Westcott takes *apostellō* as conveying the notion "of a special commission" and *pempō* as denoting "nothing more than the immediate relation of the sender to the sent" (*The Gospel according to St. John*, Grand Rapids reprint, II, 1954, p. 358; K. H. Rengstorf makes a similar distinction in *TDNT*, I, pp. 398ff.). But E. A. Abbott thinks that "*apostellō* means 'sending away into the world at large,' but *pempō* 'sending on a special errand'" (*Johannine Vocabulary*, London, 1905, 1723g). See further Chapter 4, n. 24.

22. John uses *apostellō* 28 times (next is Luke with 25) and *pempō* 32 times (Luke has it ten times). He employs the former verb for the Father's sending of the Son 17 times out of 28, and the latter 24 times out of 32. Clearly what is of central significance for him is the mission on which the Father sent the Son.

23. James D. G. Dunn goes so far as to say, "where in the Synoptics the language properly denotes a sense of divine commissioning . . . here the thought is

Throughout his Gospel he is telling us that Jesus cannot be understood simply as another earthly person. He has a special relation to the Father, a special commission from the Father, and he has come to this earth from heaven. This is to recognize that he has a very special place, a place appropriate to the only Son of God and to him alone.

If it is true that he was sent from heaven, it is also true that he will return there. Thus Jesus tells the Jews, "I am with you still for a little while, and I go to him who sent me" (7:33). On another occasion in the course of a discussion he contrasted himself with the Jews: "I know where I came from and where I am going, but *you* (emphatic) do not know where I came from or where I am going" (8:14). Even if they look for him they will not be able to find him, for they simply cannot come where he is going (8:21-22). As he introduces the narrative of the upper room John tells his readers that Jesus "had come out from God and that he was going to God" (13:3), and in the discourse that follows there is a good deal of emphasis on the thought of his going away.[24] John goes on to say that as Jesus contemplated death he said, "Now I am going to him who sent me" (16:5), which is further explained as, "I am going to the Father" (16:10). It is impossible to interpret this discourse as though Jesus meant that his death and its sequel were to be no more than what happened to any man when he died. The whole passage clearly assigns to Jesus a destiny quite unlike that which the rest of the race faces. Jesus is one with the Father in a way that they are not.[25]

---

explicitly of the Son as having been *'sent* (from heaven) into the world'" (*Christology in the Making*, London, 1980, p. 56).

24. Discussing the passage John 13:31–14:31 C. H. Dodd says, "The whole dialogue, indeed, is dominated by the ideas of going and coming. Verbs expressing these ideas (*hypagein, poreuesthai, erchesthai*) occur at least fourteen times, with Christ as subject; and the longest passage without direct reference to going and coming is not more than five verses. This dialogue in fact is occupied with the interpretation of the death and resurrection of Christ" (*The Interpretation of the Fourth Gospel*, Cambridge, 1953, p. 403).

25. C. F. D. Moule says that "the Johannine school" in common with certain other New Testament writers held that Jesus belongs "in a category other than that to which the believer hoped to belong at the end. Jesus is exalted to God's right hand, he is uniquely one with the Father and close to him, and he is the origin and the active initiator of all that the believer may hope—derivatively and by dependence on him—to become. This distinction between the divine, creative initiative

The Son and Life

There is a difficult saying in the discourse about the Son in John 5 in which Jesus says, "As the Father has life in himself, so also he has given to the Son to have life in himself" (5:26). It is the consistent teaching of the Bible that the Father is the source of all life: "with thee is the fountain of life" (Ps. 36:9). All other life is contingent. We have our existence, but, important as that is to each of us, it is alas true that everything would go on much as it is without us. The universe managed before we made our appearance, and it will doubtless survive our deaths. But we cannot say that about the life of God. His life is not contingent, but necessary. "The Father is self-existent", as Goodspeed translates 5:26 (JB prefers "is the source of life"). Augustine put it this way. God "does not, as it were, borrow life, nor, as it were, become a partaker of life, of a life which is not what Himself is; but 'hath life in Himself,' so that the very life is to Him His very self." He proceeds to give an illustration from light. We do not have physical light within ourselves, but require an external source of light: "since you remain in darkness when the candle is withdrawn, you have not light in yourselves."[26] So it is with life. We do not have life within ourselves. But God does. His relationship to life is not the same as ours.

What John is telling us is that the Son has the same "self-existent" life as does the Father. It is not separable from that of the Father, for it is the gift of the Father. But it aligns the Son with the Father over against all creation.[27] The point is important for John, and he brings it out early in his Prologue when he says of the Word, "in him was life, and the life was the light of men" (1:4). Later when Jesus speaks of himself as "the bread of life" and says that he "gives life to the world" (6:33), he is claiming to be the source of life for all the race. It is much the same when he says that he is the light of the world and that anyone who fol-

---

and human response and dependence and creatureliness seems to be clear" (*The Origin of Christology,* Cambridge, 1977, p. 103).

26. *On the Gospel of St. John,* NPNF, I, vii, p. 126.

27. F. Büchsel draws attention to 1 John 4:14, "The Father sent the Son to be the Saviour of the world", and reasons, "by His sending He who was already the Son became the Saviour, so that there is no room for doubt that the pre-existent

lows him "will have the light of life" (8:12). If anything, he goes beyond even that when he says that he is himself "the life" (11:25; 14:6). The relationship of the Son to life is not the same as that of all created beings, and this tells us something significant about the being of the Son. He belongs with God.

We should probably add here a reference to Jesus' words on the occasion when he told some of the Jews that to commit sin was to be sin's slave. He went on, "Now the slave does not remain in the house for ever; the son remains for ever" (8:35). In the context Jesus is contrasting any son with any slave. A slave has no rights. He may in fact remain in the same household all his life, but he has no guarantee. At any time he may be sold and transferred to another place. But a son of the house remains a son, whatever he may do. John is probably moving on to another meaning, as he so often does. He is surely thinking of *the* Son as well as *a* son when he says, "the Son remains for ever." In a fuller sense than any earthly son the Son of God remains forever; he is superior to the ravages of time. From another angle John is bringing out the truth that the relationship of the Son to the passing of time is not that of all the rest of us. We are creatures of time and our bodies are destined for decay. But he is Lord over time, and he "remains for ever."

John's teaching on the sonship of Jesus is thus very significant. It draws attention to the Lord's kinship with the heavenly Father, a kinship not shared with others. The Jesus of Saint John claims to be God's Son in a way that nobody else can claim, and this claim is central for an understanding of New Testament Christianity. John sees clearly that Jesus is more than an inspired man and that this "more" is the significant thing. He shares the very nature of God.[28]

Lord was already the Son" (*TDNT*, IV, p. 741, n. 16). The Son before his being sent to this earth already had the same nature as the Father.

28. Oscar Cullmann ends his treatment of this subject with these words: "In conclusion we can say that the Gospel of John as a whole penetrates more deeply than Matthew and Luke into the ultimate mystery of Jesus' consciousness of sonship as we believed we could and should infer it from the Synoptics. Although John openly proclaimed what the historical Jesus only referred to with veiled allusion, he very impressively expressed, in their very solidarity, the two sides of Jesus' Son-consciousness: obedience and oneness with the Father" (*The Christology of the New Testament*, p. 303).

CHAPTER 6

The "I AM" Sayings

A SIGNIFICANT FEATURE OF THE FOURTH GOSPEL IS a series of sayings in which Jesus uses an emphatic "I AM" to bring out important teachings about his person. In Greek, of course, the personal subject of the verb is not normally expressed: the form of the verb makes clear what the subject is. But if it is desired to emphasize the subject, then the appropriate pronoun may be used. What makes this so important in John is that we find a similar usage in the Greek translation of the Old Testament.[1] There we find that the translators used this emphatic form of speech when they were rendering words spoken by God. This sort of thing has been widely acceptable among religious people. In the not so distant past, for example, the Ten Commandments were normally cited in the form "Thou shalt not. . . ." It was a form of speech that was not much used in ordinary conversation or writing, but it seemed appropriate for the words of God. The point of all this is that when Jesus used the "I AM" construction he was speaking in the style of deity. How much this would have been perceived by his hearers is a difficult point because the construction was sometimes used in ordinary human conversation. But there is general agreement among Johannine scholars that this kind of language is a sig-

---

1. A. Deissmann holds that a similar usage is to be found in nonbiblical religion, and he can say, "Most striking of all, however, is the similarity between the utterances of the Johannine Christ in the first person, spoken with the solemnity proper to a cult, and certain ancient examples of the same style as we find it in widespread use for the purposes of non-Christian and pre-Christian religion" (*Light from the Ancient East,* London, 1927, p. 136). This means that the usage would be widely recognized in the first century, but we should not regard it as the source of John's usage. That is rather the use of the expression in the Old Testament. It is significant that, while parallels have been adduced from a variety of nonbiblical sources, no one seems to have found any real parallel to John's absolute use of "I AM".

nificant pointer to what John is telling us about the person of Jesus.

The construction is occasionally used in the other Gospels, though they lack statements with such a predicate as "I AM the bread of life" (6:35). Thus Matthew tells us that Jesus quoted the words of God: "I AM the God of Abraham . . ." (Matt. 22:32, quoting Exod. 3:6). This Old Testament usage shows us how the expression was used for divine speech. Matthew also has the expression for those who claim, "I AM the Christ" (Matt. 24:5), where solemn, divine speech is obviously appropriate, and a couple of times in the interrogative form as the disciples ask, "Is it I?" (Matt. 26:22, 25). Mark has the expression for those who claim to be the Christ, saying "I AM" (Mark 13:6), and twice on the lips of Jesus: when he came to the disciples walking on the water (Mark 6:50) and when he affirmed his messiahship before the Sanhedrin (Mark 14:62). In all three we can see why speech that accords with deity should be used. Luke has the expression on the lips of Zacharias and Gabriel (Luke 1:18, 19), and of the claimants to being the Christ (Luke 21:8). He quotes Jesus' words to the Sanhedrin, "You are saying that I AM" (Luke 22:70), and his affirmation of his identity in a resurrection appearance (24:39).[2] Again it is not difficult to understand why this manner of speech should have been used by Jesus.

Outside the Gospels the expression occurs only in Acts and Revelation. In Acts three times we read "I AM Jesus", all being the words of the risen Christ in Paul's vision at his conversion (Acts 9:5; 22:8; 26:15), once it is used of Peter's affirmation of his identity (Acts 10:21), once of John the Baptist's denial that he was "I AM" (Acts 13:25), and once of Paul's solemn affirmation that he wished that his hearers were "as I am" (Acts 26:29). In Revelation the expression occurs four times, and every time it is the utterance of the Father or the risen Christ (Rev. 1:8, 17; 2:23; 22:16).

This quick survey shows that the expression is used sparingly in the New Testament. It may be used of ordinary human life,

2. Raymond E. Brown examines this Synoptic usage and concludes that John is not "creating from nothing" in his "I AM" sayings. Rather, "Johannine theology may have capitalized on a valid theme of the early tradition" (*The Gospel according to John (i–xii)*, I, New York, 1966, p. 538).

but this use is not frequent. "I AM" mostly represents the speech of the heavenly Father or of the Son. The overtones of deity that we find in its use in the Old Testament are not lost when we move to the New.

When we turn to John, two groups of sayings must be considered. In one group Jesus adds a predicate to his "I AM", such as "I AM the Good Shepherd", while in the other the "I AM" stands by itself. We examine them in order, beginning with those with predicates. J. H. Bernard lists these passages and proceeds, "This is clearly the style of Deity. . . . Its force would at once be appreciated by any one familiar with the LXX version of the O.T."[3] Both constructions are somewhat unusual, and they form a Johannine distinctive. They have contacts with other New Testament teaching, as we have seen, but they bring before us what is fundamentally new. Leonhard Goppelt draws attention to Jesus' use of "I AM" in Mark 14:62 and proceeds: "The meaning of the Johannine formulas stood, nevertheless, in contrast to this usage. In them the 'I am' did not identify Jesus with something already known. It unveiled for man something otherwise unknown and inaccessible."[4]

"I AM the Bread of Life"

In the discourse that follows the miracle of the feeding of the multitude, Jesus tells the people, "I AM the bread of life" (6:35).[5] The saying is set in the context of a question from the people, "What sign do *you* do so that we may see and believe you?" followed by the statement: "our fathers ate the manna in the wilderness, even as it is written, 'He gave them bread from heaven to eat' " (6:30-31). Jesus pointed out two errors: it was not Moses that gave the

3. *A Critical and Exegetical Commentary on the Gospel according to St. John,* I (Edinburgh, 1928), pp. cxviii-cxix.
4. *Theology of the New Testament,* II (Grand Rapids, 1982), pp. 294-95. He also says, "In these formulas Jesus offered himself exclusively as that which man sought without knowing it: as the life!" (p. 295).
5. The expression *ho artos tēs zōēs* could mean "the bread that is alive" or "the bread that gives life" (as Goodspeed translates). The article with life ("the life", not "a life") may well point to everlasting life rather than life in general (cf. William Hendriksen, "*tēs zōēs,* qualitative genitive, referring not to any kind of life but to *spiritual, everlasting* life" (*New Testament Commentary: Exposition of the Gospel according to John,* I, Grand Rapids, 1953, p. 233).

bread from heaven, but God, and further God not only gave but "gives" the true bread from heaven. He goes on, "For the bread of God is he who (the Greek could mean 'that which') comes down from heaven and gives life to the world" (6:33). The people express a desire for this bread, and Jesus tells them that he is the bread of life. To the "I AM" saying he adds, "he who comes to me will certainly not hunger, and he who believes in me will certainly not thirst, ever" (6:35).

In the miracle of the feeding John has made it clear that Jesus is able to supply people's physical needs in miraculous fashion, and in the discourse that follows he shows that Jesus does more than that. Deep down, people have an intense spiritual hunger. John is making it clear that Jesus satisfies that hunger, and further that that hunger can be satisfied in him alone. So he turns people's attention away from their concentration on the manna that was given of old, and points out that the God who keeps on supplying the needs of his people is still at work. In that Jesus himself is the bread of life, he is the bringer of life to the spiritually dead. The definite article with "bread" ("the bread", not "a bread" or simply "bread") is perhaps unexpected because predicate nouns usually do not take the article.[6] A. T. Robertson pointed out that "when the article occurs with subject (or the subject is a personal pronoun or proper name) and predicate, both are definite, treated as identical, one and the same, and interchangeable."[7] The identity is important. If there were no article we could understand that there were others who could claim to be "bread of life": Jesus would be "a bread of life", one among others. The article means that Jesus, and Jesus only, is the bread of life. A similar comment should be made about the equivalent article in each of the other "I AM" sayings.

We should bear in mind that for the ancients bread was the principal element in the normal diet.[8] People did not have avail-

6. BDF #273.

7. *A Grammar of the Greek New Testament in the Light of Historical Research* (London, n.d., p. 768).

8. A. van Selms remarks, "Among the peasants in Palestine and elsewhere, bread is primary, other articles of solid food merely accessory. . . . 'Bread' therefore often stands for solid food in general, not only because this is the original meaning of the word but also because bread is food par excellence" (*ISBE*, I, p. 540).

able the variety of foods that we take for granted, and bread could stand for prosperity (Deut. 8:9; Prov. 12:11, etc.) and the lack of it for adversity (Lam. 1:11). On quite a few occasions it was referred to as "the staff of bread" (Lev. 26:26; Ps. 105:16; Ezek. 4:16, etc.), that is, that which supported the whole of life. It thus forms a natural simile for what is at the heart of spiritual life. Jesus is not speaking of something peripheral but of what is essential to life eternal when he refers to the "bread" of life.

The saying is repeated with variations: "I AM the bread that came down from heaven" (6:41); "I AM the living bread who (or which) came down from heaven" (6:51); and with impressive simplicity, "I AM the bread of life" (6:48). The first of these is muttered by the Jews as they complain that Jesus said these words: the quotation is not exact, but it is close enough and gives his meaning. In the Johannine manner we should understand all these slightly different sayings as meaning much the same thing. The repetition brings out the force and the importance of the saying. Jesus is making clear his heavenly origin and the fact that he alone supplies the spiritual need of his hearers.[9] Both are important for an understanding of John's thought about Jesus.

"I AM the Light of the World"

Light is one of the great concepts of this Gospel.[10] John tells us that Jesus said, "I AM the light of the world" (8:12). On another occasion he said, "I am the light of the world" (9:5), which is identical with the former saying except that it does not have the emphatic form. It conveys much the same idea, though not quite as forcefully as the first example. On another occasion Jesus said, "I have come a light into the world" (12:46; this passage has the em-

9. C. K. Barrett has an important note on the background of this and similar sayings in which he concludes, "We have here what Brown and others have described as the sapiential interpretation of the bread of life. God feeds men by his word; Jesus is his word. The Jewish and pagan elements in the background are thus joined and cemented by the Christian tradition, especially in the form of the feeding miracle and the record of the last supper" (*The Gospel according to St. John*[2], Philadelphia, 1978, p. 293).

10. O. A. Piper says that John "has a rather elaborate theology of light" in which "he stands close to the Qumran 'Hymns of Praise'" (*IDB*, III, p. 132).

phatic *egō*, though without *eimi*; it is a solemn and significant statement). Light is one of the great topics of this Gospel, for John uses the term *phōs* 23 times, more than twice as often as the term occurs in any other New Testament book (next is Acts with ten). Light is a natural figure of speech for what is good and upright, and it is often found in contrast with darkness, equally natural as a symbol of evil; John makes this contrast from time to time (e.g., 3:19). It is significant that he uses such a powerful figure of speech and one which means so much to him as a way of bringing out important truths with respect to Jesus and his mission.

John does not tell us exactly when Jesus spoke these words, but he does say that they were spoken "in the treasury" as he was "teaching in the temple" (8:20). Since Jesus was in Jerusalem at the Feast of Tabernacles for the events of chapter 7, it is a reasonable inference that that Feast is the background to the "light of the world" saying, especially as the illumination from the great candelabra was an important feature of the celebration. It is pointed out that if Jesus spoke just after the Feast, when the illumination no longer took place, the contrast between "the light of the world" and the darkness of Jerusalem would have been impressive. Another view is that the saying may contain a reference to the light given by the pillar of fire during the Exodus period. If either of these possibilities was in mind, the saying would have an interesting background. But it is scarcely necessary to look for anything of the kind. After all, "the light of the world" is a striking expression and conveys a very full meaning whenever it is spoken.[11]

The note of universality emerges as early as the Prologue. There we find that life was in the Word, "and the life was the light of men" (1:4). This does not use the "light of the world" terminology, but it conveys much the same meaning. All the light that men have comes from the life that is in the Word. The usage with light corresponds to John's teaching in other language that Christ is the significant figure in whom alone is there hope for all the human

---

11. Donald Guthrie says, "A statement like 'I am the light of the world' makes no sense except on the lips of one who was agent in the creation of the world" (*New Testament Theology*, London, 1981, p. 331). And in comparison to the creation of the world matters like the candelabra in Jerusalem and the pillar of fire in the wilderness pale into insignificance.

race. He is aware that people do not always welcome the light of the world as they should. There are people who "loved darkness rather than light because their deeds were evil" (3:19). There are evildoers who hate the light and do not come to it (3:20). By contrast the person who "does the truth comes to the light, that his deeds may be made manifest that they have been wrought in God" (3:21).

The idea that the way people react to the light is important comes out elsewhere. There is an interesting passage in the story of the raising of Lazarus. Jesus speaks of the importance of walking "in the day", and goes on: "if anyone walks in the night, he stumbles, because the light is not in him" (11:9-10). We would have expected, "because he is not walking in the light", but the reference to the light not being in him shows that we have moved from physical illumination to spiritual truth. Jesus is telling his hearers that those who reject him, who do not take him into their lives, are in grave danger. There will be something of the same thought when he later tells "the crowd" that the light is among them only for a short time (12:35),[12] surely a reference to his imminent death. He also calls on the people to "believe in the light, in order that (they) may become sons of light" (12:36). The demand for faith shows that it is not a question of physical illumination; Jesus is calling for faith in himself, and his use of "light" points to the illumination of life that he brings. The speedy withdrawal of the light points to the truth that Jesus' saving death is not far away.

The explicit phrase, "the light of the world", does not occur in these passages, but it is surely implicit. In each of them the thought is that Jesus is the only light and that people must respond to the coming of the light by giving him a welcome and believing in him. Apart from that they are lost eternally. That Jesus is the light of this whole world and that people's eternal destiny depends on their reaction to him tell us something very important about Jesus.

---

12. "The special mode of revelation embodied in Jesus' life and ministry will soon be withdrawn. If not accepted now, the chance of salvation will be lost" (Barnabas Lindars, *The Gospel of John,* London, 1972, p. 435).

"I AM the Door"

In the chapter in which he employs some vivid imagery about the sheep and the shepherd, Jesus twice speaks of himself as "the door" (10:7, 9), the first time referring to "the door of the sheep" and the second time simply to "the door". The chapter has begun with a reference to a sheepfold in which the sheep find safety and to which there is access by a door (anyone who climbs over the wall and does not use the door is up to no good, 10:1). The shepherd goes in through the door (10:2), which poses a little difficulty later in the chapter, for Jesus is spoken of both as the door and as the shepherd. But this is no great problem. We are able to understand one important truth by seeing him as the shepherd who has the right to enter by the door (in contrast to thieves and robbers who climb over the wall), and quite another by seeing him as the door through which people enter salvation.

When he says, "I AM the door", Jesus is saying that he himself is the means by which the "sheep" enter life. He says "the" door, not "a" door. There is something exclusive about the door. The normal sheepfold of the time had just one door, and Jesus is saying that the way into life goes through him, and him alone.[13] He is *the* door. When he repeats the thought he adds, "if anyone enters through me, he will be saved, and go in and go out, and find pasture" (10:9). He does not explain "saved" (which is a concept used much more often in the Synoptic Gospels than in this one), but we should understand it of the entrance into life eternal (cf. v. 10). The concepts of being "saved" and of having "life eternal" are linked in 3:16-17, and we should understand a similar linkage here. This is further brought out with the reference to going in (for security) and out (for food), further explained as finding pasture.

Thus once again we encounter the thought of an exclusive salvation, exclusive in the sense that it can be entered only through the one door, Jesus Christ. If there is but one door for all the race, then once more we are reminded of something very im-

13. W. G. Kümmel remarks, "the rarely encountered figure of the door as the entrance to the sphere of salvation says that Jesus alone provides access to salvation, to the Father. . . . Thus it emphasizes that Jesus is the exclusive mediator of salvation" (*The Theology of the New Testament,* London, 1974, p. 286).

portant about Jesus. Like the other I AM sayings, this one leads us to think of deity.

"I AM the Good Shepherd"

Following on from the conversation about the door, Jesus says, "I AM the good shepherd" (10:11). Since the word for "good" (*kalos*) has about it the notion of beauty as well as goodness,[14] some suggest that we should translate it here as "beautiful" (cf. E. V. Rieu, "I am the shepherd, the Shepherd Beautiful"). William Temple sees this meaning and proceeds, "Of course this translation exaggerates. But it is important that the word for 'good' here is one that represents, not the moral rectitude of goodness, nor its austerity, but its attractiveness. We must not forget that our vocation is so to practise virtue that men are won to it; it is possible to be morally upright repulsively!"[15] Temple's warning is one that we do well to heed, but in the present passage the emphasis is not on the way we are morally upright, but on the attractiveness of the Good Shepherd. Whatever be the case with his followers, Jesus is the Beautiful Shepherd as well as the morally Good Shepherd.

The Good Shepherd, Jesus says, "lays down his life[16] for the sheep." This is most unexpected. A shepherd was expected to live for his sheep, not to die for them. It was his task to lead them to pasture and to water, and to defend them from wild animals. Sheep are particularly vulnerable animals; through many generations they have been bred to serve the needs of the human race, and they are not much good as foragers (goats are much better). Does not the shepherd psalm say that the Lord "makes me lie down in green pastures" and that he "leads me beside still waters" (Ps. 23:2)? The sheep can be trusted to find neither green pastures

14. G. Abbott-Smith's *Lexicon* says "primarily, of outward form" and cites Cremer, "related to . . . *agathos* as the appearance to the essence"; he gives the first meaning of the word as "fair, beautiful".

15. *Readings in St. John's Gospel* (First and Second Series) (London, 1947), p. 166.

16. The expression *tēn psychēn tithenai* is unexpected. John uses it a number of times (e.g., vv. 15, 17, 18; 13:37, 38; 15:13; 1 John 3:16), but it is not easy to find examples outside his writings. Something very much like it is found in LXX (Judg. 12:3, etc.), but there the meaning is to risk the life, not to give it as here. That meaning is more usually conveyed by using *dounai*, as in Mark 10:45.

nor still waters; they depend on their shepherd. And sheep have no significant defence mechanism: they easily fall prey to predators. In early days there were wild animals in Palestine which have since died out; thus David spoke of lions and bears attacking his flock (1 Sam. 17:34-37). It is plain that the task of the shepherd was not an easy one and that it could lead the man who cared for his sheep into serious danger.

But a shepherd would reckon that he could cope with the dangers. If he thought he could not, then he would not be a shepherd. He had no intention of dying simply in order to defend some sheep. He might run into danger, but he would always be of the opinion that he would come out on top. To die for the sheep must have been very rare and seen as very tragic.

But that which is rare and tragic among human shepherds is characteristic of the Good Shepherd. "The good shepherd lays down his life for the sheep" (10:11). This is another way in which John brings out the truth that the death of Jesus was no tragic accident, but the divinely appointed way whereby salvation would be brought to those who trust him. Sheep are helpless animals, and sinners are helpless to bring about their salvation. But the Good Shepherd lays down his life, and the sheep are saved.

A second time John reports that Jesus said, "I am the good shepherd", this time adding, "and I know my own, and my own know me, even as the Father knows me and I know the Father." Then he says again, "and I lay down my life for the sheep" (10:14-15). A feature of the life of a first-century Palestinian shepherd was his knowledge of his sheep and their knowledge of him. These days when flocks may be numbered in thousands an individual sheep is unrecognizable, but people at that time had smaller numbers. Jesus spoke of a man with a hundred sheep (Luke 15:4), while the prophet Nathan referred to the irreducible minimum for a flock, "one little ewe lamb" (2 Sam. 12:3). Shepherds thus knew individual sheep, and, of course, the sheep would know the shepherds who provided for them. Earlier in the chapter Jesus had spoken of sheep who knew the voice of their shepherd and would follow him, whereas they would not follow a stranger, for they did not know his voice (10:3-5). It is important for John that Jesus has knowledge of his own, and that his own know him.

Nor should we miss the point that a second time Jesus says

that the good shepherd lays down his life for the sheep. This is not an incidental, more or less unimportant fact, but the great central truth.[17] The heart of the gospel is concerned with the provision that God has made for the salvation of his sheep, and this involves the death of the shepherd.

"I AM the Resurrection and the Life"

Thus far all Jesus' "I AM" sayings have been addressed to the Jews in general rather than specifically to his followers. But the rest of these sayings are spoken to those who have committed themselves to him. When Jesus spoke to Martha after her brother Lazarus died, he told her that Lazarus would rise, which she took as a reference to "the resurrection at the last day." Jesus then said to her, "I AM the resurrection and the life; he who believes in me, even if he dies, he will live, and everyone who lives and believes in me will certainly not die eternally" (11:23-26). Jesus does not say simply that he will give resurrection and life, but that he is resurrection and life. This is not an easy expression, but we should understand Jesus to mean that raising people from the dead and giving them life is not, so to speak, a routine activity that he performs in an uninvolved way. He is thoroughly involved in the bringing of life of which he speaks, and he identifies himself with it. That he is the resurrection means that death, which to us appears so final, is no obstacle, and that he is the life means that the quality of life that he imparts to us here and now never ceases.[18]

Jesus speaks these words in the context of the death of Lazarus, whom he was about to raise, and John clearly means us to see them in the light of that demonstration of Jesus' power over death. He is writing about one who is supremely great and who has a

17. R. H. Lightfoot says that the good shepherd's laying down of his life, "is His right and is in no way forced upon Him" (*St. John's Gospel*, Oxford, 1956, p. 207). This striking way of putting it emphasizes the voluntary nature of what the good shepherd does for his sheep.

18. Cf. G. R. Beasley-Murray, "The revelation to Martha thus is an assurance of resurrection to the kingdom of God in its consummation through him who is the Resurrection, and of life in the kingdom of God in the present time through him who is the Life. Both aspects of the 'life' are rooted in the understanding of Jesus as the Mediator of the divine sovereignty in the present and in the future" (*John*, Waco, 1987, p. 191).

breathtaking superiority to death. It is common to the human race that in the end we all face death and that there is nothing we can do about that. We may stave death off for a time, but when it takes place it is final. John writes about a Lord for whom it is not final. He is such a great person that even death gives place to him.

"I AM the Way and the Truth and the Life"

In the upper room on the eve of the crucifixion, Jesus spoke of his imminent departure, finishing with "and where I am going you know the way" (14:4). Thomas rejoined with, "Lord, we don't know where you are going; how can we know the way?" to which Jesus replied, "I AM the way and the truth and the life", adding, "no one comes to the Father except through me" (14:5-6). The "I AM" in the style of deity marks this as another very solemn statement, but it is not easy to see the precise meaning of the words. Some think that all three nouns should be given their full force, while others regard a couple of them as in effect adjectives. Thus Moffatt translates, "I am the real and living way", and Moule wonders whether "I am the Way, I am Truth, I am Life" would be better.[19] Some omit one or more of the definite articles, for example, Goodspeed, "I am Way and Truth and Life." I see no reason for such devices, and it is much better to take the words as originally written, articles and all. It seems as though Jesus is affirming three things about himself.

First he says, "I AM the way". Like the claim to be the door that we were examining earlier, there is an exclusiveness about this. He does not say that he is one of several ways, but that he is "the" way; and since he goes on to say that no one comes to the Father other than through him, it is clear that by "the way" he means "the way to God". John is insisting that Jesus is the one way to the Father. He will not allow for one moment that the way of the Jewish priestly leaders with their insistence on the place of the law and the significance of circumcision is another possible way to God. Whatever the leaders might say, John is affirming that the person of Jesus is such that he and no other can bring us

19. C. F. D. Moule, *An Idiom Book of New Testament Greek* (Cambridge, 1953), p. 112.

to the heavenly abode. He is not saying that Jesus shows the way, but that he *is* the way. This points us to the significance of his saving death. By dying for sinners he brings them to God.

"I AM the truth" brings out more than one significant piece of teaching. It reminds us first of all of Jesus' utter reliability. John has recorded a good deal of teaching which he ascribes to Jesus, and this declaration means that it is all true; it can all be relied on. And in this Gospel truth is a quality of deeds as well as of speech (3:21), so that we should conclude that Jesus' whole manner of life expresses what is true. He speaks the truth and his deeds accord with that truth. "Truth is not the teaching about God transmitted by Jesus but is God's very reality revealing itself—occurring!—in Jesus."[20] John is saying more than that Jesus proclaims the truth. Of course he does that, but to say that he *is* the truth means, as Kümmel puts it, "that he belongs to God. But then it says above all that in Jesus God has become quite personally audible and that through the encounter with this truth that has appeared personally, salvation is to be imparted to men" (Kümmel proceeds to cite 8:32).[21]

"I AM the life" takes us into the same area as the saying, "I AM the resurrection and the life". Once more Jesus is associating life very closely with himself. It is he alone whose life is unique, self-existent like the life of the Father (5:26). He is the life, and the source of life to others (3:16).

This comprehensive saying, then, claims an exclusive position for Jesus. He is the one way to God, he is thoroughly reliable, and he stands in a relation to truth such as no one else does. The same, of course, is true of his relationship to life.

"I AM the True Vine"

Twice in the discourse in the upper room Jesus declares that he is the vine. On the first occasion he says, "I AM the true vine", and adds, "My Father is the vinedresser" (15:1). On the second occasion the link with believers is stressed as Jesus says, "I AM the

---

20. Rudolf Bultmann, *Theology of the New Testament*, II (London, 1955), p. 19. Bultmann also says, "the basic meaning of 'truth' in John is God's reality, which, since God is the Creator, is the only true reality" (p. 18).

21. *The Theology of the New Testament*, p. 286.

vine, you are the vine canes", and goes on to refer to the mutual indwelling of the Savior and the saved (15:5). We should bear in mind that there are passages in the Old Testament that speak of Israel using vine imagery (e.g., Ps. 80:8-16; Jer. 2:21; Ezek. 15). Each time, however, it seems that God is pointing out Israel's sin. Thus we should understand the thought that Christ is the "true" vine as marking the contrast with faithless Israel.

In the Old Testament the vine is often a symbol of Israel, sometimes of degenerate Israel. For example, in Jeremiah we read, "I planted you a choice vine, wholly of pure seed. How then have you turned degenerate and become a wild vine?" (Jer. 2:21). We should see Jesus' claim to be the "true" vine against such a background. The people had failed to produce the fruit that would have been expected; they were false to their God, who had done so much for them. The psalmist could say, "Thou didst bring a vine out of Egypt; thou didst drive out the nations and plant it . . ." (Ps. 80:8). But although God had done so much, they had failed to live up to their vocation, or, to keep the metaphor, to produce the fruit that they should. But where Israel failed and had become a false vine, we now see the true vine, the vine in which the purpose of God would be worked out.[22]

Both verses stress the link between Christ and his people, and both bring before us the importance of fruitfulness. Salvation in Christ is not a process that leads us into magnificent laziness. Salvation in Christ is meant to result in the saved producing qualities of character that accord with their Christian profession and in their having a horror of fruitless lives. After saying that he is the true vine and the Father the vinedresser,[23] Jesus goes on to make the point

22. Cf. John Painter, "In the conflict between Jews and Jewish Christians everything turns on christology. Given that the Jewish religion was true, Jesus was a blasphemer. Given that Jesus had the significance John ascribed to him then Judaism was both false to her foundations in the Scriptures and no longer an expression of the knowledge of God. In John the emphasis is christocentric; it is Jesus against the Jews. This is nowhere clearer than in John xv" (NTS 25, 1978-79, p. 111).

23. The word is geōrgos, a general word for a tiller of the soil, a farmer. It has no necessary connection with vines; it simply means a worker on the land. But in this passage it certainly refers to a man whose business is with grapevines, so we must understand it in the sense "vinedresser".

that fruitless canes[24] on a vine are discarded. The purpose of grow-
ing vines is to produce grapes, not foliage. So, Jesus says, those canes
that do not produce fruit are taken away, and those that do are
treated in such a way that they produce more fruit. This is often understood in the sense "prunes" (as GNB, among others). But the
word does not mean "prunes", but "cleanses",[25] and this is important in the context. Jesus proceeds to say, "You are already clean on
account of the word that I have spoken to you" (v. 3). They have responded to his message and are believers. We should perhaps notice that the word for "clean" is used of those in the upper room,
with the exception of Judas, for Jesus said, "You are clean, but not
all", which John explains: "For he knew who was betraying him;
for this reason he said, 'You are not all clean'" (13:10-11). This appears to mean that the canes that are cut out are people like Judas,
those who had professed discipleship but without the commitment
that makes a genuine disciple. The first "vine" saying, then, emphasizes that those who are not "clean" are not part of the true vine.

The second saying emphasizes the importance of vital contact
with Christ. "He who remains in me, and I in him," says Jesus, "this
man bears much fruit, for apart from me you can do nothing" (15:5).
It is an error to suppose that in the energy of the flesh we are able
to do anything that pleases God. For that we need the strength that
he alone can supply. The condition of fruitfulness in Christian service is vital contact with Christ.[26] On our own we can do nothing.
In living fellowship with him all things are possible (cf. Phil. 4:13).
Exactly what the "fruit" is is not explained, but usually in the New
Testament the word means qualities of Christian character (Matt.

24. A small point is that most translations have "branches", which would normally be expressed by *klados*. *Klēma* means the flexible cane so characteristic of
grapevines.

25. The word is *kathairei*; no examples appear to be cited in which it has the
meaning "prune". It is apparently not a viticultural word, and in the context it is
important that it is related to *katharoi* in the next line.

26. Kümmel says, "the figure of the vine is not so much a description of Jesus'
relation to the Father—15:1b does this by an allusion—but rather of Jesus as the
revealer who communicates the Father's will to the disciples" (*The Theology of the
New Testament*, p. 287). This is not quite it, for more than revelation is involved.
The figure of the vine points not so much to revelation as to the communication
of life and power. John is telling his readers that fruitful lives proceed from vital
contact with the source of life. That Jesus is the revealer is true. That this is what
the figure of the vine is conveying is not.

3:8; 7:20; Rom. 6:22; Gal. 5:22, etc.) and we should probably see this as primarily in mind here. We become fruitful Christians when we remain in vital contact with Christ and manifest the effects of that vital contact in our character and our deeds.

"I AM" without a Predicate

A number of times John reports that Jesus used the "I AM" construction without qualifying it with a predicate as in the examples so far noted. This occurs, for example, in the conversation Jesus had with the woman at the well. When she says that matters of which they are speaking are matters to be dealt with by the Messiah when he comes, Jesus replies, "I AM, who am speaking to you" (4:26). Ethelbert Stauffer denies that this is "an indirect messianic affirmation", and insists "that John wishes Jesus' answer to be understood as the theophanic formula *ANI HU*."[27] Edwin D. Freed, by contrast, points out that the Baptist uses the I AM formula in his denial that he is the Christ (1:20; repeated in 3:28). Freed points out that the next occurrence of the formula is in 4:26, and he says, "Certainly one way, if not the only correct way, to convey the meaning of the Greek *egō eimi* in this context is to understand *messias/christos* of the sentence before it as the predicate with which *ho lalōn soi* is in apposition. In contrast to the Baptist's negative statement, Jesus is reported as affirming his messiahship through the use of *egō eimi*."[28] Freed's appeal to the context is certainly impressive, but Stauffer has certainly done us a service in drawing attention to the fact that the words are the solemn words of deity.[29]

27. *Jesus and His Story* (London, 1960), p. 152. *ANI HU* is the Hebrew underlying "I AM". Stauffer proceeds to give six reasons for holding this view, and concludes, "Jesus chooses intentionally the veiled formula of self-revelation from Isa. 52.6, without taking account of the messianist terminology of the Samaritans. His saying of self-revelation is a mystery, a sign, a *mashal*." Stauffer thinks that this "I AM" is "the clearest, boldest and deepest self-affirmation of Jesus" (p. 158); it means: "*where I am, there is God, there God lives, speaks, calls, asks, acts, decides, loves, chooses, forgives, rejects, hardens, suffers, dies.* Nothing bolder can be said, or imagined" (p. 159; Stauffer's italics).

28. *CBQ* 41 (1979), p. 290.

29. Stauffer is often held to take up an extreme position; therefore not many agree wholeheartedly with him. But Philip B. Harner points out that the Old Tes-

And this is surely the way we should understand the words of Jesus when he came walking on the water to the storm-tossed disciples. They were terrified at the sight as Jesus approached them (the Synoptists tell us that they thought they were seeing a phantom). He calmed them with the words, "I AM, don't be afraid" (6:20). This may be no more than a way of self-identification (as C. K. Barrett thinks),[30] but the style is the style of deity and it accords with this that Jesus came walking on the water. A somewhat similar passage is that in which Jesus says, "I AM he who bears witness about myself, and the Father who sent me bears witness about me" (8:18). It is possible that Jesus means no more than "I bear witness", but this does not seem likely. He is surely affirming in the style of deity that he stands closer to the Father than do people in general.

Jesus further said to some of the Jews, "Unless you believe that I AM, you will die in your sins" (8:24). The meaning of "dying in sins" is not spelled out, but clearly it is a dreadful fate. And people are saved from this, Jesus says, only when they come to have faith in him as I AM. Later he says to the disciples, "I tell you before it happens, so that when it happens you may believe that I AM" (13:19). In both passages we find the Johannine emphasis on the importance of believing, and in both it is linked with Jesus' own person. In both Jesus is saying that it is important that those addressed come to trust him as the I AM, which looks very much like a claim to sharing in the nature of deity. People must see Jesus as one with the Father and trust him as such. Perhaps this is the place to notice further that in his prayer in the upper room Jesus says that the Father has given him his own name (17:11), which looks like an affirmation that he shares in all that the name of God stands for.[31]

---

tament use of 'ani hu is part of the background of the use of the expression in John, and of this he says, "The phrase 'ani hu signifies that Yahweh alone is God, in contrast to the so-called gods of the various peoples of the world". He speaks of it as "This assertion of exclusive monotheism" (The "I Am" of the Fourth Gospel, Philadelphia, 1970, p. 8).

30. The Gospel according to St. John, p. 281. He goes on to say, "If in the present passage there is any hint of the epiphany of a divine figure it is not because the words egō eimi are used but because in the gospel as a whole Jesus is a divine figure."

31. Brown finds examples of the use of "I AM" as the name of God in the Old Testament (as Isa. 43:25) and rabbinic sources, and goes on, "The use of 'I AM' as a divine name in late Judaism may explain the many Johannine references to the

It is not easy to escape something of the same conclusion when Jesus says, "then you will know that I AM" (8:28),[32] and especially when he says, "Truly, truly, I tell you, before Abraham was, I AM" (8:58).[33] The claim to have been in existence before Abraham must be either delusion or a statement that the speaker was sovereign over time. In both passages John is telling us something about the nature of Jesus. He is not to be thought of as simply another man. He was a man, but he was more, and passages like these bring out the "more". It is significant that when the Jews heard Jesus say, "before Abraham was, I AM", they tried to stone him (8:59); they regarded the statement as blasphemous. Harner links this with the attempt to stone Jesus in 10:31: "They attempt to stone Jesus when he has said *ego eimi* in 8:58, and also when he has said 'I and the Father are one' in 10:30. In this way John indicates that the two statements are identical in meaning. As in 13:19, the absolute *ego eimi* in 8:58 expresses the unity of the Father and the Son."[34] Since stoning was a serious business, it is not easy to see why the Jews should have attempted it on these two occasions unless, as Harner suggests, they thought Jesus guilty of blasphemy. His claim was far-reaching.

We should also notice the series of references to "I AM" at the time of the arrest. Jesus twice elicited from the soldiers the information that they were looking for "Jesus of Nazareth" (18:5, 7),

---

divine name that Jesus bears" (*The Gospel according to John (i–xii)*, p. 537; he cites passages like 5:43; 10:25; 17:11, 12).

32. On 8:28 C. H. Dodd remarks, "The *egō eimi* carries with it the solidarity of Christ with God" (*The Interpretation of the Fourth Gospel*, Cambridge, 1953, p. 96). Barrett, however, finds the expression to mean no more than "Jesus is the obedient servant of the Father, and for this reason perfectly reveals him. *Egō eimi* does not identify Jesus with God, but it does draw attention to him in the strongest possible terms" (*The Gospel according to St. John*, p. 342).

33. On this verse Dodd points to "the contrast of the verbs, *genesthai*, to come into being, in the aorist, and *einai*, to be, in the continuous present. The implication is that Jesus does not stand within the temporal series of great men, beginning with Abraham and continuing through the succession of the prophets, so as to be compared with them. His claim is not that He is the greatest of the prophets, or even greater than Abraham himself. He belongs to a different order of being" (*The Interpretation of the Fourth Gospel*, p. 261). F. Büchsel says of 8:58, "This is the only passage in the NT where we have the contrast between *einai* and *genesthai*. The verse ascribes to Jesus consciousness of eternity or supra-temporality" (*TDNT*, II, p. 399).

34. *The "I Am" of the Fourth Gospel*, p. 39.

and both times he responded with, "I AM". In between John has another "I AM", in which he tells his readers that when Jesus "said to them, 'I AM', they went away backward and fell to the ground" (18:6). John pictures a scene in the gloom of the garden, imperfectly lit by the torches carried by the arresting posse. But instead of the terrified fugitive they expected would be hiding in the shadowy recesses of the garden, the soldiers find themselves confronted by a majestic figure who advances to meet them and addresses them in the language of deity. Once again John is saying something to his readers about Jesus' kinship with the heavenly Father. This is not the speech or the action of one who is nothing more than just another man. The falling to the ground seems to be John's way of saying that there was a special significance in the words; the soldiers reacted like men in the presence of deity.

John has "I AM" again when Jesus says, "where 'I AM', there also will my servant be" (12:26), and when the blind man to whom Jesus had given sight affirms his identity (9:9). But neither of these seems to be significant for our present inquiry. They are the normal human response in the situations described, and we should not look for more. But in the other passages it certainly seems that John's use of the expression is distinctive. We get nothing like it anywhere else in the New Testament (except for a handful of passages in the Synoptics); thus we must recognize that John is using the hallowed expression to bring out the truth that his Master was one with a special relationship to the heavenly Father, a relationship in which he must be thought of as partaking in the nature of deity,[35] and a relationship which does not compromise the truth that there is but one God.[36]

35. G. E. Ladd can say, "Most scholars think that Stauffer defends an extreme position, but it seems beyond question that in the use of the absolute *egō eimi*, Jesus is in some real sense identifying himself with the God of the Old Testament" (*A Theology of the New Testament*, Grand Rapids, 1974, p. 251).

36. Cf. Harner, who claims that in the *egō eimi* passages John "expresses his belief that Christian faith does not violate the integrity of monotheism in holding the Son to be one with the Father" (*The "I Am" of the Fourth Gospel*, p. 57).

CHAPTER 7

God the Father

JOHN HAS A GOOD DEAL TO SAY ABOUT GOD. HE USES the word "God" 83 times, which, of course, is much less than in some other New Testament writings. Thus Luke has the word 122 times in his Gospel and another 166 times in Acts, while in the much shorter Romans Paul has it 153 times. But when we add that in addition to the word "God" John speaks of the same Being as "Father" more than 120 times, we see that he has a strong interest in the deity. When he speaks of "God" John almost invariably means the Father, but we should notice that he includes the words of Thomas to the risen Jesus, "My Lord and my God!" (20:28).

For John God is a great person; he is "the only true God" (17:3), which separates this Evangelist from the many polytheists of his day. God, he says, "is spirit" (4:24), which makes it clear that he is not to be understood as the idolaters saw him or as just another being like us, only greater. He is a being of a different order, and that must be borne in mind when we approach him in worship. Precisely because God is spirit, those who worship him must worship him "in spirit and truth" (4:23, 24); access to God is not always and everywhere open to people who presume that they may approach at any time and in their own way.[1] That worship is to be "in truth" as well as "in spirit" points to the impor-

---

1. G. S. Hendry points out that the passage "has commonly been taken to mean that God, being Spirit, is present everywhere and can be worshiped anywhere; the important thing is not where men worship, but how they worship." This he denies. The meaning, he holds, is rather: "God is present in his own realm, to which man as such has no access. To worship God in spirit is not a possibility that is always and everywhere open to man. . . . The meaning is that the location has been redefined, and God is now to be worshiped in the place where he is present, i.e., in Him who is the truth incarnate" (*The Holy Spirit in Christian Theology,* London, 1957, pp. 31-32).

tance of sincerity and reality in worship. We are not to think that a great God is honored by a shallow, materialistic approach.

It accords with this that no one has ever seen God (1:18).[2] He has chosen to reveal himself in the incarnate Word, but that is his choice. Created beings are unable to encounter him with the use of the physical eye. The Word (spoken of as *monogenēs theos*, "only-begotten God") has declared what he is (1:18). But his greatness and his transcendence are plain for John. A little illustration of this is the reference to "the angels of God" who go up and down on the Son of man (1:51). At one and the same time we see the greatness of God (whose angels these are) and his willingness to have dealings with those he has created (the angels come to this earth).

God Was in Christ

A point that John emphasizes is that this great God has revealed himself in Jesus Christ. He has many ways of bringing out the unity of the two. Thus he starts his Gospel with some statements about a being he calls "the Word". He never explains the term, but as his Gospel unfolds it becomes clear that this is a designation of Jesus Christ. It points to him as divine (1:1) and as the revealer of the Father (1:18). By saying "the Word was with God" (1:1), John makes it clear that he is not equating the Word with the Father. They stand in the closest connection, but they are not identical. When we read of him as "a teacher come from God" and are informed that God is "with him" (3:2), this tells us something about God as well as about Christ.[3] The God of whom John writes is a God who chooses to reveal himself; he does not leave those he has created without guidance and help. There is teaching that comes from God (7:17; 8:40). Jesus quotes the prophet to the effect that they will be "all taught by God" (6:45; cf. Isa. 54:13), and

2. F. L. Godet remarks, "One can know everything else, not God! The perfect, *heōrake, has seen*, denotes a result, rather than an act, which would be indicated by the aorist: 'No one *is in possession* of the sight of God, and consequently no one can speak of Him *de visu*.' The full truth does not exist on earth before or outside of Jesus Christ; it truly *came* through Him" (*Commentary on the Gospel of John*, I, Grand Rapids, n.d., p. 280).

3. Floyd V. Filson says, "Nicodemus was convinced that only by God's active power could Jesus do such signs" (*Saint John*, London, 1963, p. 45).

proceeds to say that everyone who has heard and learned from God comes to him. The God who has always willed to make his teaching known to his people has brought all this to its consummation in the coming of Christ. Thus we often hear that he is "from God" or a similar expression (6:46; 8:42; 9:33; 13:3, etc.).

The tragedy of so many in John's day (and in ours) is that they have been so wise in their own estimation that they have rejected the ways of God and have set up their own way as the way to life. Jesus pointed out that some of his hearers did not really "seek the glory that is from the only God" (5:44); they did not "have the love of God in themselves" (5:42).[4] Their own ideas of the way to God were so clear to them and so strongly held that they were sure that God was their Father (8:41), but their deeds denied this (8:42). Indeed, their deeds showed that the devil was their true father (8:44). They did not receive the one who came to them with the words of God, and they did not listen to him because they were not God's people (8:47). In the last resort they valued the approval of people more highly than the approval of God (12:43).

But the God of whom John writes does more than reveal. Revelation and teaching, if that was all, could lead to despair as people come to realize that they do not live up to the standard that God demands. But John is writing about a God who brings salvation, not a God who brings despair. John insists that God loves the world and that he took action in giving his Son so that all who believe in him might be saved (3:16). Jesus speaks of his death in terms of glorification (12:23), and this seems still to be in mind when he goes on to refer to God's glorifying of his name (12:28). The death of Jesus was God's glorious action in bringing salvation to people who could never obtain it, left to their own devices. God sent the Son, not so that people would be condemned but so that they would be saved (3:17). This is the point of earlier statements which bring out the truth that people cannot by their own efforts

4. I have taken *tēn agapēn tou theou* to mean "the love they had for God" rather than "the love God had for them". The Greek is, of course, open to either interpretation, but even if the latter be accepted, the people in question are blamed for "not having it in them", which must mean that they had refused to respond. That God loved them is clear, but they did not respond to that love with an answering love, so however we translate, they are blamed because they had no real love for God.

enter the heavenly family (1:12-13) and that rebirth by water and the Spirit is the only way to enter the kingdom of God (3:3-8). In this vein Jesus speaks of "the free gift of God" (4:10).

Some people once asked Jesus what they must do "to work the works of God" (6:28), a question that clearly showed that they thought that their salvation depended on their working works that would be acceptable to God. But Jesus told them that "the work of God" (the singular is important) is that they "believe in him whom he sent" (6:29). The way into God's salvation is not the way of human merit or human achievement of any sort, but rather of trust in the one whom God sent. And this is the point of the passages which speak of believing in Christ or in God or in both (e.g., 3:18; 9:35; 11:27; 14:1). God is acting in Christ to bring salvation, and this is received by simple trust, not by some difficult human achievement. That sin is a serious matter is brought out in this Gospel, and that "the wrath of God" abides on the disobedient sinner is clear (3:36). But John's great teaching about God is that he has taken the initiative in bringing about salvation. It is God who has made the way whereby the sinner may be saved. It is God who has sent "the Lamb of God" (1:29, 36) to be offered for the salvation of sinners. This whole Gospel was written so that people might believe and thus enter life (20:31).

Father

That God is the Father of his people is not commonly taught in the Old Testament. We do find it, as when the psalmist says that God looks for a time when "He shall cry to me, 'Thou art my Father . . .'" (Ps. 89:26) or when the prophet says, "Yet, O LORD, thou art our Father" (Isa. 64:8; cf. Isa. 63:16; Jer. 3:19; 31:9, etc.). But "Father" tends to be applied to the nation as a whole rather than to the individual Israelite. There is nothing in the Old Testament writings to match the way the word is used in the New. Specifically, John consistently speaks of God as Father, and there is no Old Testament equivalent.[5]

---

5. There is no equivalent in a good deal of modern writing either. Thus in his book *Concepts of Deity* (London, 1971), H. P. Owen sets forth classical theism as teaching such things as "the unity of God", "God the Creator", etc. He has 12 such

John's great advance over everyone else in the New Testament in his teaching about God lies in the emphasis he gives to the truth that God is Father, the Father of our Lord Jesus Christ, and the Father of believers. "Father" has become the typical Christian word for God, and it is a priceless gain that we have come to think of God as our Father. James Moffatt points out that "a religion may call God by several names, but there are titles for God without which it would not be itself, and for Christianity the supreme title is that of 'Father.' "[6] He goes on to point out that this is not something Christians took over from Judaism, for it is not found there. It is a way of looking at God that we owe to Jesus. And in the New Testament writings it is John who gives it emphasis.

We have seen that he uses the word "God" 83 times; we should also notice that he has the word "Father" 137 times, of which no less than 122 refer to God. No one in the entire New Testament has this habitual reference to the divine fatherhood. Paul has a strong emphasis on the place of God, and in the Pauline writings this word occurs no less than 548 times. This is a staggering total and reminds us that Paul was a God-centered man. But, although he has some striking and significant passages about the Father, all told he uses this term only 63 times and many of these refer to human fathers. Thus in Romans he refers to God as Father only four times, in 1 Corinthians three times, in 2 Corinthians five times, and in Galatians four times. The highest total in any Pauline writing is eight in Ephesians. The only New Testament writer who may be linked with John in this respect is Matthew, who has the word 64 times, of which 45 refer to the heavenly Father. For John clearly it was of central importance that our God is our heavenly Father. We should appreciate more than we

---

points, but he does not include any such heading as "God the Father". In fairness it should be said that he is not trying to expound the biblical revelation, but it is interesting that in a book on God written from a Christian perspective there is nothing about God as Father.

6. *The Theology of the Gospels* (London, 1928), p. 99. Cf. Joseph Bonsirven, "This idea of the divine Fatherhood occupies a central position in the Revelation that Jesus brought to us. . . . Jesus contributed to this an unexpected novelty: he was the only Son of God. He became incarnate so that we should share his sonship . . ." (*Theology of the New Testament*, London, 1963, pp. 107-108).

do the truth that our habit of speaking of our God simply as "the Father" is a habit we owe to John.

In discussing the way in which he uses the term we must retrace some of the ground we covered when we were thinking of his teaching about God, but perhaps it would be true to say that in each case there is more on the subject under "Father" and the subject is treated more fully and from a different angle. First, let us notice that the Father is a great person. Jesus appears throughout this Gospel as a most important being, but he says, "the Father is greater than I" (14:28). What this says about the place of the Son must be understood with some care,[7] but the passage certainly ascribes the highest possible place to the Father.

A passage with some difficulties is that in which RSV and others translate some words of Jesus as "My Father . . . is greater than all" (10:29). There is a problem in that some good MSS read "What my Father has given me is greater than everything" (GNB). In the former case we have a clear affirmation that the Father is superior to everyone and everything that exists; in the latter it is usually agreed that "what" refers to the church, since it is "that which the Father gave" to Jesus and is greater in the Father's eyes than anything else on earth. We should probably accept this second reading, but in doing so we should not overlook the fact that it has significant implications for the greatness of the Father.[8] Jesus is saying that the Father is so powerful that nothing and no one can pluck his people from his grasp.

We should put with these passages those that speak of honoring the Father. When Jesus speaks of the Father as committing all judgment to the Son "so that all may honor the Son, even as they honor the Father" (5:23), the implication is that the Father is certainly to be honored by all. And when Jesus says that he honors

---

7. The words are spoken in a context of the completion of the incarnation with all its implications of Jesus' lowliness. His coming to earth involved a certain subordination, but the church seems never to have regarded this passage as teaching that the Son is inferior by nature to the Father.

8. E. C. Hoskyns sees little difference in the ultimate meaning whichever of the possible readings we accept. He says that the passage means: "The Father is the only source of the ultimate security of the believers in Jesus. They belong to Jesus because they have been given to Him by the Father" (*The Fourth Gospel*, London, 1947, p. 389).

the Father (8:49), the thought is that if such a great person as the Jesus of whom John writes renders honor to the Father, then the Father is supremely important.

The Father is not accessible to ordinary mortals, for no one has seen him, other than Christ (6:46; cf. 1:18). The Father "has life in himself" (5:26) and may be called "the living Father" (6:57). Heaven may be spoken of as "my Father's house" in which there are many places of residence (14:2). The use of such varied expressions shows us something of the ease with which John uses the term "Father" and of the greatness of him to whom it refers. We are not to think of the Father in terms appropriate only to people like ourselves. John conceives of him as a very great being indeed.

The Father and the Son

The complement of "Father" is "Son" and, while John speaks of God as the Father of his people, the principal way in which he employs the term is to relate the Father to Christ. The Jews were incensed that Jesus "called God his own Father, making himself equal with God" (5:18). They were not upset that Jesus spoke of God as Father in the manner of Isaiah or Jeremiah. They were upset that, because he spoke of him as his own Father, he related himself to God in a way in which he related no one else.[9] And the tense of the verb is continuous. He did it habitually. They were not complaining because of an isolated, perhaps untypical slip. They were complaining because of what they saw as a settled attitude. It accords with this that Jesus could say, "I live on account of the Father" (6:57), and again, "I and the Father are one" (10:30), and "the Father is with me" (16:32). Repeatedly he is said to be in the Father, and the Father in him (10:38; 14:10, 11; 17:21). To have seen him is to have seen the Father (14:9); to know him is to know the Father (8:19; 14:7). People are blamed who know neither the

---

9. Barnabas Lindars regards "*his own* Father" as "in contrast with the sense in which God is the Father of all men"; of Jesus' suggestion that he was equal with God Lindars says, "Nothing could be more provocative to Jews who did not accept his claim. It was not only the ultimate folly to put oneself on a level with God, but absolute blasphemy" (*The Gospel of John*, London, 1972, p. 219).

Father nor the Son (16:3). The Father knows him, and he knows the Father (10:15). The things the Father does the Son does too (5:19). Such statements point to a close relationship to the Father, such a close relationship indeed that it is shared with no one else.

This is seen also in a variety of things the Father is said to do with respect to the Son. Thus Jesus is one "whom the Father sanctified, and sent into the world" (10:36; cf. "I went out from the Father", 16:28). The Father has "sealed" the Son (6:27), or set his seal of approval on him. He has given all things into his hands (13:3), a staggering claim. The Father has "given" him the works that he does (5:36), and it is the people the Father has given him who come to him (6:37; 17:24). The Father has spoken to him, and it is what the Father has said that he speaks (12:50). The Father has taught him, and these things he speaks (8:28). His "word" is the "word" of the Father (14:24). It means much the same to say that it is what he has seen with the Father that he speaks (8:38), and that it is what he has heard from the Father that he makes known (15:15). Over and over John tells us that the Father sent the Son (5:36, 37; 6:44, etc.).[10] Hans Conzelmann brings out some of the significance of this by saying, "The key-words 'sending', 'the one who is sent' (emissary) mean that God himself is responsible for salvation".[11] Jesus' deeds are good works from the Father (10:32), indeed they are the works of the Father (10:37), for the Father, living in him, does his works (14:10). Jesus speaks of his capacity to lay down his life and to take it again, and explains, "this command I received from my Father" (10:18). His departure from this life is several times said to be a going to the Father (13:1; 14:12, 28; 16:10, 17, 28). The great movement from heaven to earth and back again is put in one verse: "I came out from the Father and have come into the world; again I leave the world and go to the Father" (16:28). This verse does not use the verb "send", but it follows a statement that the Father loves the disciples because they have loved Christ and have believed that he came out from God (v. 27). Whatever verb is being used, there is not the slightest

10. John uses *apostellō* 17 times and *pempō* 24 times for the Father's sending of the Son, a total of 41 times, a considerable total in a book of 21 chapters. See further pp. 102ff.

11. *An Outline of the Theology of the New Testament* (London, 1969), p. 341.

133

doubt that Jesus is speaking of the divine love that sent him to this earth and of the fact that when his mission was accomplished he would return to the Father.

It is not surprising that John speaks of the Father's love for the Son (3:35; 5:20; 10:17; 15:9), and of the Son's love for the Father (14:31). It is perhaps surprising that this is the one place in the New Testament in which the Son is explicitly said to love the Father. Throughout the New Testament, of course, the Son's love for the Father is everywhere implicit; it is significant that the one passage in which it comes to expression is in John.

The Father and the Children

That God is Father means, for John, in the first instance that he is the Father of our Lord Jesus Christ. It is in this relationship that we see what divine fatherhood means. But it is also important for John that believers enter the heavenly family and may call God "Father". As we have noted elsewhere, John does not call them "sons of God". As it relates to the heavenly family he reserves "son" for Christ; when he is speaking of believers, he calls them "children" rather than "sons". This is a Johannine usage; Paul, for example, does not hesitate to speak of human members of the heavenly family as "sons". But John's usage distinguishes between Christ's sonship and that of anyone else. Jesus *is* God's Son; believers *become* God's sons. He belongs to God's family because of what he is; we may be adopted into that family despite what we are. As J. I. Packer puts it, "The gift of sonship to God becomes ours, not through being born, but through being born again."[12] John is quite clear that our membership in the heavenly family is not to be taken for granted; it is sheer miracle.

We should take this seriously. The New Testament nowhere teaches that the whole human race belongs to the heavenly family as though being born on earth meant being enrolled in heaven. As Alan Richardson says, "There is therefore something original and distinctive in the teaching of Jesus about God as the Father of each individual disciple. Jesus did not, of course, teach the

12. *Knowing God* (London, 1973), p. 181. He says later, "Our first point about adoption is that it is *the highest privilege that the gospel offers*" (p. 186).

134

liberal protestant notion that God is Father of all men *qua* men and that all men are therefore brothers (Harnack's 'essence of Christianity'); God is Father only of those who have by faith and repentance entered into his reign and accepted the obedience of sons."[13]

G. E. Ladd emphasizes this point and holds that in respect of the scope of God's fatherhood "a radical change" has come over New Testament criticism. Certainly in an earlier day it was common to have it said that there is a divine fatherhood over the entire human race, but it is now widely recognized that it is difficult to find this in the New Testament. Ladd draws attention to "two exegetical facts: (1) Jesus never grouped Himself together with His disciples as the sons of God, since His messianic sonship is different from the sonship of His disciples; (2) Jesus never applied the category of sonship to any but His disciples. People become children of God by recognizing His messianic sonship".[14] On one occasion at any rate in this Gospel Jesus almost goes out of his way to distinguish between his sonship and that of his disciples (20:17), and John has what amounts to the classic way of describing how people become children of God (1:12-13).

The Father Works

"My Father works up till now," Jesus said, "and I work" (5:17). Jesus spoke these words in a situation wherein the Jews were accusing him of breaking the Sabbath, and in doing so he drew attention to the fact that the Father works even on the Sabbath. If this were not so, the whole universe would cease to function. It is not a question of whether work of some kind is permitted on the Sabbath, but what kind of work is allowed. But for our present purpose the thing to notice is that the Father is active. John is not writing about an absentee God who allows the universe to go on

13. *An Introduction to the Theology of the New Testament* (London, 1958), p. 149.
14. *ISBE*, II, p. 511. C. F. D. Moule draws attention to the use of "Abba" (Mark 14:36; Rom. 8:15; Gal. 4:6) and reasons, "there is no need to doubt that it is a genuine word of Jesus; and, representing a form of address to human fathers, it reflects in Jesus an unprecedented simplicity and directness of approach to God" (*IDB*, II, p. 433). While the word itself is not recorded in John, this Gospel certainly gives evidence of this "unprecedented simplicity and directness of approach to God."

all by itself. The Father is at work sustaining it all and working out his purposes.[15]

Elsewhere Jesus draws attention to God's work in salvation. The Father keeps giving the true bread from heaven (6:32), the bread that sustains spiritual life. And in an important saying Jesus tells his hearers that no one can come to him "unless the Father who sent me draws him" (6:44). The initiative in salvation does not come from the sinner; it comes from God. John does not depict a God who is kindly enough disposed towards sinners to accept them if and when they turn to him. He depicts a God who loves people, even sinful people, so much that he seeks them out and draws them to himself. Without that drawing they cannot be saved. In the same context we find that all are taught by God, and that only as they learn from him do they come to Christ (6:45). The same truth may be expressed in Jesus' words: "No one can come to me unless it be given him of the Father" (6:65). This truth was repeated in the upper room when Jesus said, "No one comes to the Father except through me" (14:6).[16] He also said that the person who loves him will be loved by the Father, and that he himself will love him too (14:21; cf. 14:23). Such passages make a strong link between the Father and the Son, specifically in the working out of salvation. We also find that the Father bears witness to Jesus (8:18), a statement that we should probably understand in something of the same way. It is Jesus who brings the salvation of which we have been talking, and that salvation is God-appointed. So the Father bears his witness to Jesus and to

15. Cf. Ronald A. Ward, "God is the Sustainer of the universe. To use a word common in Canada, He is its Operator. Jesus does not live in a naturalistic universe: the sun indeed rises regularly, but the uniformity is not self-working. God may work according to law, but it is He who works, not a substantial law. *He* causes His sun to rise . . . and *He* causes it to rain" (*Royal Theology*, London, 1964, p. 26).

16. W. F. Howard sees in these words "the theme of the Gospel." He goes on, "It underlies all the teaching of the Epistles. The words are not to be understood as a disparagement of all the soaring imaginations of seekers after God in any age or race of men. Still less should we read into them a repudiation of all that had been spoken by prophetic seers in their fragmentary witness to Israel. Many had sought God, and had been found by Him. The uniqueness of the revelation in Christ is that in him we have the Way to the *Father*" (*Christianity according to St. John*, London, 1943, pp. 181-82).

what he is doing. From another angle we see the importance of the divine initiative in bringing salvation into being.

With this we should take Jesus' words, "In my Father's house are many dwelling places (if it were not so I would have told you), for I am going to prepare a place for you" (14:2).[17] There is an air of assurance about these words; Jesus is speaking of something about which he has certain knowledge. And it conveys to the disciples the certainty of ultimate triumph. For the moment they were in trouble from the opposition of the world, and they would soon be plunged into gloom when what they saw as the tragedy of the crucifixion took place. But Jesus looks beyond all that to the fact that the salvation he had come to bring would carry right on into the life beyond this one.

There is also an activity of the Father of a more severe kind. As we saw in an earlier chapter, when Jesus speaks of himself as the true vine he speaks also of the Father as the vinedresser and explains the meaning of this in these terms: "Every cane in me that does not bear fruit he takes away, and every one that bears fruit he cleanses so that it may bear more fruit" (15:2). We should probably not understand the cane that does not bear fruit as an imperfect believer. Jesus goes on to speak of his followers as being "clean" (the adjective corresponding to the verb just used of the Father's activity), and a little earlier he had said of those in the upper room, "you are clean, but not all," a statement John explains by adding, "for he knew who was betraying him; for this reason he said, 'You are not all clean' " (13:10-11). When the Father purges the vine of the "unclean" canes, he is ridding it of people like Judas, those who profess membership while in fact betraying all that Jesus stands for.[18] Such have no place in the church.

There is also an activity in those who really are abiding in the

---

17. It is possible to take the passage in the way RSV does: "In my Father's house are many rooms; if it were not so, would I have told you that I go to prepare a place for you?" But since John has not recorded any saying about Jesus preparing a place, it seems better to take the words "if it were not so, I would have told you" as a parenthesis or a plain statement.

18. C. K. Barrett has a twofold application: "The original branches in God's vine were the Jews; these, being unfruitful (unbelieving), God removed . . . but *en emoi* shows that his primary thought was of apostate Christians" (*The Gospel according to St. John*[2], Philadelphia, 1978, p. 473).

vine. Those who bear fruit are cleansed so that they will bear more fruit. The grapevine, left to itself, will produce a few grapes and a riotous mass of foliage. The result may be interesting and decorative, but it is not fruitful. Jesus is telling us that the Father looks to those saved in Christ to live fruitful lives, not to produce flashy, ornamental achievements barren of effect. God's pruning away of what is barren (no matter how aesthetically satisfying we find it) may well be painful. But it is a necessary part of living out the fulness of our salvation. We are saved not in order to indulge in spiritual hobbies of our own, but in order to produce fruit.

Worship

Early in his Gospel John tells the story of Jesus' driving the traders from the temple. As he does so, he quotes the words of Jesus: "Take these things away from here; do not make my Father's house into a house of trade" (2:16). From the beginning John lets his readers see that there is a dignity attaching to God and to the house of God. We are not to take lightly the place that is linked to the name of God.

Nor should we take lightly the way we worship. When the woman at the well puts her emphasis on the place where God is worshipped, Jesus tells her that a time is coming when God will be worshipped in neither of the places she is discussing. He goes on, "You worship you know not what. We worship what we know, for the salvation (i.e., the messianic salvation, not salvation in general) is from the Jews" (4:22).[19] It is not enough to have a spirit of devotion, as doubtless many of the Samaritans did. It is important to take notice of what the Father requires of those who approach him. Jesus goes on to point out that the Father actively seeks those who worship "in spirit and in truth" (4:23). Indeed, those who worship "must" worship in this way (4:24). We should

19. R. C. H. Lenski comments, "Though in the Greek abstract nouns may have the article as a matter of course, here 'the salvation' denotes the specific and only salvation contemplated in God's promises and to be realized in his incarnate Son. This salvation is in no way promised to the Samaritans, so that it would emanate from their midst, but to the Jews alone. The Messiah could not be a Samaritan, he had to be a Jew" (*The Interpretation of St. John's Gospel*, Columbus, 1956, pp. 320-21).

not pass over too quickly the fact that the Father "seeks" worshippers of this kind. This is a new note. Judaism knew of a God who would welcome the penitent sinner when he returned. But the thought that God actively seeks people who will worship in the right way is not to be found there. Judaism has no equivalent of this passage on worship or the Synoptic parable of the man with a hundred sheep.

On more than one occasion John records that Jesus prayed. He records his thanksgiving at the tomb of Lazarus (11:41-42) and the interesting occasion when Jesus looked at one possible prayer and prayed another. He asked, "What shall I say?" and suggested, "Father, save me from this hour." He rejected this because "for this reason I came to this hour." So he prayed, "Father, glorify your name" (12:27-28).[20] The passage shows us something of Jesus' prayerfulness, of the difficulty in the way of the Son's understanding quite what he should do, and of his recourse to prayer as the way out of the difficulty.[21]

There are some interesting references to prayer during Jesus' conversation with his disciples in the upper room on the eve of the crucifixion. He said to them, "I will pray the Father, and he will give you another Paraclete, so that he may be with you for ever" (14:16). The parts played by the Father and the Son in the sending of the Spirit are difficult to untangle, for a little later Jesus said that he would send the Paraclete from the Father (15:26).[22]

20. There are some who hold that Jesus actually prayed, "Father, save me from this hour", then added, "for this reason I came to this hour"; he then changed his prayer to "Father, glorify your name." See William Hendriksen, *New Testament Commentary, Exposition of the Gospel according to John,* II (Grand Rapids, 1954), pp. 198-201. But it is better to see a consistency of purpose in the sequence I have outlined.

21. William Barclay brings out something of the courage of Jesus as he prayed this prayer: "No one wishes to die; no one wishes to die at thirty-three; and no one wishes to die upon a cross. There would have been no virtue in Jesus' obedience to God at all, if it had come easily and without cost. Real courage does not mean not being afraid. There is no virtue in doing a thing if to do it is an easy thing. Real courage means to be terribly afraid, and yet to do the thing that ought to be done" (*The Gospel of John,* II, Edinburgh, 1956, p. 146).

22. Gary M. Burge speaks of John as placing the two views, that the Father would send the Spirit and that the Son would send him, "in direct tension." But, "As Brown comments, there is no theological tension here. Jesus and the Father are one (10:30), and John's point is the divine agency of the Paraclete" (*The Anointed Community,* Grand Rapids, 1987, p. 203).

We can certainly say that the sending of the Spirit involves them both, and that the Son's prayer is important in this connection. And so is the Father's consideration for the people saved by his Son. He would not leave them without the help they needed and would certainly respond to the Son's prayer. We should probably understand Jesus' later words, "I do not say to you that I will pray the Father for you" (16:26), in much the same way, since he adds, "for the Father himself loves you" (v. 27). Jesus is affirming in strong terms that the disciples may approach the Father in prayer with the greatest confidence. They might perhaps expect that Jesus would pray for them, and the passage is such that we cannot for one moment doubt that he would be ready to do this. But he assures them that the Father's love makes this unnecessary. The Father and the Son are at one.

The prayer of the disciples is mentioned elsewhere in the same conversation. "Whatever you ask the Father in my name, he will give you", said Jesus (15:16; almost the same words are used in 16:23). Interestingly, this is preceded by Jesus' statement that he had chosen them and appointed them so that they should bear fruit in order that whatever they should ask the Father. . . . We usually think that we should pray in order that we may be fruitful, but here we have the thought that we should be fruitful in order that we may pray. We are prone to downgrade the importance of prayer. We say the right words about it, but so often use it as a means to an end, that of being better servants of God. These words of Jesus remind us both that we do not pray well unless we are fruitful and that the prayer that results from fruitfulness is important.

We should also, of course, bear in mind that the conversation in the upper room ends with the great prayer that John records in chapter 17.[23] This prayer covers a wide range and embraces such thoughts as the glorification of the Son and the glorification of the

23. G. A. Turner and J. R. Mantey comment, "We now come to the 'throne room,' to the 'holy of holies' of this 'Spiritual Gospel' ", and go on to remark that "This chapter is to the Fourth Gospel what the central spire is to a Gothic cathedral; it unifies and dominates the whole. Here, more than any other one spot, the reader is truly on 'holy ground' " (*The Gospel according to John*, Grand Rapids, n.d., p. 332). This may be a trifle exuberant, but it draws attention to the fact that this chapter is very important.

Father as the Son's work on earth comes to its consummation. The intimacy between the Father and the Son is reflected in the repeated use of "Father". A noteworthy feature of the prayer is its stress on giving. The verb *didōmi*, "to give", is used 17 times in this prayer, with 13 of them referring to gifts the Father gave to the Son. From another point of view we see that the Father and the Son are involved together in the work of salvation for which the Son came to earth. The prayer contains petitions for the disciples who were there with Jesus, for they were about to face a terrible trial, and it is interesting that as Jesus faced the cross he gave thought to the effect this would have on his followers. He prayed also for those who would believe through their preaching, for the church through the ages.

The World

In a striking and well-known passage John tells us that God loved the world and gave his Son for it (3:16). But throughout this Gospel the world is pictured as not understanding what the Father has done. It is true that the world, in its religious form, claims that God is its Father (8:41), but Jesus points out to such "religious" people that if God were really their Father they would love him (8:42). It is the thought we see running right through this Gospel, that the Father has acted in Christ for the salvation of the world. When then people oppose and hate the Son, it is obvious that they belong to the world, that they are not really children of God. So it is that when the Pharisees ask Jesus, "Where is your Father?" Jesus replies, "You know neither me nor my Father; if you had known me, you would have known my Father too" (8:19). Since Jesus is in the world on a mission from the Father, and since he constantly does the Father's will, it is not possible really to know God and yet to oppose him. The attitude of the Pharisees towards Jesus made it impossible to think that they really knew the Father.

Some scholars these days are sure that the Jesus of Saint John was not interested in those outside the little Christian group. Such writers often maintain that Jesus in this Gospel refuses to pray for the world, and cite 17:9 as evidence for this contention. Thus H. W. Montefiore says, "In the Fourth Gospel Christ does not pray for the world, only for his disciples and those who will believe through them. In the Fourth Gospel Christ does not die for the world. He lays down his life for his friends."[24] But this is to overlook two considerations. One is that it is not easy to see how Jesus could pray for "the world" as "world". Could Jesus possibly pray that the world should be blessed in its worldliness? That it should go on from strength to strength in its opposition to God and its persecution of God's people? Surely the only prayer that he could pray for "the world" is that it should cease to be "the world". The second consideration is that that prayer he did pray, twice. He prayed that "the world may believe that you sent me" (17:21) and that it "may know that you sent me" (17:23). Both times he is praying that the world may come to recognize the Father's hand in what he was doing, and that, of course, means that it ceases to be the world and comes to be numbered among the followers of him whom God sent.

"The Name"

In an earlier chapter we noticed that "the name" of Jesus was very important. Now we take notice of the fact that "the name" of the Father is also a very significant concept. As in the case of Jesus, "the name" stands for the entire person, so that in the passages we now consider it means the Father's essential being, all that the Father is and does.

Sometimes we find that this concerns the mission of the Son (in this Gospel it is impossible to separate the work of the Son from that of the Father).[25] The tragedy of the Jews was that, although Jesus had come "in the name" of his Father, they did not receive him (5:43). At the triumphal entry into the city of Jerusalem Jesus was greeted as him "that comes in the name of the Lord" (12:13). In line with this the works he did were works

24. *Awkward Questions on Christian Love* (Philadelphia, 1964), p. 106. So also E. Käsemann complains that "It is not even universally recognized that John demands love for one's brethren, but not for one's enemies, and correspondingly that Jesus loves his own, but not the world" (*The Testament of Jesus*, London, 1968, p. 59). This is surely a perversion of the teaching of this Gospel (cf. 3:16).

25. Cf. R. Abba, "Christ's claim to have come in his Father's name means as the Father's representative (John 5:43). His works done in that name bear witness to the Father's authority, which he shares (10:25). In him there has been given to men the complete revelation of the divine nature: he has manifested and declared the name of God (12:28; 17:6, 26)" (*IDB*, III, p. 506).

done "in the name of my Father" (10:25), so that at the end he could say, "I have manifested your name to the men whom you gave me" (17:6). With this we should take the words, "While I was with them, I kept them in your name" (17:12), and the prayer that the Father would keep them in his own name (17:11). It accords with the idea of revelation which runs through this Gospel that Jesus could also say, "I have made your name known to them, and I will make it known, so that the love with which you have loved me may be in them, and I in them" (17:26). This is a complex passage, but at the least we can say that Jesus' making known of the name leads to the love of the Father being a reality in the inner being of the disciples.

We should add a couple of passages that speak of the Father's concern. One occurs when he says that the Father will send the Spirit in his (the Son's) name (14:26), and the other assures them that whatever they ask the Father in his (again, the Son's) name the Father will give them (15:16). Both bring out the concern the Father has for his people and the provision he makes for them as they go forward on their earthly pilgrimage.

Eschatology

This Gospel is not noteworthy for an emphasis on the last time. John is more interested in the fact that the last time has been made present in the life and death and resurrection of Jesus. But he does not overlook the fact that the Father is Lord of the end as well as of the beginning. The Father raises the dead and gives them life (5:21), which probably refers to the spiritually dead and denotes an act in the here and now, but which may also apply to the end time. Again, Jesus says, "If anyone serves me, him will the Father honor" (12:26). This is true of the here and now, but it will reach its climax at the end of time. We should not overlook either the implications of Jesus' words in the upper room: "I am coming again, and I will receive you to myself" (14:3), a passage on which Donald Guthrie comments, "this certainly appears to demand a future event to complement the statement about a going away".[26]

---

26. *New Testament Theology* (Leicester, 1981), pp. 800-801.

The words emphasize the activity of the Son rather than the Father, but in the context the two are combined and we should see this here.

We should not overlook the fact that now and then this Gospel refers to judgment at the end time. This may refer to the action of the Son, as in the recurrent "I will raise him up in the last day" in the bread of life discourse (6:39, 40, 44, 54), though even here we cannot say that all action by the Father is excluded. Certainly he is involved elsewhere. Thus Jesus says that the Father judges no one but has committed all judgment to the Son (5:22), which certainly looks forward to what the Father has determined for Judgment Day. This is also in mind when Jesus says to some Jews, "Do not think that I will accuse you to the Father" (5:45). There is, of course, a sense in which Jesus is a standing witness against unbelievers in the present life, but this passage seems to point forward to final judgment. We should probably discern something of the Father's action also in the firm prediction that Jesus' "word" will at the last day judge anyone who despises him (12:48). This also seems to be part of the meaning of the statement that the wrath of God "abides" on the disobedient sinner (3:36). The saying clearly points to what happens here and now, but it gives no hint that it is confined to this life.

CHAPTER 8

The Holy Spirit

RUDOLF SCHNACKENBURG ISSUES A WARNING TO anyone who studies what the New Testament in general and the Fourth Gospel in particular have to say about the Holy Spirit that in this twentieth century: "consciousness of the presence of the Spirit has to a very great extent disappeared, even in the believing community, and has therefore to be aroused as a prior condition." He adds, "It is possible to say that the only person who will understand the words about the Spirit is one who has already experienced the presence of the Spirit."[1] We cannot assume that anyone who lays a casual claim to being Christian will really understand what the work of the Holy Spirit is, and the teaching of John on the subject will accordingly not necessarily be obvious. But anyone who genuinely submits to the lordship of Jesus will understand what John is saying. As we approach this subject, then, we must bear in mind that John is writing for believers, not for nominal adherents of the Christian religion.

John has a good deal to tell us about the Holy Spirit, and he does it in his own way. He speaks of the Spirit as "the Spirit of truth" (14:17; 15:26; 16:13) and uses the unusual designation *paraklētos* of him (14:16, 26; 15:26; 16:7). He associates the Spirit with the beginning of Jesus' ministry and with the beginning of the spiritual life of believers. He links the gift of the Spirit with the declaration of forgiveness and retention of sins (20:22-23). Even to list such things is to show that John has his own individual contribution to make to our understanding of the Spirit of God.

Some of his references to "spirit" are not important for our purpose. Thus he speaks of Jesus as deeply moved in spirit (11:33)

---

1. *The Gospel according to St John,* III (New York, 1982), p. 153.

and as troubled in spirit (13:21). These passages refer to Jesus' human spirit and tell us nothing about the Holy Spirit. The same is probably true of the passage that says that Jesus "gave up his spirit" in death (19:30), although some have found here the thought that the dying Jesus gave the Spirit to the disciples at the cross.[2] It is an unusual way of referring to death and may indicate that there was an element of voluntariness about the way Jesus died, perhaps "he handed over his spirit to the Father." We should also here not give serious consideration to the statements that the worshipper must worship "in spirit and truth" (4:23) and that "God is spirit" (4:24). The former tells us about the involvement of the human spirit in worship (there may well be in addition an allusion to what the Holy Spirit does in true worship, but the primary reference is to the worshipper), and the latter tells us something about the nature of the Father.[3] Neither is directly concerned to give information about the Holy Spirit.

But there are several other passages with important teachings about the Spirit. Thus at the beginning of this Gospel's narrative we have information about John the Baptist. Among other things we read: "John bore witness saying, 'I saw the Spirit coming down like a dove from heaven, and it remained on him. And I did not know him, but he who sent me to baptize in water said to me, *On whomever you see the Spirit coming down and remaining on him, this is he who baptizes in Holy Spirit.* And I have seen, and I have borne

---

2. E. C. Hoskyns translates "He handed over the Spirit", and thinks the words were "directed to the faithful believers who stood below." He speaks of "The outpouring of the Spirit here recorded", and says that 1 John 5:8 "seems to make this interpretation not only possible, but necessary" (*The Fourth Gospel,* London, 1947, p. 532). So also R. H. Lightfoot, "to them primarily, when the Lord inclines His head to rest, in the peace of His union with the Father and of His accomplished work, He hands over the new dispensation of the Spirit" (*St. John's Gospel,* Oxford, 1956, p. 320). But this is an improbable exegesis.

3. J. D. G. Dunn holds that this verse refers to God's "relationship to men" rather than to "the being of God": "Spirit is God's mode of communication with men. Consequently he looks for men to respond in the same manner—to worship in Spirit and truth" (*Jesus and the Spirit,* London, 1975, p. 353). We may agree that God does communicate with us by the Spirit, but that does not mean that John 4:24 is not telling us something about the nature of God. Cf. J. H. Bernard, "It is the Essential Being, rather than the Personality, of God which is in question" (*A Critical and Exegetical Commentary on the Gospel according to St. John,* I, Edinburgh, 1928, p. 150).

witness that this is the Son of God'" (1:32-34). When Jesus first came to him, the Baptist saluted him as "the Lamb of God, who takes away the sin of the world" (1:29), and then reminded his hearers that he had spoken previously about the one who would come after him and who had come to be before him (1:30-31). Next come the words about the Spirit, so the saying comes very early in the Baptist's acquaintance with Jesus. For him it was important to be clear that Jesus and the Holy Spirit were connected.

He says that he saw the Spirit coming down on Jesus, and there is no real reason for thinking that he meant that he had seen a vision. In this Gospel the verb employed here is used of seeing with ordinary physical sight, and that appears to be the meaning in this passage. John is saying that there was an outward manifestation that looked like a dove[4] when the Spirit came on Jesus. From the other Gospels we learn that this was at Jesus' baptism, but in the Fourth Gospel we do not read of that baptism (the Baptist in this Gospel does one thing only—he bears witness to Jesus). At that time Jesus heard the heavenly voice, "You are my Son, the Beloved, in you I am well pleased" (Mark 1:11). From there he went on to the temptation and to the beginning of his mission.

This means that the Holy Spirit came on Jesus as he began his public ministry. Thus it is a fair inference that the human Jesus needed the divine Spirit as he began his work for God and for sinners. In an earlier chapter we saw that the Fourth Gospel puts some emphasis on the reality of Jesus' humanity; the coming of the Spirit underlines this. We all, being human, need the help and the guidance of the Spirit of God, and in that Jesus underwent the experience of which we read at his baptism we see that he is one with us.

Perhaps we should here look at another of the difficult sayings about the Spirit, this one involving a comment about Jesus: "He whom God sent speaks the words of God, for he does

---

4. It is perplexing that the Spirit came in the form of a dove. It is often said that the dove was a symbol of the Holy Spirit, but there seems no evidence of this (see C. K. Barrett, *The Holy Spirit and the Gospel Tradition*, London, 1947, pp. 35-39). Among the Rabbis the dove symbolized Israel (see SBk, I, pp. 123-25; I. Abrahams, *Studies in Pharisaism and the Gospels*, I, New York, 1967, p. 48). If this is in mind here, Jesus is depicted as the true Israelite as he received the Holy Spirit. But this is conjectural.

not give the Spirit by measure" (3:34). The precise understanding of the expression is much more difficult than appears on the surface. First, it is not completely certain who it is who gives the Spirit. It could possibly be the one whom God sends, that is, Jesus, but most agree that it is the Father. Some MSS indeed clear the difficulty up by inserting "God" or "the Father" (and JB translates, "God gives him the Spirit without reserve"). But even without such an addition it seems that this is the way the passage should be understood. If we think of Christ as giving the Spirit to believers, there is the problem of "not . . . by measure". It is true that when the Spirit is given to believers there is always the thought of abundant supply, but we cannot think that believers receive the Spirit in the same degree as Christ did.[5] Augustine and Calvin both draw attention to the fact that grace is given to believers "according to the measure of Christ's free gift" (Eph. 4:7). This does not specifically mention the Spirit, but it may well have relevance to the Spirit's presence with believers.

We could think of the Father as giving the Spirit to Christ or to believers. But while we need not doubt that God the Father gives the Spirit to believers,[6] it seems that his giving without measure applies better to his gift of the Spirit to Christ. Rieu translates, "God bestows the Spirit on him with no grudging hand", and this appears to be the sense of it. We should bear in mind that the very next verse tells us that "the Father loves the Son, and he has given all things into his hand" (3:35). The context makes it clear that it is the gifts the Father makes to the Son that are in mind.

It would be possible to take the Greek in the sense, "he whom God sent speaks the words of God, for the Spirit does not give by measure." While this points to an important truth, it scarcely fits the context, and most agree that it is an unlikely meaning for the passage.

It seems, then, that we are take the words as indicating that God the Father gives the Spirit to the Son unstintingly. The Spirit

5. Cf. Edwin H. Palmer, "To us God gives the Spirit in part and never in fullness, but to Christ he gave him not by measure, but without measure, limitlessly, in completion and fullness" (*The Holy Spirit*, Grand Rapids, 1958, p. 67).

6. H. B. Swete argued for this view: "God gives His Spirit to men ungrudgingly; there is no limit to His bounty but that which comes from the incapacity of the recipient" (*The Holy Spirit in the New Testament*, London, 1910, p. 136).

is to be seen in all his fulness in the ministry of Christ. We need not doubt that this is true also, though to a lesser extent, in the ministry the Lord commits to Christ's followers. But the primary application is to Christ. The passage reinforces those earlier ones which speak of the Spirit as coming on Jesus for the work of his ministry.

Baptism in the Spirit

John the Baptist goes on to contrast the baptism in which he was engaged, "baptism in water", with what Jesus would do, "baptize in Holy Spirit" (1:33). The exact significance of the expression is not easy to discern,[7] but the main thrust is clear: Jesus would bring people a new life, a life characterized by the presence of the Holy Spirit. There is the thought of a richness that could not be brought by such a ministry as that of John the Baptist. John's baptism was no more than a baptism of repentance; there was something essentially negative about it. It was an important negative and one that is fully taken over into the Christian way. For Christians as well as for the followers of John the Baptist repentance is a necessity; evil must be forsaken. But Jesus does what the Baptist could never do: he brings the gift of the Holy Spirit with all that that means in terms of newness of life.

This truth is further brought out in Jesus' conversation with Nicodemus, which speaks of the necessity of a rebirth. Jesus first tells the Pharisee that "unless one be reborn from above, he cannot see the kingdom of God" (3:3).[8] We have already learned in

---

7. John speaks of Jesus as baptizing *en pneumati hagiōi*. This might conceivably signify being "in" the Spirit (with "in" having some such sense as it has in being "in Christ") or as the Seer who came to be "in the Spirit" (Rev. 1:10; 4:2, etc.). Again Christians are to pray in the Spirit (Eph. 6:18), they have love in the Spirit (Col. 1:8), they are sanctified in the Holy Spirit (Rom. 15:16). But it is usually accepted that in the present passage the parallelism with baptism "in water" shows that we should take "Spirit" as the means or the agency of the baptism in question. Cf. J. H. Bernard, "the contrast of 'water' and 'spirit' in the Baptist's references to his ministry of baptism is intended to convey that it was only preparatory to, and symbolical of, a greater ministry that was at hand" (*A Critical and Exegetical Commentary on the Gospel according to St. John*, I, p. 52).

8. The meaning of *gennēthēi anōthen* is not obvious. The verb strictly denotes the action of the male parent, "beget", rather than that of the female, "give birth

the Prologue that the children of God are born "not of bloods, nor of the will of the flesh, nor of the will of man, but of God" (1:13), and there is something of the same truth here. The way into the kingdom is not that of putting forth the best human effort; it requires a completely different life, which can be spoken of as a new birth. It is a new start, freed from all the handicaps of the old life.

Nicodemus responded with the question, "How can a man be born when he is old?" and added another, "He cannot enter his mother's womb a second time and be born, can he?" (3:4). It may be that he did not like the way the conversation was going and accordingly chose to be deliberately obtuse. Since a proselyte to Judaism was sometimes spoken of as a child newly born, Nicodemus may have thought it inappropriate that such a term be used of a leader like himself. Or he may have been wistful. His reasoning may have been something like this: "I am today the result of my heredity and then of all that has happened to me through the years. It would be nice to break away from the heavy hand of the past with all its bad habits, fears, prejudices, and the like and to make a completely new start. But the lesser miracle of a physical rebirth is quite impossible; how much more that of giving a man a new start in life! Regeneration would be wonderful, but it is quite impossible."

Jesus replies, "Truly, truly, I say to you, unless one is born of water and Spirit, one cannot enter the kingdom of God" (3:5). The "truly, truly" with which the saying begins shows that it is very important and very solemn. The introduction of being born "of water" is somewhat perplexing. Some have thought that we should understand it in terms of purification, perhaps the baptism of John with its stress on repentance. The way into the kingdom would then embrace the negative, the cleansing from sin, and the positive, the work of the Holy Spirit within.

---

to" (we have the same terminology in 1 John 3:9), but we should probably not insist on this; "be born" gives the sense of it. The adverb may mean "from above" or "again". Elsewhere in this Gospel it means "from above" (cf. v. 31), but in this context Nicodemus clearly understood it in the sense "again". But this is certainly wrong; if we decide against "from above" we should understand the sense "anew", for Jesus is certainly not speaking of a repetition of one's physical birth. He was speaking of something completely new.

Others remind us that among the Jews anything damp, such as "water", "dew", "drop", or "rain", was a euphemism for the male semen. If we understand it here in this sense, the saying may mean "unless one is born of natural seed and also of the Spirit . . .", that is, "naturally and spiritually. . . ." We should also notice that "water" and "Spirit" are closely connected in this saying.[9] Thus, it may well be that the two should be taken closely together in the sense "of spiritual seed". In that case the meaning will be much the same as "born of the Spirit" (3:8). This would give a very satisfactory meaning.

In modern times it is often taken for granted that the reference is to Christian baptism: a person must be reborn in baptism in order to enter the kingdom. The point strongly urged in favor of this meaning is that when this Gospel was circulating in the early church, this meaning might well have been favored (actually we have no way of knowing whether it would have been favored or not).[10] But against it is the impossibility of Nicodemus's making sense of such a meaning. Christian baptism had not yet been begun, and would not be for a matter of years. It is not easy to see why Jesus would perplex the Pharisee with a reference to a not-yet-existent Christian sacrament. The only way one can hold this position is by surrendering any view that this conversation is historical. John, it is said, is giving us his view of baptism and doing so by manufacturing this conversation.

Of the three views it seems that the second is the best, and in the form "born of spiritual seed". Jesus is surely affirming that the way into the kingdom is not by any human device. It is by regeneration brought about by the Spirit of God. We should perhaps notice the plural "you" in the expression "you must be reborn from above" (3:7). Jesus is not speaking of something

---

9. The Greek is *ex hydatos kai pneumatos*, not *ex hydatos kai ek pneumatos*. The use of only one *ek* and the absence of the definite article bring the two terms together. The expression seems to mean "of water-and-spirit" rather than "of water and of spirit".

10. Cf. J. D. G. Dunn, "Besides assuming that we know when the Gospel was written, and the sacramental understanding of the readers to whom it was addressed, it assumes also that it was John's intention to fit his writing into the context of that understanding and not to challenge or alter it in any radical way" (*Baptism in the Holy Spirit,* London, 1970, p. 190).

private to Nicodemus but of what applies to everybody. There is no way into God's kingdom by our own energies or devisings. We enter when the Spirit of God remakes us.[11]

In his discourse in the synagogue in Capernaum Jesus has a further saying of interest in the present connection. Towards the end of that address he says, "The Spirit is the life-maker; the flesh profits nothing at all. The words that I have spoken to you are spirit and they are life" (6:63). The contrast between "Spirit" and "flesh" might lead us to think of the human spirit, but that spirit cannot be said to give life. It is the Holy Spirit who is the giver of life. Jesus is saying to a different audience what he has said to Nicodemus, namely that real life comes from the working of the Holy Spirit and in no other way. It is important to realize that life is a good gift of God.[12] When Jesus goes on to speak of his words as Spirit and as life, we should probably understand a further reference to the Holy Spirit. He is saying that his teaching is not to be interpreted in a wooden, literalistic manner, but as the Holy Spirit enlightens. There is a strong emphasis on the connection with real life and the Holy Spirit.

We see, then, that John has a good deal to say about the work of the Holy Spirit in initiating spiritual life. The life Jesus calls on people to live is not attained by a desperate human attempt to bring it into being. It is not something meritorious; it does not earn God's favor. It is the result of the Holy Spirit at work within the believer in such a way that the person is regenerated by divine power. The Holy Spirit brings such a person to a level of living that could never be attained by any human effort. John is clear throughout his Gospel that it is this sort of living that is significant. The gospel summons people to enter a wonderful way of life, a life characterized by the presence and power of the Spirit of God.

11. Perhaps we should notice here Eduard Schweizer's contention that "The only miracle . . . is the Spirit's gift of faith in Jesus as the Son sent by God" (*The Holy Spirit*, London, 1981, p. 107). It is only the Spirit of God that can bring sinners to believe in Jesus, and without that there would be no Christianity.

12. This was not always appreciated by Jewish teachers. We read in the Mishnah, "Great is the Law, for it gives life to them that practice it both in this world and in the world to come" (*Aboth* 6:7). On this view it is practising the law that is important, not the gift of God.

The Era of the Spirit

Another of John's difficult sayings is found at the climax of Jesus' words to the people when he went up to the temple at the Feast of Tabernacles. On the last day, the great day of the Feast, he stood and cried, "If anyone is thirsty, let him come to me and drink. He who believes on me, as the Scripture said, rivers of living water will flow from his inner being." John adds the comment, "This he said about the Spirit, whom those who believed in him would receive; for it was not yet Spirit because Jesus was not yet glorified" (7:37-39). There is a problem about punctuation, and for example NEB renders the first part of the passage, "If anyone is thirsty, let him come to me; whoever believes in me, let him drink." This is possible, and it is accepted by a number of commentators, but it seems that the other way of taking it is better. It is the thirsty rather than the believer who is invited to drink.[13] Jesus is calling on his hearers to come to him and find their spiritual thirst satisfied, and he is doing so in terms of Old Testament concepts.

But our concern is basically with John's explanation. The words I have rendered "it was not yet Spirit" are usually understood to mean "as yet the Spirit had not been given" (RSV; so NEB, NIV, GNB, etc.) or "there was no Spirit as yet" (JB). The trouble with such translations is that the Spirit had been given, and there was a Spirit. John has spoken of the Spirit as coming down on Jesus (1:32), and he has said that Jesus would baptize with the Spirit (1:33). He has said that people must be "born of the Spirit" if they would enter the kingdom of God (3:5, 6, 8). He has quoted Jesus as saying that the Spirit gives life, and that his words are Spirit and are life (6:63). It cannot be said that in John's view there was no Spirit or that the Spirit had not been given.

We may be helped if we look at the reason he gives for it being not yet Spirit, namely "because Jesus was not yet glorified." John has had glory before him ever since "we saw his glory" (1:14), but this is his first use of the verb "glorify", a verb he will use 23 times in all (no other New Testament writing has it more than Luke with

13. I have discussed the passage and given reasons for my position in *The Gospel according to John* (Grand Rapids, 1971), pp. 422-27.

nine times). It is a significant concept for John. Glory is usually understood in terms of majesty and splendor, but John has the profound idea that real glory is to be seen in lowly service. When someone who is entitled to a high and lofty eminence leaves all that to render lowly and loving service, that for John is real glory. He sees this in the way Jesus lived in lowliness when he came to earth to save us, and especially when he died on the cross. John views the crucifixion as the glorification of Jesus.[14] In this willing acceptance of a shameful death with sinners and for sinners, John sees the supreme glory. It is in this that Jesus is "glorified".

John is explaining, then, that the death of Jesus is the necessary preliminary to the full work of the Spirit. We may profitably reflect that Calvary preceded Pentecost, and John is saying that in the divine economy this is necessarily the order. There could be preliminary manifestations of the Spirit, but the full working of the Spirit of God depended on the accomplishing of the atoning work of Christ. To use the language of later theologians, justification precedes sanctification. As we have seen in the earlier passages we have noted, John does not minimize the importance of what the Spirit was already doing. But he looks forward to a time when the "glorification" of Jesus would prepare the way for a fuller manifestation of the Spirit.[15]

The Spirit of Truth

In the Farewell Discourse Jesus refers to the Holy Spirit as "the Spirit of truth" (14:17; 15:26; 16:13). This is a very unusual expression, found nowhere else in the New Testament and not common in Jewish writings. It is found in the Qumran scrolls and

14. Cf. E. F. Harrison, "The word 'hour' in the Fourth Gospel points regularly to the death of Christ. Jesus was not seeking to invest the cross with an aura of splendor which it did not have, in order to conjure up a psychological antidote to its pain and shame. Rather, glory properly belongs to the finishing of the work which the Father had given him to do, since that work represented the perfect will of God" (Walter A. Elwell, ed., *Evangelical Dictionary of Theology,* Grand Rapids, 1984, p. 444).

15. Donald Guthrie remarks that the words here "mark a clear line of distinction between the Spirit's activity in the ministry of Jesus and his subsequent work in the church" (*New Testament Theology,* London, 1981, p. 529).

in the *Testament of Judah* 20:1, 5 (and does not appear to be attested elsewhere), but John's usage is not that of either. In the Qumran writings "the spirit of truth" is set in opposition to "the spirit of falsehood". Here, for example, is an extract from *The Community Rule:*

> He has created man to govern the world, and has appointed for him two spirits in which to walk until the time of His visitation: the spirits of truth and falsehood. Those born of truth spring from a fountain of light, but those born of falsehood spring from a source of darkness. All the children of righteousness are ruled by the Prince of Light and walk in the ways of light, but all the children of falsehood are ruled by the Angel of Darkness and walk in the ways of darkness.[16]

Clearly this "spirit of truth" differs greatly from "the Spirit of truth" in John's Gospel. In the Qumran writings there are two more or less equal spirits ("God has established the spirits in equal measure until the final age, and has set everlasting hatred between their divisions"[17]); they are engaged in a continuing battle which sometimes appears to be a battle for people and sometimes a battle within people as the "spirit of truth" tries to get people to do what is right and the "spirit of falsehood" tries to enlist them in the ways of evil.

It is fairly clear that John is not writing about the same thing as the author of the Scroll. While there is an arresting similarity of language, there is an impassable gulf between their meanings. John is telling us about a very great Being, one who stands with the Father and the Son, whereas the Scrolls refer to a created being on a much lower level, one who is perpetually at war with a spirit who is his equal.

The *Testament of Judah* also refers to two spirits: "So understand, my children, that two spirits await an opportunity with humanity: the spirit of truth and the spirit of error. In between is the conscience of the mind which inclines as it will."[18] A little later this document assures us that "the spirit of truth testifies to all

16. Cited from G. Vermes, *The Dead Sea Scrolls in English* (Harmondsworth, 1968), pp. 75-76.

17. *Ibid.*, p. 77.

18. 20:1, cited from James H. Charlesworth, ed., *The Old Testament Pseudepigrapha*, I (New York, 1983), p. 800.

things and brings all accusations."[19] Clearly this is a dualism not unlike that which we see at Qumran. In many Jewish writings there is the thought of two Yetzers, one good and one evil, that strive within mankind, and the Qumran use, that of the *Testament of Judah*, or both may well be a development of this concept. But it is clear that despite the similarity of terminology these writings tell us nothing about the Spirit of truth in John.

In 1 John there is a contrast between two spirits: "From this we know the Spirit of truth and the spirit of error" (1 John 4:6). This could be understood in the same sense as the Qumran writings,[20] but it is more likely that here as in the Gospel by "the Spirit of truth" John means the Holy Spirit and that "the spirit of error" is a way of referring to Satan.[21] The evil one is not called by this title elsewhere, but a similar expression is used of him when he is called "the deceiver of the whole earth" (Rev. 12:9).

John does not tell us why the Holy Spirit is called "the Spirit of truth" in these passages, but it is not unlikely that he means that the Spirit characteristically bears witness to the truth. In 1 John we find that the Spirit "is the truth" (1 John 5:6), which in the context seems to mean that the Spirit's testimony is thoroughly reliable; it must be accepted because the nature of the Spirit is truth. The Spirit speaks God's truth.[22] In John 14:17 the thought that the Spirit is in believers is stressed. The world cannot receive this Spirit; it neither sees nor knows him. But it is different with believers, for the Spirit lives in them. The Spirit of truth "proceeds from the Father",[23] and he will bear witness about Christ (15:26).

---

19. 20:5, *ibid*.

20. J. L. Houlden cites the passage from Qumran and comments, "The similarity with the doctrine of our present passage is striking" (*A Commentary on the Johannine Epistles*, London, 1973, p. 106).

21. So Raymond E. Brown, *The Epistles of John* (New York, 1982), p. 501. He translates the title of the evil one as "the Spirit of Deceit", which links it more firmly with Rev. 12:9.

22. Cf. I. H. Marshall, "it is possible that John is thinking here of the activity of the Spirit who witnessed in the past to Jesus as the Son of God and who still bears his testimony, confirming to the believer what he has already said" (*The Epistles of John*, Grand Rapids, 1978, p. 235).

23. This verse is the scriptural support for the position of the Eastern Church that the Spirit proceeds from the Father only, not the Father and the Son, as is held in the West. But the passage will scarcely support the weight that is placed upon it. The preposition is *para* rather than *ek*. On this point B. F. Westcott comments,

The combination emphasizes that the Spirit's testimony about Christ is to be accepted.

The Spirit of truth, Jesus says, "will guide you in all the truth" (16:13). The verb "guide" (*hodēgeō*, here only in John) is connected with the word for "way" (*hodos*); just as Jesus is the Way, so he is the Truth (14:6) to whom the Spirit of truth leads people. The work of the Christ and that of the Spirit are thus seen to be closely related. It is not certain whether Jesus is saying that the Spirit will lead them "into (*eis*)" or "in (*en*)" the truth. Some commentators think the meaning to be that the Spirit leads people so that they come to know the truth, others that the Spirit leads people who do in fact know the truth in the ways of truth. But the two prepositions were not sharply enough distinguished in the New Testament period for us to make much of this. Both of the suggested meanings are true, and we may thankfully accept both. But in this place where Jesus is speaking to believers the emphasis is on the Spirit's work in leading us in the knowledge of the truth.

Jesus goes on to say that the Spirit will not speak from himself but what he hears, which is a way of saying that the Father and the Spirit are at one in what the Spirit will do in the way of leading in the truth. Jesus says further, "he will declare to you the things that are coming." This is probably to be understood as a reference to the whole body of Christian truth, most of which lay in the future at the time Jesus spoke.[24] It is scarcely possible to take it to mean that the Spirit will unveil the future to believers, for Christians through the ages, even deeply spiritual Christians, have been as bad at foretelling what will happen as unbelievers have been. But the Spirit has been active in leading people on and on into the entire body of Christian truth. All the more is this the

"The use of *para* in this place seems . . . to show decisively that the reference here is to the temporal mission of the Holy Spirit, and not to the eternal Procession" (*The Gospel according to St. John*, II, Grand Rapids, 1954, p. 213). The context is not concerned with intra-Trinitarian relationships but with the coming of the Spirit to believers. It is the way the Spirit will continue the ministry that Jesus has had among believers, not the origin of the Spirit, that is in mind.

24. Cf. Swete, "He will carry forward the revelation of Christ and complete it. *He will declare the coming things:* the things of that great and untried life which was about to open before the Church at the Pentecost and to reach its perfection at the Second Coming; the things of the new age, the dispensation of the Spirit" (*The Holy Spirit in the New Testament,* p. 163).

likely meaning in that Jesus goes on to say, "He will glorify me, for he will take of mine and declare it to you" (16:14). The work of the Spirit is in no sense in opposition to that of the Son: it is what the Son has that the Spirit will declare.[25] "The Spirit of truth" thus proves to be a very illuminating way of referring to the Holy Spirit. It does not cover all his activities, but it does make plain a number of important truths. The Spirit who fulfils all that is involved in being the Spirit "of truth" is a very significant being.

The Paraclete

Another title used of the Spirit in the Farewell Discourse is the Greek term *paraklētos*. There is no real English equivalent for this term, so we transliterate it as "Paraclete".[26] The Greek term means "called to the side of", which is understood as being for the purpose of helping. It was often used in legal contexts, so that the meaning "advocate" is often found.[27] But we should understand this in a wide sense. It might denote the functionary we call "the counsel for the defence", but it was not confined to him. Any friend who could come to court and speak in defence of the accused was his paraclete. The significant points are that the word has a legal air about it and that it means someone who helps.

The term occurs four times in the Farewell Discourse and nowhere else in the Fourth Gospel. The only other occurrence of the word in the New Testament is in 1 John 2:1, where we learn that if we sin we have "an Advocate with the Father, Jesus Christ the righteous". Here "Advocate" is clearly the right word, as

25. Cf. Donald Guthrie, "The Spirit is essentially self-effacing. . . . He does not seek his own glory; only that of Christ. This was to prove a valuable test; for any movement claiming the possession of the Spirit, and yet which glorifies the Spirit instead of Christ, would be seen to be alien to the teaching of Jesus about the Spirit" (*New Testament Theology,* p. 531).

26. The meaning given in Liddell and Scott's *Greek-English Lexicon* (rev. H. S. Jones and R. McKenzie) is *"called to one's aid,* in a court of justice: as Subst., *legal assistant, advocate"*; they add "summoned" and "intercessor" as other possible equivalents. J. Behm says, "the history of the term in the whole sphere of known Greek and Hellenistic usage outside the NT yields the clear picture of a legal adviser or helper or advocate in the relevant court" (*TDNT,* V, p. 803).

27. We get "advocate" from the Latin *advocatus,* which is the exact Latin equivalent of *paraklētos.*

Christ is envisaged as pleading for us before the Father's throne when, since we have sinned, we are in real need.

There appears to be a reference to Christ in the first use of the term in the Gospel, where Jesus says, "I will pray the Father, and he will give you another Paraclete, that he may be with you for ever, the Spirit of truth . . ." (14:16-17). "Paraclete" is here applied to the Spirit of truth, but in that he is "another" Paraclete there is room for the thought that the first such helper is Jesus. This is strengthened by the fact that every function assigned to the Holy Spirit in this Gospel is elsewhere said to be performed by Christ. Thus the Spirit teaches believers (14:26), and so does Jesus (7:14); the Spirit is the Spirit of truth (14:17), and Jesus is the truth (14:6); the Spirit is in the disciples (14:17), as is Jesus (14:20; cf. also 1 John 2:24); the Spirit bears witness (15:26), and Jesus does the same (8:14). Both come from the Father (15:26; 16:27-28); the world knows neither (14:17; 16:3). We could go on, but this is enough to show that John takes seriously the idea that Jesus and the Spirit can be linked under the concept "Paraclete".[28]

As John sees it, the Spirit is the divine presence when Jesus' physical presence is taken away from his followers. The passages we have just looked at have made it clear that there is a very close relationship between Jesus and the Spirit: the Spirit is the continuing presence of Jesus with his followers. As J. D. G. Dunn puts it, "The lengthening time gap between John and the historical Jesus, and the continuing delay of the parousia do not mean a steadily increasing distance between each generation of Christians and the Christ. On the contrary, each generation is as close to Jesus as the last—and the first—because the Paraclete is the immediate link between Jesus and his disciples in every generation."[29] In view of

---

28. Stephen S. Smalley concludes that the Paraclete in this Gospel is to be identified with the Spirit, "But the Paraclete in John is not just the Spirit with another name, even if 'Paraclete' and 'Holy Spirit' appear together as synonymous in John 14:26. For the Johannine doctrine of the Paraclete adds to what we know of the Spirit from elsewhere. In particular, the Paraclete is not only . . . like Jesus in nature; he is also like Jesus in activity" (*John: Evangelist and Interpreter,* Exeter, 1978, p. 231).

29. *Jesus and the Spirit,* p. 351. Cf. Raymond E. Brown, "In all that John says of this figure, the intimate relation of the Paraclete to Jesus is what is dominant" (*NTS* 13, 1966-67, p. 126). Cf. also J. M. Boice, "His revelation is an extension of Christ's revelation. The Spirit is the revealer of Jesus" (*Witness and Revelation in the Gospel of John,* Exeter, 1970, p. 152).

this it is important that the Spirit "abides" or "dwells" in believers (1 John 3:24; cf. 4:13).

The Paraclete is here identified with "the Spirit of truth" (14:16-17) and later with "the Holy Spirit" (14:26), connections that point us to an intense moral purpose. As E. A. Abbott put it, "emphasis is laid on the Paraclete, or Advocate, as not being one of the ordinary kind—the kind that takes up a client's cause, good or bad, and makes the best of it—but as being 'holy,' and—which is twice repeated—'a Spirit *of truth*' ".[30] Indeed, it is well to bear in mind that not only in the Paraclete passages but throughout the New Testament the characteristic way of referring to the Spirit is "the *Holy* Spirit", not "the powerful Spirit" or "the wise Spirit" or any such expression. We should not miss the strong moral note that is connected with the Spirit's work.

It is the Father who sends the Spirit (14:26), and sends him to teach (cf. 1 John 2:27).[31] This is clearly an important function, but it is not clear how it is to be carried out. Does Jesus mean that the Spirit will be at work within believers so that each will have teaching direct from God? Or does he mean that the Spirit will so guide the church's teachers that they will convey divine teaching to those they instruct? Perhaps we should not make too sharp a distinction, for surely the truth is that the Spirit may use either method. The important thing is that the kind of teaching John is giving he can rightly attribute to the work of the Spirit working as Jesus had said he would.[32]

The Spirit is also to bring to the disciples' remembrance what Jesus had taught them (14:26). This indicates that the teaching the Spirit will carry out is in the fullest harmony with what Jesus taught: we are not to think of the Paraclete as instituting new

30. *Johannine Grammar* (London, 1906), p. 40.

31. R. Schnackenburg finds this "an original Johannine view about the Spirit, since 'teaching' as a function of the Holy Spirit is encountered elsewhere only in Lk 12:12" (*The Gospel according to John*, III, pp. 141-42).

32. Cf. D. G. Vanderlip, "It appears valid, therefore, to say that one function of the Paraclete doctrine in John is to give a defense for the validity of the deeper insights and understanding which the Fourth Gospel gives. The Paraclete, in other words, is both the source and the endorsement for the developed perspective on the life and ministry of Jesus contained in John" (*Christianity according to John*, Philadelphia, 1975, p. 172).

doctrines that contradict or replace what the Savior taught.[33] The two are in perfect harmony, and indeed things that the disciples may well have forgotten will be recalled to their memories by the Spirit (a truth well worth bearing in mind when we are considering what is included in our Gospels).

Allied to the thought of the Spirit as a teacher is that of him as a witness (15:26). He comes from the Father, and he bears witness. John does not explain in what way he bears this witness, but it would seem that it is in the way the Spirit indwells believers and leads them in the right way.[34] As the Spirit leads and directs them, they are led into a fuller understanding of who and what Jesus was and to a firmer commitment to his cause. This saying goes right on to affirm, "you also bear witness" (15:27), and since the witness of the disciples is to outsiders it would appear that this is part of the Spirit's witness as well. The thought is probably that what the Spirit does in believers forms a witness to those not yet Christian. It is part of the way the world is to be won for Christ. The thought recurs in 1 John, where we find the Spirit linked with "the water" and "the blood" in bearing witness (1 John 5:8). There are problems here, but our best understanding is that "the water" refers back to Jesus' baptism and "the blood" to his death on Calvary.[35] This means that the Spirit's witness is linked with the critical points of Jesus' ministry. Again we see that the Spirit directs people to Jesus. Something like this is also the thrust of the passage in which John urges his readers to test the spirits (1 John 4:1) and tells them that this is the way they know "the Spirit of God": "every spirit that confesses that Jesus Christ has come in the flesh is of God, and every spirit that does not confess Jesus is not of God"; he adds, "this is the spirit of the anti-

33. F. D. Bruner says of the sayings about the Paraclete in this Gospel, "When one arranges the several sayings the most pervasive mark is Christocentricity. The Holy Spirit appears to have as not only the center but as the circumference of his mission the witness to Jesus" (*A Theology of the Holy Spirit*, London, 1971, p. 277). Similarly J. D. G. Dunn, "The dominant theme is the continuity between the ministries of Jesus and the Paraclete" (*Baptism in the Holy Spirit*, p. 175).

34. Cf. W. G. Kümmel, "Here it is clearly stated that the disciples, who can tell of Jesus because they have joined themselves to him, disseminate the Paraclete's witness to Jesus in that the Paraclete is speaking through them" (*The Theology of the New Testament*, London, 1974, p. 318).

35. The alternative is to see a reference to the sacraments of baptism and holy communion. This is not as probable, but if it be accepted it still points us to Jesus.

christ" (1 John 4:2-3). Plainly the work of the Spirit and the work of Christ are related in the most intimate fashion.

The final reference to the Paraclete is Jesus' saying, "If I do not go away, the Paraclete will not come to you; but if I go, I will send him to you" (16:7). This reinforces what we saw earlier about the Spirit reminding disciples of what Jesus had taught, and even more of the truth that during the time of Jesus' ministry "it was not yet Spirit, for Jesus was not yet glorified" (7:39). The ministry of Jesus necessarily preceded that of the Spirit, and it was not until he went away from earth, his mission of salvation completed, that he would send the Spirit.[36]

The passage goes on to speak of the Paraclete as convicting the world of sin, of righteousness, and of judgment. The work of the Spirit is usually concerned with believers; indeed, this is the one place where he is said to do a work in the unbelieving world. Again, his work is usually said to be that of helping, but here he is convicting the world. It is an important work, for in the first place people do not easily come to see themselves for what they are, sinners. They need a work of the Spirit of God in their hearts to bring this about. He will also convict the world of "righteousness", which surely means the righteousness that Christ brought about by dying for needy sinners. Only as the Spirit works in their hearts do people come to see that they cannot be righteous in God's sight by their own puny efforts. And it takes the work of the Spirit for anyone to discern righteousness in that dreadful miscarriage of human justice that put Jesus on the cross. Jesus adds, "because I go to the Father and you see me no more" (16:10), a statement that points forward to the cross and to the ascension. In both of these (though in different senses) Jesus would be taken from them. But the Spirit at work in them would teach them the meaning of it all. Finally, Jesus speaks of convicting of "judgment, because the prince of this world has been judged" (16:11). The defeat of the evil one is not merely a military victory, but an act of judgment. There is justice in what happened at the cross even if that is not apparent other than to those to whom the Spirit of God gives enlightenment.

---

36. So Swete: "The mission of the Spirit could not begin till the mission of the Son was ended; Jesus could not come in the Spirit till He had ceased to live in the flesh" (*The Holy Spirit in the New Testament*, p. 157).

So far we have noted that "Paraclete" is a term with a legal background, although it is not quite as definite a term as our "counsel for the defence". We should notice that a number of attempts have been made to give the term a more precise meaning. The King James Version translated it by "Comforter", a translation that might be supported by the fact that the context has some indications of trouble: "Let not your heart be troubled" (14:1); "I will not leave you as orphans" (14:18); "Let not your heart be troubled or be cowardly" (14:27); "a little while and you will no longer see me" (16:16); "you will wail and lament . . . you will be grieved . . . you therefore now have grief" (16:20-22). The King James translators could also have enlisted support from a number of the early Greek commentators who, for reasons not apparent to us, saw the term as meaning something like "Consoler".[37] This meaning, however, is not supported either by Greek usage generally or by that in the Greek Old Testament.[38] Despite Davies it seems that the only way we could defend "Comforter" is by taking seriously its derivation from the Latin *con* ("with" or intensive) and *fortis* ("strong") and by seeing it as meaning "Strengthener". But this is not what we mean by "Comforter". A number of modern translations render the term as "Helper" (e.g., Goodspeed, GNB). To this it is objected that it scarcely does justice to the passive idea in the term (it means "called alongside").

The legal background leads many to regard "Advocate" (NEB, Rieu) or "Counselor" (RSV) as the right translation. This is supported by the usage in 1 John 2:1, where few would doubt that "Advocate" is suitable, as well as by the fact that in the context there are several references to keeping commandments (14:15, 21,

37. J. G. Davies, however, examines the LXX uses of the term and concludes: "We may conclude therefore that, despite its passive form, *paraklētos*, set by the author of the fourth gospel in the same complex, has assumed an active significance and that its primary meaning is 'comforter'" (*JTS*, n.s. 4, 1953, p. 38). Alan Richardson is impressed by the connection of the word with *paraklēsis* and *parakalein*, but understands this in terms of "the consolation of Israel" (Luke 2:25) and similar passages. Paraclete, he says, "bears a markedly eschatological sense" (*An Introduction to the Theology of the New Testament*, London, 1958, p. 114).

38. J. M. Boice finds an objection to the idea of Comforter: "the difficulty lies in reconciling the idea of comfort with the revelational and judgmental aspects of the Spirit's witness" (*Witness and Revelation in the Gospel of John*, p. 145).

23, 24). Because sinners do not always obey God's commands, they need an Advocate. It could also be pointed out that judgment is one of the great themes of this Gospel. Against this view is the fact that an advocate addresses himself to the court, or speaks to others on behalf of his client, whereas in John he speaks rather to the client (cf. 16:7-11). If the Spirit speaks on behalf of anyone, it is neither the disciples nor the unbelieving world, but Christ; he is Christ's advocate.[39] We should also bear in mind that in this Gospel much of the Paraclete's work, for example teaching or bearing witness, is not specifically related to judgment or to our failure to keep the commandments.

The legal background is undoubted, but perhaps we should bear in mind that the term could be used of anyone who was a friend in a legal dispute; it was not confined to the counsel for the defence. It is perhaps this that leads to translations like "Friend" (C. K. Williams; cf. R. Knox, "another to befriend you"). The objection to such renderings is that the term does not denote friendship in general; there is a legal background to be borne in mind. Perhaps something like "Friend at court" gives the idea as well as we are able to recover it. The Spirit is the Friend of sinners who are in no good case when they face the judgment of God. They need help. This may come in a variety of ways, as reminding them of Christ's teachings, bearing witness, convicting of sin, teaching, and other activities. There appears to be no one term in English that covers all these activities. We must either use a term that draws attention to one of them, or use different terms in different contexts, or retain "Paraclete".[40]

---

39. Raymond E. Brown reminds us that "the Fourth Gospel is written in a legal atmosphere where Jesus is put on trial. This theme runs from the opening scene in John where official interrogators challenge the Baptist, through the many interrogations of Jesus about his witnesses (v.31-40; viii.13-19), to the dramatic trial before Pilate. In this background the forensic function of the Paraclete is to show the disciples (and through them to show the world) by his witness that Jesus was victorious in the trial. . . ." Brown proceeds to reject "advocate" and "counsellor" as translations and to point out that a purely forensic translation "does not do justice to his role as teacher" (*NTS* 13, 1966-67, pp. 116-17).

40. Schnackenburg examines a number of ideas about the source of the term "Paraclete" (*The Gospel according to St John*, III, pp. 144-50).

"Receive Holy Spirit"

There is a very important but very difficult passage towards the end of the Gospel in which Jesus commissions his followers and equips them with the Holy Spirit for their task in the world. On the evening of the day that Jesus rose from the dead the disciples were gathered together when Jesus came and stood in their midst. He gave them the greeting of peace and showed them his hands and his side. Then he said, "Peace to you; as the Father has sent me, I also send you." John tells us that he then breathed into or upon them and said, "Receive Holy Spirit; if you forgive the sins of any, they have been forgiven them; if you hold the sins of any, they have been held" (20:21-23).

There has been a good deal of discussion about the relationship of this passage to the sending of the Spirit at Pentecost as related in Acts 2. Not a few scholars hold that Luke and John are referring to the same thing and that John sees the definitive gift of the Spirit to the church as made on Easter Day whereas Luke locates it several weeks later. Bultmann goes further and says that for John "Easter, Pentecost, and the parousia are not three separate events, but one and the same."[41] This is surely an exaggeration. It seems best to think of John as referring to a gift of the Spirit other than that of which Luke speaks.[42] Where that Evangelist refers to the outpouring of the Spirit to equip the church for its continuing ministry throughout the world, John is speaking of the way the Spirit enables believers to declare what sins are forgiven and what sins are not. John is not writing with what Luke says in mind, either by way of correcting him or supplementing him.

First, let us notice that Jesus sends the disciples on their mission. One of the key thoughts of this Gospel is that the Father sent the Son into the world; reminding them of that truth, Jesus

41. *Theology of the New Testament*, II (London, 1955), p. 57.
42. Although G. E. Ladd holds that "There is no substantial objection to taking the Johannine incident as an acted parable that was actually fulfilled at Pentecost" (*A Theology of the New Testament*, Grand Rapids, 1974, p. 289). James Moffatt points out that John connects the gift of the Spirit very closely to Jesus, which is not the case with Acts, though he does not give attention to the significance of Acts 2:33 (*The Theology of the Gospels*, London, 1912, p. 187).

goes on to send the disciples, indeed to send them in the same way: "as the Father . . . I also. . . ." We cannot say that they were sent to do the same thing as Jesus did, for his saving work was unique and far beyond the power of any created being. But we can say that their work proceeds from his. Jesus lived and died and rose that our sins might be dealt with, and the disciples go out with the gospel message that there is salvation in Jesus for all who turn to him. The one mission is closely linked with the other.

For that mission they will need all the help they can get. Thus Jesus proceeds to equip them with the Holy Spirit. First he "breathed", where the compound *emphysaō* may mean that he breathed into them or that he breathed upon them. We should notice that there is no mention of individual gifts: Jesus is not said to have gone round the little group, breathing on each one of them individually. The gift that he gave as he breathed was a gift for the group as a whole. It was a gift to the church rather than to individual members. It is sometimes urged that the gift was made to the apostles and thus to the ministry of the church. But nowhere do we read that the group consisted only of apostles. There is every reason for thinking that this was the group of which Luke 24:33ff. speaks, and that group included Cleopas and an unknown person. In any case this group is called "disciples" (20:19), not apostles. They surely represent the church as a whole rather than the ministry of the church.[43]

The words that accompanied the gift were "Receive Holy Spirit." From the fact that there is no definite article some have drawn the conclusion that what is meant is not the Holy Spirit, but some gift of the Spirit or even "a holy spirit". But this seems to put too strong an emphasis on the lack of the article. It probably means no more than that an emphasis is put on the fact that the gift is nothing less than Holy Spirit. The idea that an impersonal gift of the Spirit is in mind here, whereas the Spirit comes fully personally on the Day of Pentecost, runs into the difficulty that there is no definite article with Holy Spirit in Acts 2:4. There

43. E. Schweizer holds that if they are regarded as office-bearers, "then the Parting Discourses (including, e.g., the commandment of love) must be completely restricted to them" (*TDNT*, VI, p. 442, n. 753).

and here we should understand the expression to refer to "the Holy Spirit" and not "a holy spirit".

Jesus proceeds to speak of forgiveness and the reverse: "if you forgive the sins of any, they have been forgiven them; if you hold the sins of any, they have been held."[44] Some sections of the church have held this to mean that certain individuals have the power to forgive or to withhold forgiveness, but it is not easy to see this in the words used. First, in the forthright words of William Barclay, "One thing is quite certain—no man can forgive any other man's sins." He immediately goes on, "But another thing is equally certain—it is the great privilege of the Church to convey the message and the announcement and the fact of God's forgiveness to men."[45] Keeping these two facts in balance is the real problem for us. We should notice that the gift was made to the group as a whole, not to individual members. It may be argued that the church must act through individual members, but this is not necessarily so. The church has often acted through synods and congregations, and it is at least arguable that a matter as important as the forgiveness of sins cannot be left to the decision of an individual. Jesus did not speak of individuals, and we must have strong evidence if we are to transfer the words from the church as a whole to some individual members of it.

Then we should notice the plural "any" (*tinōn*). Just as the gift was made to the church as a whole, so it refers to classes of sinners, not to individuals. It may well be argued that what refers to classes has its application to individuals, but we should be clear that Jesus did speak of classes only. He did not say "the sins of what individual sinner you forgive. . . ." Inspired by the Holy Spirit the church may say, "Such and such sins are forgiven, whereas such and such are not." The words do not mean more.

We should not overlook the fact that the verbs "forgiven" and "held" both seem to be in the perfect tense. Some MSS have the present tense with "forgiven", and a few even have the future, but most have the perfect. And the perfect is practically universal with "held". If we take the tense seriously, the meaning is "they

44. I have taken the *an* to mean "if", but it could be the suffix "-ever", as in ASV, "whose soever sins. . . ." But there is no real difference in meaning.

45. *The Gospel of John*, II (Edinburgh, 1956), p. 318.

have been forgiven . . . they have been held."[46] In other words, it is not a case of the church actually doing the forgiving. That is a divine prerogative. All that the words indicate is that the Spirit-filled church may say authoritatively, "Such and such sinners have been forgiven . . . such and such sinners have not been forgiven." It is a declaration of what God has done, not of what the church is currently doing. It may be difficult for us to understand how that is going to work out in practice, but that is no reason for denying the force of the language used.

Nor should we forget that the power to forgive and the power to withhold forgiveness go together. Those who see Jesus as conferring authority on chosen individuals within the church (priests?) to forgive do not always give sufficient attention to the fact that these two powers go together. It gives us no great problem that an individual priest might say to a sinner, "I forgive your sins". But if that is what the words mean, then that same individual priest might say to another sinner, "I refuse to forgive your sins", and those sins would be retained. Now individual priests, even godly priests, sometimes make mistakes, but it is impossible for us to hold that God will retain sins that should have been forgiven. But the one right goes with the other. B. F. Westcott comments, "It is impossible to contemplate an absolute individual exercise of the power of 'retaining'; so far it is contrary to the scope of the passage to seek in it a direct authority for the absolute individual exercise of the 'remitting.'"[47] That must remain an insuperable difficulty in the way of seeing the words as conveying to individuals a personal power to forgive sins.

There can be no doubt that these words refer to forgiveness and the withholding of forgiveness. But our best understanding of the passage is not to see a definitive giving or withholding of this great gift as residing in fallible human hands. Jesus is saying

46. Nigel Turner points out that the perfect tense "has to express two truths at once: the previous inception of the condition and the present continuance of it." In the present passage he rejects the idea that the perfects can be understood in the sense of the present or the aorist and translates, "whose soever sins you forgive, they have been forgiven (perfect); whose soever sins you retain, they have been retained" (*Grammatical Insights into the New Testament,* Edinburgh, 1965, pp. 80, 81).

47. *The Gospel according to St. John,* II, p. 352.

that the Spirit-led church has the authority to say which sins have been forgiven and which not. John Marsh has a useful comment: "There is no doubt from the context that the reference is to forgiving sins, or withholding forgiveness. But though this sounds stern and harsh, it is simply the result of the preaching of the gospel, which either brings men to repent as they hear of the ready and costly forgiveness of God, or leaves them unresponsive to the offer of forgiveness which is the gospel, and so they are left in their sins."[48] We should bear in mind further that in recounting what happened in a post-resurrection appearance of Jesus to his disciples, the Lord reminded them that "so it is written, that the Christ should suffer and that he should rise from the dead on the third day, and that there should be proclaimed in his name repentance for the forgiveness of sins . . ." (Luke 24:46-47). This may be much what Jesus is saying in our present passage.

John thus has a singularly rich and significant understanding of the work of the Spirit of God. Some of the things he has said are difficult for us to comprehend, and there remain some passages where exegetes must agree to differ. But the main thrust of the teaching is plain enough. The Spirit continues the work of Christ. In the divine economy it was Christ who gave the definitive teaching and made the atoning sacrifice, and it was Christ who rose triumphant over death. Then when Christ returned whence he had come, it was the Spirit who lived in the hearts of God's people, the Spirit who would lead and guide and strengthen them for service. The life of the people of God is a life enriched by the never-failing presence of the Spirit of God.

---

48. *The Gospel of St John* (Harmondsworth, 1968), pp. 641-42. Cf. Lesslie Newbigin, "The Church, consecrated in the truth by the promise of the Spirit, is sent into the whole world to be the bearer of that effective action. It will be insofar as it manifests in its corporate life the marks of Christ's passion. And as the effective presence of the light it will also bear the dread responsibility of being the occasion of judgment upon those who prefer the darkness to the light" (*The Light Has Come*, Grand Rapids, 1982, p. 269).

CHAPTER 9

"That You May Believe"

THE AUTHOR OF THIS BOOK TELLS US THAT HIS WHOLE
Gospel was written "that you may believe that Jesus is the
Christ, the Son of God" (20:31).[1] It accords with this that, as we have
seen in earlier chapters, there is a great concentration on the figure
of Jesus. John takes pains to show that he is indeed the Christ, the
Son of God. But he has not done this out of some historical or anti-
quarian interest. His aim is to bring people to believe, and in believing to have life. This means that believing is very important for him,
and in fact he makes the idea ring through his whole book. He uses
the verb "to believe" 98 times, far and away the most in any New
Testament book. We generally think of Paul as a teacher who put
great emphasis on faith, and of course he did this. But the most frequent use of the verb in any one of his letters is 21 (in Romans), and
in the entire Pauline corpus it occurs only 54 times (he has the noun
"faith" 142 times, but John far surpasses him in the use of the verb).
Interestingly, the book that has the most occurrences after John is
Acts, which is probably accounted for by the fact that that book
records some very effective preaching of the gospel, with the result
that many people believed.

A fact that has never been satisfactorily explained is John's
concentration on the verb "to believe" coupled with his total ne-
glect (in the Gospel) of the noun "faith". This term does not occur
even once in this Gospel (and only once in all three Johannine
epistles; Revelation has it four times). John never gives a hint as

---

1. H.-J. Hermisson and E. Lohse link this passage with that which tells us that
the Baptist was sent by God to bear witness to the light "so that all might believe
through him" (1:7), and draw the conclusion that "Jesus' effect is thus represented
from the beginning to the end as a proclamation which calls one to faith" (*Faith*,
Nashville, 1981, p. 160).

to why he has avoided the word. It may be that he preferred the verb as more dynamic, but this is simply speculation.[2]

The verb can denote a belief that is lightly held and with little in the way of valid reason (e.g., Luke 8:13). But in the characteristic usage of the New Testament writers it points to a firm trust, solidly based, and affecting the entire life of the believer. It points to "relig. belief in a special sense, as faith in the Divinity that lays special emphasis on trust in his power and his nearness to help, in addition to being convinced that he exists and that his revelations or disclosures are true" (BAGD). This is so throughout the New Testament, and specifically in the Fourth Gospel. For John it is a concept of central importance.

He uses the concept in a variety of ways, some of which are very occasional. Thus once he has the accusative after the verb when Jesus asks, "Do you believe this?" (11:26). When he wants to express this meaning he more usually employs the dative (e.g., 2:22), but this passage shows something of his flexibility. Again, he once uses the verb in the sense "entrust": "Jesus did not entrust himself to them" (2:24; cf. Luke 16:11; Gal. 2:7, etc.). On occasion he can use the preposition *peri*, "about", as when he says that the Jews did not believe "about" the man before them that he had been born blind and been given sight by Jesus (9:18). John can speak of believing "through" someone (1:7) or something (17:20), or again of believing "on account of" the word (4:41-42) or the deeds (14:11). Such constructions show something of John's versatility in handling this verb, but they represent no more than occasional uses.

More significant is the fact that we may sum up most of John's usage under four headings corresponding to the Greek construc-

2. W. A. Whitehouse comments, "The efficacy of faith for salvation and for right relationship with God is not to be sought in the act itself, but rather in that to which a man holds firm by believing. The Fourth Gospel, by the very fact of not using the noun, makes this plain" (A. Richardson, ed., *A Theological Word Book of the Bible*, London, 1950, pp. 75-76). It is sometimes suggested that John avoided the noun because of its Gnostic associations, and it is pointed out that he similarly avoided *gnōsis*. But there is no real evidence for the existence of Gnosticism as early as this Gospel, and in any case W. F. Howard finds "no reason to suppose that it (i.e. *pistis*) had acquired a meaning in contemporary Hellenistic mysticism which put the word under the ban" (*Christianity according to St. John*, London, 1943, p. 155).

tions he employs: (1) the simple dative, (2) following the verb with "that" (*hoti*) which indicates the content of the belief, (3) following it with "in" (more exactly "into") which points out the person trusted, and (4) the absolute use. We shall look at these in turn.

The Simple Dative

The use of the simple dative[3] conveys the idea of giving credence to someone or something, of accepting a statement as true. A good example of this early in the Gospel is when John says that the disciples "believed the Scripture, and the word which Jesus spoke" (2:22). The words of Jesus in question were "Destroy this sanctuary, and in three days I will raise it up" (2:19). John records them early in Jesus' ministry when the disciples knew little about him and when they could not be expected to fathom such an enigmatic statement. But after the resurrection, John says, they came to believe. He does not identify the particular passage of Scripture, and it is possible that he means the general tenor of our Old Testament rather than any one specific passage (it is notoriously hard to pin down passages predicting the resurrection, but the New Testament writers were clear that this took place "according to the Scriptures", 1 Cor. 15:4). What is clear is that the verb *pisteuō* is here used in the sense of giving credence, first to Scripture and then to Jesus' saying which is linked with Scripture. There is a not dissimilar use of the construction when we read that Jesus said to some opponents, "If you believed Moses, you would believe me, for that man wrote about me" (5:46). In both clauses the meaning is "accept as true". This is the case also when the royal officer "believed the word that Jesus spoke to him" (4:50); he accepted it as true and acted on it.

John reports a number of times that people believed Jesus, or did not believe him, or were urged to believe him. Thus Jesus said to the woman at the well, "Believe me, woman, that an hour is coming . . ." (4:21), where the construction points to an invita-

---

3. E. C. Blackman comments, "The Johannine usage is very distinctive. It is clearly rooted in the primitive usage of the church, as is seen from the reappearance of the use of the verb followed by the dative, with a *hoti* clause, and from the absolute use" (*IDB*, II, p. 224).

tion to the woman to accept as true a prophecy that Jesus was making. A similar use of the construction occurs when we find some hearers of Jesus asking, "What sign do you do so that we may see and believe you?" (6:30).[4] They were not sure of his teaching. If he were to do a sign, they reason, they would see it and it would accredit him. They would then believe him. Whether they would is, of course, doubtful, but that is what they are suggesting.

Again, John refers to some Jews who "had believed him" (8:31). Since this follows a statement that "many believed in him" (8:30), some students hold that the same people are referred to and that the two constructions are accordingly being used more or less synonymously. Others take the opposite position; for example, J. H. Moulton holds that "the variation from the previous *p. eis* cannot be merely accidental". He later says, "The really important matter [i.e., in the New Testament, not merely in John] is the recognition of a clear distinction between *believe on* or *in* and *believe* with the dative simply."[5] It is certainly important to recognize that there is a significant difference between accepting that what someone says at a given moment is true and trusting that person, but it is not so clear that John always stresses the difference. It seems probable that we should not make a hard and fast distinction between the two constructions as they are used in John, but that here the construction with the dative points to people who had not really committed themselves wholeheartedly to Jesus (as their subsequent conduct shows). They accepted as true what he had said, but did not act on it as they should. So a little later Jesus asks, "If I speak truth, why do you not believe me?" (8:46).

The Father and the Son are very close throughout this Gospel, so it is not surprising that sometimes the thought of believing the Father is linked in some way with the Son. In a notable saying, Jesus declares, "he who hears my word and believes him who sent

4. C. K. Barrett comments, "*hina* is not incorrectly used: the sign is to be done *in order that* we may see it." He cites a passage from *The Gospel of Thomas* that reads, "Tell us who thou art so that (*hina*) we may believe (*pisteuein*) in thee" (*The Gospel according to St. John*, Philadelphia, 1978, p. 288).

5. *A Grammar of New Testament Greek, I, Prolegomena* (Edinburgh, 1906), pp. 67, 68.

me has life eternal" (5:24).[6] The thought of his having been sent by the Father is linked with believing Jesus in another saying, "You do not have his word abiding in you, because you do not believe him whom he sent" (5:38). And in a reference to his "works", combining the miraculous with the nonmiraculous, Jesus said, "If I do not do the works of my Father, do not believe me; but if I do them, even if you do not believe me, believe the works, so that you may come to know and keep on knowing that the Father is in me, and I am in the Father" (10:37-38). Running through such sayings is the thought that the Father is at work in and through the Son. He has sent the Son on a mission to this world, and the works the Son does are evidence that the Father is accomplishing his purpose. The reference to hearing Jesus' word and believing the Father is instructive: the two are not to be separated. And Jesus' word is not so very different from the Father's word; their failure to believe Jesus leads to a failure to take the Father's word into themselves.

In these passages "believing" and "believing in" are not so very far apart. The two concepts are distinct, and on occasion John can make effective use of the difference, as we have seen. But in the end, if we really believe Jesus and his Father, we will trust, trust them both.

Believing That—

Several times John speaks of believing that (*hoti*) something that follows is true. Indeed, his whole Gospel is written "in order that you may believe that (*hoti*) Jesus is the Christ . . ." (20:31). The construction is important, for it underlines the truth that for John faith has content. He is not writing in order that his readers may somehow become trustful people, that and no more. He wants them to be trustful, but in such a way that their trust is directed to the Christ. So it is that throughout his Gospel we keep coming across

6. This passage heads the list of those of which W. F. Howard says, "Faith in the sense of credence, that is, accepting someone's word without the waverings of doubt, is given a high place where the authority is self evident, or where spiritual insight should discern the self-authentication of the message" (*Christianity according to St. John*, p. 157).

statements that emphasize the importance of a right content in faith.[7]

Such statements refer in one way or another to Christ. An interesting example occurs at the end of the "bread of life" discourse. Some of Jesus' hearers, who were scandalized at what he had said, "went away backwards, and no longer walked with him" (6:66). Jesus asked the Twelve whether they, too, would go away, to which Peter made the firm retort: "*We* (emph., '*we* over against others') have believed and have known that *you* are the Holy One of God" (6:69). Both verbs are in the perfect tense and indicate a continuing state. Peter is saying not only that he and his companions have come to believe in Jesus but that they continue in that state, not only that they had a passing glimpse of knowledge about him but a continuing certainty. "The Holy One of God" is a rare expression in Scripture. In the New Testament it is used elsewhere only of the demoniac who cried out to Jesus in the synagogue, "I know who you are, the Holy One of God" (Mark 1:24; Luke 4:34).[8] It is rare also in the Old Testament (though it is used of Aaron in Ps. 106:16). We should understand it to point to Jesus' consecration by the Father (cf. 10:36) and see this as an important ingredient in believing as John understands it. The link with knowledge is also important. Faith is not concerned with pious fancies, but with a real knowledge of Christ and his relationship to the Father.

This is brought into the content of believing in other ways. Thus Jesus addresses a series of questions to Philip in the upper room when that disciple has said it will be enough for them if Jesus simply shows them the Father: "Have I been with you for such a long time and you do not know me, Philip? He who has seen me has seen the Father; how do *you* say, 'Show us the Father'?" Then, "Do you not believe that *I* am in the Father, and the Father is in me?" (14:8-10). Part of believing, as John under-

―――――――――

7. "John does not think of faith as a vague trust, but as something with content. . . . Faith means believing that—" (Leon Morris, *The Gospel according to John,* Grand Rapids, 1971, p. 856).

8. C. E. B. Cranfield points out that the expression "is not a known messianic title. . . . It is as the divine Son of God rather than as Messiah that the demoniacs address Jesus." In John 6:69 he thinks the title is used "to designate Jesus as from beyond this world and belonging to God" (*The Gospel according to Saint Mark,* Cambridge, 1959, p. 77).

stands it, is acknowledging that the relationship between Jesus and the heavenly Father is so close that to have seen one is to have seen the other. We should also notice that people like Philip who had been so close physically to Jesus throughout his ministry still know his essential being only through faith.[9]

The closeness of the Father and the Son comes out later in the same discourse. Jesus assures his followers there gathered together that the Father loves them "because *you* have loved me, and have believed that *I* came out from God" (16:27). The divine origin of Jesus is important, and as we have seen believing linked earlier with knowledge, now it is joined with love. There is a warmth about believing that finds expression in love.[10] A little later we find the disciples saying that they are aware that Jesus "knows all things", so that there is no need for him to ask them questions. "In this," they go on, "we believe that you came out from God" (16:30). Now we may well say that the disciples' faith was inadequate (R. H. Lightfoot points out that they had not advanced beyond Nathanael at the beginning or the woman at the well [1:47-50; 4:29], both of whom had faith resting on knowledge, whereas "a faith which has now seen greater things than these [1[50]] should have a deeper basis"[11]). But at least they had come to see something important about Christ's person, and as they went on in his service this knowledge and this faith would deepen and grow.

Essentially the same point is made in connection with the Father's "sending" of Jesus. Jesus concludes his prayer at the tomb of Lazarus with the petition that the bystanders "may believe that *you* sent me" (11:42). The theme is found in another

9. Cf. Walther Lüthi, "So fundamental is faith where the Lord is concerned that even these men who have seen everything with their own eyes, heard everything with their own ears, touched Him with their own hands, and have eaten and walked with Him, can conceive who Christ is only through faith. Hence the question to Philip, 'Believest thou not that I am in the Father, and the Father in me?' And the words to all the disciples, 'Believe me that I am in the Father, and the Father in me' " (*St John's Gospel,* Edinburgh and London, 1960, p. 190).

10. Cf. Hermisson and Lohse, "that faith which trusts in Jesus' words in full confidence shows its overcoming power in love. Thus one can recognize Jesus' disciples by the fact that there is love among them (13:35)" (*Faith,* p. 167).

11. *St. John's Gospel* (Oxford, 1956), p. 290. B. F. Westcott points out that in this confession the disciples had not advanced as far as John the Baptist (*The Gospel according to St. John,* II, Grand Rapids, 1954, p. 236).

prayer when, as he prays on the eve of the crucifixion, Jesus includes the words, "they have known truly that I came out from you, and they have believed that *you* sent me" (17:8). He later prays for the world, "that it may believe that *you* sent me" (17:21). In earlier chapters we have seen that the divine mission, the fact that it was the Father who sent Jesus, is important. This is brought out in Jesus' prayers. It is interesting that in most of the instances his *you* is emphatic: "it was none less than *you*, the Father, who sent me" is the force of it. For John it is important that believing include the profound conviction that in Jesus we see more than simply another Galilean. He had come into the world on a mission. He had been sent by God.[12]

Twice Jesus speaks of the importance of believing "that I AM", where he uses the very language of deity. In the first of these passages the alternative to the faith of which he speaks is to die in one's sins, so that the believing in question has soteriological significance (8:24).[13] To believe in Jesus as "I AM" means salvation; not to believe means loss. In the second passage Jesus points out that his prophecy of the betrayal would, when it came to fulfilment, lead his followers to believe "that I AM" (13:19). It would convince them that what he was doing showed conclusively that he could not be explained on purely human premises.

Then we should notice Martha's great confession: "I have believed that *you* are the Christ, the Son of God, he who comes into the world" (11:27). This certainly gives a rich and full content to faith, with its threefold acknowledgment of who Jesus is.[14] We

12. Keith W. Clements understands faith as "a personal trust in the gracious God known in Jesus. It is reliance upon the God who moves in love towards us" (*Faith*, London, 1981, p. 25). Cf. also n. 22 below.

13. R. Schnackenburg points out that the I AM "is the Old Testament revelation formula which the Johannine Jesus, as the revealer of the New Testament, claims for himself. In him, he is saying, God is present to reveal his eschatological salvation and offer it to men" (*The Gospel according to St John*, II, New York, 1982, p. 200).

14. Cf. John Marsh, "Martha's reply seems at first sight to be off the mark; but a closer examination shows that it is not. Martha has perceived that what Jesus has said is not a series of two propositions about living and dead men, but rather a statement about himself as the real life of all who love and believe in him. So her answer when it comes is not in the form of assent to the propositions stated, but a confession of her belief in the Lord's special relationship to the Father" (*The Gospel of St John*, Harmondsworth, 1968, p. 428).

may well say that Martha seems not to have understood fully all that her words meant, for a little later she was found protesting when Jesus asked that Lazarus's tomb be opened. But it can scarcely be denied that she had made significant progress in understanding what believing means and that John's inclusion of her affirmation is meant, among other things, to draw attention to a very significant part of the way his readers should understand believing.

We should add that the connection of knowledge and believing is sometimes brought out with other constructions. Thus Jesus told some Jews who "had believed him" (dative) that if they abode in his word they would know the truth, and the truth would set them free (8:31-32). The same construction is used in the passage which speaks of believing the works, so that "you may come to know and keep on knowing" that the Father is in Christ, and he in the Father (10:38). So, too, the father of the boy Jesus healed at a distance came to believe (the absolute use) when he knew that the healing took place at the time Jesus spoke the words of power (4:53). Believing is connected with testimony (an important concept in John) in 19:35. Such passages underline the truth that John is not advocating faith in faith, so to speak. The belief for which he looks is grounded on fact, specifically on the fact of what God has done in sending his Son to be the Savior of the world.[15]

Believing and knowing are closely connected in John, but the manner of the connection is not easy to work out. We can say that believing sometimes seems to come before knowledge and to lead to it (e.g., 6:69; 8:31-32). This makes an important sequence: first we put our trust in Christ and then we are led further and further in the way of knowledge of Christ and of the Father and of our fellows. But it is also possible to say that knowledge often precedes believing (e.g., 16:30; 17:8). This, too, is an important sequence, for faith is not groundless: first the knowledge of God or of Christ is revealed to us, and that leads us to trust him. We

15. H. L. Jackson says that faith and knowledge are "interchangeable ideas" in this Gospel, "or rather they express the same truth looked at from different sides. 'To know' (*gignōskein*) in the Johannine language expresses the perception of eternal truth; 'to believe,' its temporal discovery and appropriation" (James Hastings, ed., *A Dictionary of Christ and the Gospels*, I, Edinburgh, 1906, p. 570).

should not try to separate the two too sharply; in Johannine thought they go together.[16]

Believing "In" or "On"

A very important construction and one that John uses often is that in which he follows the verb "believe" with the preposition *eis*, which normally means "into". It is interesting that John uses this preposition rather than *en*, "in". In English we normally speak of believing "in" Jesus rather than believing "into" him, but John prefers the more dynamic expression. There is a possible exception in 3:15,[17] but against this John never elsewhere uses "in" (*en*) with "believe" (whereas he uses "into" [*eis*] very often) and, further, the absolute use of "believe" is common in this Gospel. The passage should surely be understood in the sense, "in order that everyone who believes may have in him life eternal."

J. H. Moulton pays attention to the importance of the construction "to believe in" (*eis*) in the New Testament generally. He points out that in classical Greek there is not a great deal of difference between "believing" and "believing in", and he cites Liddell and Scott for the view that in the classical writings these two notions "run into each other". But this was not the case with the Christians: "To be unable to distinguish ideas so vitally different in the scheme of Christianity would certainly have been a serious matter for the NT writers."[18] Outside John the construction *pis-*

16. R. Bultmann well remarks, "it is apparent that knowledge can never take us beyond faith or leave faith behind. As all knowledge begins with faith, so it abides in faith. Similarly, all faith is to become knowledge. If all knowledge can only be a knowledge of faith, faith comes to itself in knowledge. Knowledge is thus a constitutive element in genuine faith" (*TDNT*, VI, p. 227).

17. The passage reads *hina pas ho pisteuōn en autōi echēi zōēn aiōnion*. It is quite possible grammatically to take *en autōi* with the preceding *ho pisteuōn*, but this would be unexampled in John despite the frequency of his use of the verb. On the other hand there is good reason for taking it with what follows, for John has the concept of abiding "in" Christ (6:56; 15:4, etc.; cf. also 12:46), and sometimes the concept of "life in–" (5:39). Nigel Turner here rejects the meaning "everyone who believes in him"; he finds the passage to mean "every believer whose life is hid in Christ possesses eternal life" (*Grammatical Insights into the New Testament*, Edinburgh, 1965, p. 121).

18. *Prolegomena*, p. 67. Cf. also O. Michel, "The frequency of *pisteuō eis*, believe in . . . in the vocabulary of mission, is a striking departure from ordinary Gk. and the LXX" (*NIDNTT*, I, p. 599).

teuein epi is more common than that with *eis*, but Moulton finds little difference between them: "we may freely admit that it is not safe to refine too much: the difference may amount to little more than that between our own *believe on* and *believe in*." He goes on, "The really important matter is the recognition of a clear distinction between *believe on* or *in* and *believe* with the dative simply."[19] It is possible that as far as Johannine usage is concerned Moulton makes the distinction too sharp, but his main point is incontestable. For the New Testament writers it was important to be able to distinguish between simply accepting a statement as true, and trusting a person. There cannot be the slightest doubt that when John uses the expression *pisteuein eis*, he is conveying the idea of wholehearted trust in Jesus Christ.[20]

The object of the faith in mind when John uses this construction is almost invariably Jesus. We do have "Believe in God" (14:1), though we should notice that it is immediately followed by "believe also in me." But since faith in Christ is unthinkable apart from trust in the Father, we should not make too much of this.[21] In several passages Jesus says things like "he who believes in me . . ." (6:35), but in the Gospel as a whole the most frequent construction uses the third person and refers to believing "in him". Thus after the first miracle in Cana of Galilee John tells us that his disciples "believed in him" (2:11). It is not easy to see the precise meaning in this early passage. That the disciples exercised some form of faith is clear, and since it is not said that anyone else believed in Jesus at this time, they certainly committed themselves to him in a way that nobody else did. But because they were at the beginning of their walk with Jesus, their faith must have been somewhat undeveloped at this time. Perhaps we would not be unfair in saying that their faith indicates some understanding of who Jesus was and some element of commitment, though both were capable of development and growth and both did develop and grow in later times.

19. *Ibid.,* p. 68.
20. Of this construction E. C. Blackman says, "This usage is as prominent in John as it is rare elsewhere in the NT, and seems to have no parallel in the LXX or nonbiblical Greek" (*IDB,* II, p. 225). It is a Johannine distinctive.
21. Cf. D. M. Baillie, "To believe in Christ, according to the Fourth Gospel also, is to find God revealed in Him" (*Faith in God and its Christian Consummation,* London, 1964, p. 260).

John further tells us that God loved the world, and that he "gave his only Son, that everyone who believes in him should not perish but have life eternal" (3:16). This is the heart of the Christian gospel. John is saying that God was active in the death of Jesus on Calvary's cross, and that because of what that death accomplished anyone who believes in him will be the possessor of eternal life.[22] The negative side of this comes out a verse or two later: "He who believes in him is not condemned", and that this is serious is made clear with the addition, "He who does not believe has been condemned already, because he has not believed in the name of the only Son of God" (3:18). Believing in Jesus is the critical thing.

A variety of people are said to have believed in Jesus. Early we find that the "signs" that he did caused many in Jerusalem to believe in his name (2:23), and at other times "many" came to believe (e.g., 7:31; 8:30; 10:42). In this Gospel "the Jews" generally means the opponents of Jesus, but on occasion "many of the Jews" believed (11:45; 12:11), even "many of the rulers" (12:42). Indeed, there was an occasion when the enemies of Jesus feared that unless they took action "all men" would believe in him (11:48; they mean a large number of Jews, for they express the fear that the Romans will come and take away their "place" and their nation). Samaritans are also numbered among those who believed in Jesus (4:39). By contrast, Jesus' brothers did not believe in him (7:5), and there was an occasion when the Pharisees asked, "Have any of the rulers or of the Pharisees believed in him?" (7:48), using a form of question that expects a negative answer. Those who do believe have life eternal (6:40). In an unusual and very interesting passage John speaks of the Holy Spirit, "whom those who believed in him (i.e., in Jesus) would receive" (7:39). Believers are not meant to live out the life of Christian service in their own strength; thus the gift of the Spirit is very important. And this passage says that believers as such, that is, all who believe, receive the Holy Spirit. The thought

22. R. Bultmann points out that this produces love in the believer. "Faith sees in Jesus the Revealer of the divine love (3:16). Hence it is itself the reception of this love, and from the reception of this love there springs forth love in believers" (*TDNT,* VI, p. 228).

is not developed in this Gospel, and indeed it scarcely could be, for the Spirit could not be given in this sense until after Jesus had been "glorified". The crucifixion must take place before the Spirit could be given in all his fulness.[23]

Believing may be connected with Jesus' mission, as when he said that "the work of God" is "that you believe in him whom he sent" (6:29), or even more strikingly when he equates believing in him with believing in him who sent him (12:44). There is probably not a great deal of difference when he speaks of believing in "the Son of man" (9:35), for this is the title by which he chose to refer to himself in the exercise of his mission. We could say the same about believing "in the light" (12:36), for Jesus is "the light of the world" (8:12). Or he may speak of believing in "the Son" (3:36). On one occasion people were so impressed by the raising of Lazarus that "many of the Jews went off and believed in Jesus" (12:11). A number of times John refers to believing "in the name" of Jesus, and this will be another way of referring to all that Jesus is and stands for (1:12; 2:23; 3:18).[24] So important is believing of this kind that not to believe in Jesus is sin (16:9; cf. 12:37). But to believe in him means the supply of all that is needed, for the believer will "certainly not thirst, ever" (12:35).

We saw earlier that Jesus sometimes says things like "he who believes in me . . ." (6:35; 7:38; 11:25, 26; 12:44, 46; 14:1, 12). In one such passage he refers to people who believe in him "through the word" of his followers (17:20). We notice accordingly that people did not have to see Jesus of Nazareth in order to believe in him. It was possible for them to come to a place of faith on the basis of the word preached. It would seem that by the time John wrote his Gospel this was the way the majority of believers had come to exercise faith.

23. John Marsh points out that the gift of the Spirit "is a gift which includes all the benefits of the incarnation of the Son, and requires that his work on earth be complete and full. That the Spirit cannot come until Jesus be glorified is a theological, not a chronological fact. John is as aware of the activity of the divine nature in the lives of the disciples during the incarnation as are the synoptists" (*The Gospel of St John*, pp. 342-43).

24. "For those 'who received him,' who 'believed in his name' in this complete sense, faith acquired an entirely new scope; it signified the unique attachment which gathered around the Person of Jesus" (*DB*, p. 289).

The Absolute Use

Sometimes there are questions which employ the absolute use of the verb. Thus when Nathanael affirmed that Jesus was "the Son of God" and "the King of Israel", Jesus replied, "Because I said to you, 'I saw you under the fig tree', do you believe?" (1:50). Jesus does not say what it was that Nathanael believed, but in the context we may fairly say that it was what he had just said that indicates the content of his belief. Nathanael found himself attracted to the person of Jesus, and he had come under the conviction that he was no ordinary man. Rather, he was "the Son of God" and "the King of Israel".

On other occasions the use of questions brings out the failure of people to believe. We see this at the end of the conversation with Nicodemus when Jesus asked, "If I have told you earthly things and you do not believe, how will you believe if I tell you of heavenly things?" (3:12). The question points to a wrong attitude, and one that was inhibiting belief. It is not quite the same with the disciples in the upper room, for they affirmed their belief: "we believe that you came out from God".[25] But Jesus responded to this with, "Do you now believe? Look, an hour is coming, indeed it has come, when you will be scattered . . ." (16:30-31). The disciples thought they trusted Jesus, and to be sure in some measure they did. But their trust was not such that it would sustain them in the time of trial they were about to face. The belief for which Jesus was looking was something more than the facile words that the disciples uttered so easily. Still this was better than the complete rejection of Jesus that we find in an earlier question addressed to some opponents, "How can *you* (the pronoun is emphatic) believe, receiving as you do glory from one another, and you do not seek the glory that is from the only God" (5:44). It is possible to be so preoccupied with what other people say and

25. B. A. Mastin holds that this "is belief in only a part of what Jesus was declaring at verse 28, though their faith is sincere and as far as it goes it is correct. It is perhaps also defective in that the word *God* is used instead of the more expressive term 'Father' . . ." (J. N. Sanders, *A Commentary on the Gospel according to St John*, edited and completed by B. A. Mastin, London, 1968, p. 363). That their faith was as yet defective I agree, but the use of 'God' does not indicate this. They are simply repeating the word Jesus has used in verse 27.

think that we cut ourselves off from a right relationship with God. These people not only did not, but could not, believe.

The importance of right belief is that this is the way into real life. Jesus puts this very simply: "He who believes has life eternal" (6:47). There is nothing that we can bring to the quest for life; it comes as God's good gift. All that we do is receive it trustingly. To believe is to have life. We should see this in the case of the nobleman whose boy Jesus healed in distant Capernaum while he was in Cana, and of whom we are told that he himself believed, and so did his whole household (4:53). Trust in Jesus brought the wonderful cure. But it did more. It brought the nobleman into a fuller faith which he shared with his household, and it brought both him and his household into that life which is life indeed.[26] Faith like this is in mind when Jesus stands at the tomb of Lazarus and says to Martha, "Did I not tell you that if you believe, you will see the glory of God?" (11:40). A wonderful miracle is about to be performed, one that will be seen by all those present. But those with faith will see more: they will see the glory of God.[27] It is probably this of which Jesus speaks when he says to the disciples at the time he was told of Lazarus's illness, "Lazarus has died, and I rejoice for your sake, so that you may believe . . ." (11:14-15). What was about to happen would be a stimulus to real faith on the part of the disciples. Perhaps we should add at this point a reference to the gathering in the upper room when Jesus' predicted his "departure" from them and said, "And now I have told you before it happens, so that when it happens you may believe" (14:29). In all these cases what is looked for is a firm trust in Jesus, even though there is nothing outward to justify it. It is a trust in Jesus, not in favorable circumstances.

26. G. H. C. MacGregor comments, "Again we are reminded that in our Gospel the word 'believe' covers many gradations of faith. In this man's case faith had been present even before the certification of the miracle (50); now that faith is confirmed. Previously he had trusted in a promise; now he believes in the absolute sense, that is, that Jesus is the Christ" (*The Gospel of John*, London, 1928, pp. 122-23).

27. "The real meaning of what He (i.e. Jesus) would do is accessible only to faith. All there, believing or not, would see the miracle. But Jesus is promising Martha a sight of the glory. The crowd would see the miracle, but only believers would see its real significance, the glory" (Leon Morris, *The Gospel according to John*, p. 560).

There are several references to believing in the resurrection narratives. The first comes when the Beloved Disciple ran to the tomb. At first he did no more than peep into it, but after Peter came and entered, so did this Disciple, "and he saw and believed" (20:8). It is not easy to determine what he believed. At first sight we are inclined to say, "believed that Jesus had risen". That may possibly be the meaning, but we should bear in mind that John does not say so much. In the next verse we find that they did not yet know the Scripture that he must rise from the dead, which does not look very much like an affirmation of belief in the resurrection. But certainly the Beloved Disciple's faith was deepened in some way. At the very least he recognized that something wonderful had happened.[28]

Then we should notice the story of Thomas (20:24-29). That disciple was absent when Jesus first appeared to the group. His response to the news that Jesus was alive was the affirmation that unless he saw the nail prints and put his hand into the wound in Jesus' side, he would not believe. In the context "believe" evidently means "believe that Jesus has risen from the dead". Then a week after the first appearance Jesus came again, showed that he knew what Thomas had said, and exhorted him, "Don't be faithless (*apistos*) but believing (*pistos*)." Thomas reacted with the exclamation, "My Lord and my God!"[29] No one has given expression to such a high view of Christ's person up till this point (or for that matter after it in this Gospel). Jesus responds with, "Because you have seen me, you have believed? Blessed are those who have not seen and yet have believed." Here believing is clear-

28. John Marsh comments, "This can hardly be read save in the light of what John has to say about the word of the Lord to Thomas later in the chapter. The beloved disciple saw the empty tomb and the abandoned cloth lying in it. On that sight, he believed. So does the evangelist begin to make it clear that it is not by seeing the earthly Jesus that one 'sees' the Lord. He can be 'seen' in this profounder sense through the witness of an empty grave" (*The Gospel of St John*, p. 634).

29. Barnabas Lindars interprets the passage in the light of Jesus' statements "I and the Father are one" (10:30) and "He who has seen me has seen the Father" (14:9). He goes on, "It is in this sense that 'my God!' is an appropriate expression of faith in Jesus as the exalted Lord. The act of belief not only puts Thomas into relation with the risen Lord, but also with the Father himself" (*The Gospel of John*, London, 1972, p. 615). He further sees Thomas's words as "a summary of the Gospel as a whole" (p. 616).

ly connected not only with accepting the fact of the resurrection, but also with a high view of Jesus' person. Belief is belief in one who came from God and who is God.

Perhaps we should notice here that the writer of the Gospel puts special emphasis on the actual death of Jesus. He tells us that someone who was there saw the piercing of Jesus' side and the coming out of water and blood, "and he who has seen has borne witness, and true is his testimony; and that one knows that he speaks truth, so that you also may believe" (19:35). There are several problems relating to this passage, but for our present purpose it is important to notice that believing is connected with a knowledge of the fact of Jesus' death. Without that death there could, of course, be no resurrection. Believing, as John understands it, certainly includes a recognition of the significance of Jesus' rising from the dead.

In many passages in this Gospel notice is taken of people who did not believe. We have seen that a benediction is pronounced on Thomas because he saw and believed, but earlier Jesus spoke of people who had seen and had not believed (6:36). There is the problem that exactly what they did not believe is not said. But they had been spectators of what Jesus had done in the early part of his ministry, and they had heard his teaching. They could have responded to that by believing as far as they were able, but they did not. They did not respond to Jesus; they rejected him. They may have had something of the same attitude as that of those who were castigated because they would not believe unless they saw "signs and wonders" (4:48).

Unbelief is serious. "He who does not believe", we read, "has been condemned already, because he has not believed in the name of the only Son of God" (3:18). Here "does not believe" is explained as "has not believed in the name of the only Son of God." As we have seen before, faith has content: those who believe, believe in God's Son, and their trust is placed in One who is the highest of all. Failure to believe in such a one must inevitably result in condemnation. The fact that what this means is not spelt out does not mean that it should not be viewed with the utmost seriousness.[30]

30. A. M. Hunter remarks, "John declares that the man who personally trusts Christ is lifted out of the realm of God's judgement. But there is another and dark

Sometimes John's predestinarian strain is connected with believing. Thus on the occasion of the Bread of Life discourse, Jesus pointed out that there were some of his hearers "who do not believe" (6:64). John goes on to point out that Jesus knew from the beginning who would not believe and who would betray him. He then reports Jesus' words: "For this reason I told you that no one can come to me unless it were given him by my Father" (6:65). Not dissimilar is the passage wherein people complain to Jesus in an expression of uncertain meaning, which most translate as RSV, "How long will you keep us in suspense?" (10:24).[31] Jesus replies, "I told you, and you do not believe", and refers his questioners to the deeds he has done. Then he says, "But *you* (emphatic) do not believe, because you are not of my sheep" (10:26). In line with such passages John tells us, towards the end of Jesus' public ministry, that there were people who "could not believe", and he proceeds to cite a prophecy of Isaiah to support this (12:39-40). John does not gloss over the truth that those who do not accept Jesus are blameworthy, but neither does he gloss over the complementary truth that God is active in the process whereby people believe and come into salvation. Believers do not congratulate themselves on their spiritual perspicacity in that they succeeded in believing where others do not. They recognize that apart from the miracle of grace within them they would never have believed. But that grace is a reality, and those who do not believe seem not to have it.

Now and then reasons are assigned for believing, though this is not common. But after Jesus had talked with the woman at the well, she went into her village and brought the men out to meet him. John tells us that many of them "believed" on account of what the woman told them (4:39). But when they had come to

---

side to the medal. Face to face with Christ, we cannot be neutrals, balanced between belief and unbelief; and so, *the unbeliever has already been judged in that he has not given his allegiance to God's only Son.* If a man refuses to trust in the Son of God, no further verdict is needed, for his own conduct finds him guilty" (*The Gospel according to John,* Cambridge, 1965, p. 41).

31. The words might mean "How long do you plague us?" or "Why are you taking our life away?" The former is supported by modern Greek usage, the latter by the fact that the verb is used in the sense "take (life) away" no farther back than verse 18. See further pp. 85-86 above.

know Jesus for themselves, they no longer believed on account of her words but because "we ourselves have heard, and we know that this is truly the Savior of the world" (4:42). A specific reason is not assigned, but it is worth noticing that the man born blind made his confession, "I believe, Lord" (9:38), after he had spoken with Jesus.

A Basic Unity

It is important to look at the constructions John uses and to try to discover what may be learned from each of them. But it is important also to understand that John does not press the distinctions hard. It is clear that his use of the "believe" terminology includes quite a range of meaning, but it is also clear that when he uses a particular construction he may not mean to exclude what may be conveyed by other constructions. For example, in the case of the man born blind at which we were just looking, Jesus asks, "Do you believe in (*eis*) the Son of man?" The formerly blind man asks, "Who is he, sir, that I may believe in (*eis*) him?" Finding that it is the one to whom he is talking, he says, "I believe, Lord" (9:35-38). It is not easy to think that the meaning has changed dramatically from the beginning to the end of this short conversation.

We should make a similar remark about some earlier words. John tells us that "He who believes in (*eis*) him is not condemned, but he who does not believe has been condemned already" (3:18). It is the same with John's statement of the purpose of his Gospel. "These have been written," he says, "so that you may believe that Jesus is the Christ, the Son of God, and that believing you may have life in his name" (20:31). It is impossible to find a good reason for differentiating between the two uses of the verb in passages like these.

Or we might notice that "believing in" is the distinctive construction, and one that is often connected with the gift of life. But we should not overlook Jesus' words, "He who hears my teaching, and believes him who sent me, has life eternal" (5:24). Here it is plainly faith that matters and is the means of entering into eternal life, but the verb is followed by the simple dative and refers to the Father rather than to the Son.

We may say that God has acted in the mission of his Son, and that people receive this salvation when they believe in the Son. We may say that the construction with *eis* expresses this most adequately. But in the end we cannot differentiate this too sharply from other ways of looking at the process. If we believe God or Christ (the use of the dative), if we really believe him, then we will further believe "that" he has acted for salvation and we will believe "in" him. And so fundamental will faith be to us that we will quite easily refer simply to "believing". In the end what is meant by all these constructions is joined together in one satisfying spiritual experience.

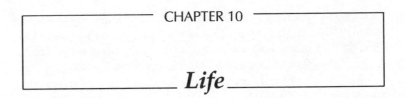

CHAPTER 10

Life

JOHN HAS A GREATER INTEREST IN LIFE THAN OTHER
New Testament writers, at least insofar as his use of the "life" terminology goes.[1] He has the verb *zaō* 17 times (Romans has it 23 times,
but next is John, then Revelation with 13), and the noun *zōē* 36 times
(next is Revelation with 17). If we combine the totals for noun and
verb, Romans has 37 occurrences and Revelation 30, but these are
well behind John's 53. Clearly for John life is a major topic. It is worth
noticing that nearly half of his references to "life" qualify it as "life
eternal" (17 out of 36). Even when he does not use this adjective, the
context often shows that eternal life is what he has in mind.

Physical Life

Sometimes life seems to mean the ordinary physical life of the
here and now, though even then there may be something very unusual about it. For example, when the father of a seriously ill boy
in Cana came to Jesus in Capernaum for help, Jesus said, "Your
son lives" (4:50),[2] and as the word of power was spoken the boy's
physical life was restored. The repetition of the essential expression (4:51, 53) gives emphasis to the fact that it was a word of
power and brings out the truth that Jesus is Lord of life, physical
as well as eternal. Death cannot defeat him.

1. A. M. Hunter gives three reasons why this Gospel continues to "speak to
the condition" of so many Christians, the first of which is "It is the Gospel of Life".
He later says, "between this prelude and this coda [i.e., 1:4 and 20:31], 'life' is John's
dominant theme" (*According to John*, London, 1968, pp. 107, 108).
2. Translations like "your son will live" (RSV, GNB) reduce the saying to a
prophecy of the outcome. This overlooks the tense of the verb and the fact that
John is recording a "sign" (4:54). It is the overcoming of death by Jesus' powerful
word that John records, not a soothing saying assuring the father that there is nothing to worry about.

190

But when this ordinary physical life is in mind, John mostly employs the word *psychē* (he uses it ten times).[3] More often than not, he uses this term when he is speaking of laying down his life and the like. It is this word that we encounter, for example, in the references to the Good Shepherd laying down his life (10:11, 15, 17). In this passage there is no question of the term pointing to "eternal life" or the like: Jesus is saying that he will die to bring salvation to his sheep. He is referring to the end of his earthly life, an end that would be accomplished on the cross. And it is this same death that is in mind when Jesus says, "No one has greater love than this, that one lay down his life for his friends" (15:13). The statement is quite general, but there can be no doubt that Jesus is referring particularly to the death he would shortly accomplish on the cross.

It is this word that is used in the discussion about Peter's readiness to die for Jesus. Peter said to Jesus, "Lord, why can't I follow you now? I will lay down my life for you" (13:37). He gives the word emphasis by putting it first in its clause, "My life for you I will lay down." Jesus responds by using Peter's word and Peter's emphasis, "Your life for me will you lay down?" after which he goes on to prophesy Peter's threefold denial (13:38). That Peter did not in fact die in this way for Jesus is beside the point. The fact is that it is the surrendering of the physical life of which the two are speaking.

This term occurs also in the passage in which Jesus says, "He who loves his life (*psychē*) loses it, and he who hates his life (*psychē*) in this world will keep it into life (*zōē*) eternal" (12:25), a strong statement with parallels in the Synoptic Gospels. The thought here is that the person who concentrates on his own success in the here and now loses life in all that matters, whereas the person who

---

3. Alf Corell says, "Consistently *zēn* and *zōē* are used to signify the 'spiritual' life—life in and through Christ as opposed to the purely physical life. The latter is mostly covered by the term *psychē*; e.g. in 10.15, 17, Jesus lays down his life for his sheep. . . . The difference between *psychē* and *zōē* is clearly shown in 12.25: 'He that hateth his life (*psychē*) in this world shall keep it unto life eternal' (*eis zōēn aiōnion*)" (*Consummatum Est*, London, 1958, p. 139). It is doubtful whether this distinction is always strictly observed (there does seem to be a reference to physical life in the use of *zēn* in 4:50, 51, 53). But that *zōē* often means "spiritual life" and *psychē* "physical life" is undoubted.

does not seek personal advantage (who trusts the Lord?) has that life which is life eternal.[4] The use of the two words for "life" is interesting. The first and second occurrences plainly refer to this ordinary physical life with its varied interests and opportunities. The person who concentrates his efforts and his interests on this life, who lives in and for himself, in the end loses it all. It is the person who is ready to lose all that this life means for Christ's sake who comes into the possession of the life that matters, life eternal.[5] John uses the word once more, namely when he tells us that Jesus said, "Now is my soul troubled" (12:27). This is a reminder that in his human life Jesus could be troubled just as we can, and indeed more, for we never know the trouble of soul he experienced as he contemplated his death for sinners. But the word is here used in the sense "soul" rather than "life", so it is not directly relevant to our present inquiry.

Jesus Is the Life

Of major interest is the way John links life with Jesus. Twice he tells us that Jesus said that he *is* life. To Martha Jesus said, "I am the resurrection and the life" (11:25), and to the disciples in the upper room, "I am the way, and the truth, and the life" (14:6). Both sayings link life with Jesus in the closest fashion, but it is not easy to go beyond this.[6] To say that someone is living is easily understandable; to say that he is life is not. Since in both passages "life" has the definite article, "I am the life", we may possibly say that

4. Cf. W. Barclay, "only by spending life do we retain life. The man who loves his life is moved by two aims. He is moved by selfishness and he is moved by the desire for security. His own advancement and his own safety are the two things which are the driving force of life. Not once or twice but many times Jesus insisted that the man who hoarded his life must in the end lose it, and the man who spent his life must in the end gain it" (*The Gospel of John*, II, Edinburgh, 1956, p. 144).

5. "The man will keep his *psychē* not indeed for physical life, which he may well surrender, but for eternal life, of which he can never be robbed" (C. K. Barrett, *The Gospel according to St. John*,[2] Philadelphia, 1978, p. 424).

6. G. R. Beasley-Murray holds that "the truth" and "the life" explain how Jesus is "the way": Jesus is the way "because he is the truth . . . and because the life of God resides in him (in the context of the Gospel that includes life in creation and life in the new creation . . .)". A little later he says, "as the Life he is the mediator of the salvation which is life in God" (*Word Biblical Commentary: John*, Waco, 1987, p. 252).

this points to the truth that he is the real life, the genuine life, over against all false claimants to being or having life. There have always been people who have claimed that those they despise are not really living, but that they themselves are really vital, genuinely alive. Sometimes they have been religiously inclined and have held that their particular way is the way to a life for God, though interestingly they have often been worldly-minded folk who dismiss faithful men and women, alleging that they live narrow and circumscribed lives and miss out on the debaucheries and the like which in their opinion make life worth living.

Over against all such claims Jesus is the life. When we reflect that after so many centuries he still inspires people of a wide variety of races and social stations in almost every country in the world to give him their supreme loyalty and use their whole lives in his service, we perhaps glimpse a little of the vitality, the life, that Jesus is. We could say the same about those countless numbers who, in his name, delight to serve in thankless tasks in lowly places throughout the world's mission fields, in the slums of the world's great cities, and among the outcasts of society.

From a very different point of view half a century back Beverly Nichols made much the same point. Replying to a radical New Testament critic who would say no more about Jesus than "the outline of a man and the traces of an individual activity are still to be distinguished", Nichols wrote:

> Ye gods! If you have ever done any writing you may have a faint idea of the immense difficulty of making a character *live* even for a single publishing season, in a single language. And if you have ever done any reading, the remotest acquaintance with European literature will inform you that there are no "characters", not even Don Quixote (the most lifelike evocation of an individual in literature) which are more than tiny shadows against the immense reality of the character of Jesus.
>
> You cannot deny the reality of this character, *in whatever body it resided*. Even if we were to grant the Professor's theory that it is all a hotch-potch of legend, *somebody* said "The Sabbath was made for man, and not man for the Sabbath"; *somebody* said "For what shall it profit a man if he shall gain the whole world and lose his own soul"; *somebody* said "Suffer the little children to come unto me, and forbid them not: for of such is the Kingdom of God"; *somebody* said "How hardly shall they that have riches

enter into the Kingdom of God"; *somebody* said "All they that take the sword shall perish with the sword".

Somebody said these things, because they are staring me in the face at this moment from the Bible. And whoever said them was *gigantic*. And whoever said them was *living*, because we are in the year 1936 and I am "modern" and you are "modern", and we both of us like going to the cinema and we can both drive a car and all that sort of thing, and yet we cannot find in any contemporary literature any phrases which have a shadow of the beauty, the truth, the individuality, nor the *indestructibility* of those phrases.

And remember, I have only quoted five sentences at random.[7]

I am not, of course, suggesting that Jesus lives simply in the sense that a character in a literary work lives. I am saying that Nichols, from a point of view rarely considered in theological circles, brought out the truth that Jesus is *"living"*; there is a vitality about Jesus which we do not encounter elsewhere and to which John gives special emphasis. Jesus is life.

Jesus Gives Life

And he is the source of life. Right at the beginning of his Gospel John says, "In him was life" (1:4), a statement that follows an earlier affirmation that it was the Word through whom all creation took place. We may fairly deduce that he is the source of all life on earth, though John does not develop that thought. He is much more inclined to talk about Jesus as the source of spiritual life, as when he quotes him as saying "I give them life eternal" (10:28) or "I came in order that they may have life, and have it abundantly" (10:10).[8] He tells us that in his great high-priestly prayer Jesus prayed, ". . . even as you have given him authority over all flesh, in order that all that you have given him, he may give to them life eternal" (17:2). This last passage links the Son with the Father in a way with which we have become familiar in our earlier studies.

7. *The Fool Hath Said* (London, 1936), pp. 126-27 (Nichols's italics).

8. R. F. Bailey renders the passage, "I am come that they may have life and may have it to overflowing", and proceeds, " 'I am the way,' we shall find later, leads on to 'I am the Life' " (*Saint John's Gospel*, London, 1957, p. 136).

194

There is a sense in which the Son gives life, but there is also a sense in which life belongs to the Father.

In an earlier discourse Jesus spoke of the Father as having "life in himself" and as having given to the Son "to have life in himself" (5:26). This unusual expression is rendered by Goodspeed "the Father is self-existent", while GNB has "Just as the Father is himself the source of life, in the same way he has made his Son the source of life." Clearly John is telling us that Jesus does not have the same relationship to life as we do. Our life is contingent, whereas his is necessary. Our life has a point of origin, while his does not.[9] Elsewhere Jesus refers to God as "the living Father" (life is his characteristic), and goes on, "and I live on account of the Father (*dia ton patera*)" (6:57). Such statements make it clear that Jesus does not see his life as on all fours with the life that the rest of us live. He came where we are, certainly, and lived our human life. But that does not tell the whole story. In his essential being he shares the life of the Father. But because of what he is, he is able to make a gift of life to those who come to him: "because I live, you will live too" (14:19).

Earlier in the discourse after he healed the lame man Jesus said, "Truly, truly, I say to you that an hour is coming, and now is, when the dead will hear the voice of the Son of God, and those who hear will live" (5:25). It is possible to take this in the sense that Christ will call the dead from their graves at the last day, a thought which he goes on to express (vv. 28-29). But at this point he seems to be speaking rather of life here and now, as the words "and now is" indicate. Jesus is saying that right now he calls the spiritually dead out of their lost state and gives them life. Life in this sense is not a natural possession: it is a divine gift. He has just said that the believer "has passed out of death into life" (v. 24), and, while the saying has eschatological overtones as is indicated by the assurance that he will not come into judgment,[10] Jesus is surely saying that the life he gives will be effective even on the great day of judgment. The recipient of his gift need not fear that

9. Cf. Augustine, quoted on p. 105 above.
10. In the Johannine manner there is probably the thought of a present judgment: the believer does bring down judgment on himself. But it seems impossible to empty the saying of eschatological force. Not only is the believer not subject to present judgment; he is delivered from future judgment, too.

it will be found wanting on Judgment Day. Even there and even then he will have life.

The Bread of Life

An important passage on life begins with Jesus saying to his Jewish hearers, "Do not work for the food that perishes, but for the food that abides unto life eternal, which the Son of man will give you; for him did God the Father seal" (6:27). These words are uttered when people who had been numbered among the 5,000 who were miraculously fed from the five loaves and two fish sought Jesus out on the other side of the lake. They were looking for Jesus, indeed, but not because of any profound spiritual perception. They had been well fed and apparently looked for a continuation of this kind of expertise on the part of Jesus. They wanted to make him a king.[11] He was not prepared to go along with their idea and immediately pointed them away from the material food that had impressed them so greatly. He urged them to look for the food that would sustain them "unto life eternal". They should be concentrating on eternal life, not on the kind of sustenance they had so recently received from him, no matter how wonderful it was.

In the section on the "I AM" sayings we noticed that Jesus calls himself "the bread of life" (6:35, 48), an expression that draws attention to the truth that Jesus is the sustainer of real life. The first use comes in response to his hearers' demand for a sign, their reminder to Jesus that "our fathers ate the manna in the wilderness", and their citation of Psalm 78:24, "He gave them bread from heaven to eat". Clearly they were saying to Jesus that the Messiah would do much more than they had seen him do. There was a widespread Jewish expectation that the Messiah would reproduce the miracle of the manna,[12] and goodness knows what

11. Lesslie Newbigin comments, "The enthusiasm of the crowd rises; they will seize him forthwith and make him their leader." He goes on, "This is not faith but unbelief. They have not understood who Jesus is. Jesus will not be the instrument of any human enthusiasm or the symbol for any human program" (*The Light Has Come,* Grand Rapids, 1982, p. 76).

12. Thus the *Midrash Rabbah* informs us that "R. Berekiah said in the name of R. Isaac: As the first redeemer was, so shall the latter Redeemer be. . . . As the

fantasies they had in mind when they spoke of the giving of "bread from heaven". John is making it clear that Jesus' hearers lacked spiritual perception: no matter what Jesus did and taught they would find some way of rejecting him. But John's interest is in what Jesus said, and specifically in what he said about life. This runs through the entire discourse.

We must bear in mind that bread was the most important item of diet for Jesus and his hearers. References to "your staff of bread" (Lev. 26:26;[13] Ezek. 4:16; 5:16; 14:13) show its central importance for sustaining life. When Jesus then says that he is "the bread of life", he is pointing to the truth that without him there is no life worth the name. He gives life and he sustains life, and the saying comes very close to repeating what we have seen elsewhere, that he *is* life.

Jesus also speaks of "the bread of God" which his hearers had mentioned, and he tells them that the bread of God "is that which (or he who) comes down from heaven and gives life to the world" (6:33).[14] His hearers doubtless took this to refer to something material like the manna or perhaps even some special variety of the bread they commonly used, for they go on to say, "Sir, always give us this bread" (6:34). It is this that leads up to Jesus' saying, "I am the bread of life", so that clearly he understood the words to mean "he who comes down from heaven. . . ." It is another way of referring both to his heavenly origin and the truth that he and only he gives life to the world. Again there is the claim that it is Jesus and only Jesus who gives life to this troubled world. It will be this that is in mind when he goes on to say, "He who comes to me will certainly not hunger, and he who believes in me will certainly not thirst, ever." Neither "bread" nor "life" occurs in this

former redeemer caused manna to descend, as it is stated, *Behold, I will cause to rain bread from heaven for you* (Ex. XVI,4), so will the latter Redeemer cause manna to descend, as it is stated, *May he be as a rich cornfield in the land* (Ps. LXXII,16)" (*Ecclesiastes Rabbah* 1.9; Soncino edition, p. 33).

13. Martin Noth explains, "food is like a staff to lean upon in order to walk more securely; cf. the expression 'to support oneself with a morsel of bread' = 'to fortify oneself (with a meal)' " (*Leviticus*, London, 1965, p. 199).

14. J. H. Bernard points out that "the bread of God" is not only "such as 'comes down from heaven,' for that was said of the manna . . . but such as coming down imparts life and not merely bodily nourishment" (*A Critical and Exegetical Commentary on the Gospel according to St. John*, I, Edinburgh, 1928, p. 195).

expression, but it is the same essential thought that is conveyed, with the addition that the life he gives is infinitely satisfying.

The Jews proceed to mutter about Jesus (the word usually seems to convey the meaning of a hostile utterance spoken in a low voice which would make the actual speakers difficult to identify). They maintain that he said, "I am the bread that came down from heaven" (6:41). This is not an exact quotation of anything that Jesus is recorded to have said, but that need not worry us since it reproduces the gist of his claim. John's insertion of this saying into his narrative keeps the focus on Jesus' heavenly origin, and we should not miss the implication that the life he gives is not a superior version of the best life on earth but something different, the life of heaven, or, as John prefers to put it, "life eternal" [15]

Towards the end of the discourse Jesus repeats the saying that he is the bread of life (6:48), and goes on to remind his hearers that their fathers "ate the manna in the wilderness, and they died" (6:49).[16] They had been insistent in drawing his attention to the manna and implying that what he was doing was nothing wonderful, certainly nothing like the giving of the manna to a whole generation of people for 40 years. But Jesus was concerned with much more than sustaining this physical life, which was all that the manna could do. He is talking about "the bread that came down from heaven, in order that one might eat of it and not die" (6:50).[17] This brings him to the point where he says plainly, "I am the living bread who came down from heaven" (6:51); there is to be no doubt that he himself is the bread that will give people that

15. Peder Borgen agrees with the viewpoint that this chapter teaches "that the eternal life is a present reality which unfolds itself in time up to the final close at the bodily resurrection on the last day" (*Bread from Heaven*, Leiden, 1965, p. 172).

16. U. E. Simon says of "Your fathers . . . died" (6:48, 58), "this is the incontrovertible evidence which testifies to the nothingness of existent religions. The pagan hope certainly does not avail in the Fourth Gospel." Earlier he has said, this Gospel's "stark realism again continues in the best tradition of what Cullmann has called the 'pessimistic conception of death' which rests, however, on the the optimistic regard for the living God" (F. L. Cross, ed., *Studies in the Fourth Gospel*, London, 1957, p. 99).

17. Bertil Gärtner holds that John "makes a clear distinction in this section between the three 'ages' and their 'bread': the manna in the desert for the Mosaic ?eding of the people in the desert, and the bread appropriate to the

life in which they will not die. Jesus goes on, "if anyone eats of this bread, he will live for ever; and the bread that I will give is my flesh, for the life of the world." It does not surprise us that this produced strife among the Jews, with questions being raised about how they were going to eat his flesh. But John's readers would be expected to discern that Jesus was referring to his atoning death. People would get life indeed, but the cost of their life would be his death.

We should notice that a new thought is introduced at the end of this discourse. In the earlier part of the address the references to the bread that came down from heaven might well be taken to direct us to the incarnation. They point to the truth that to bring us life the Son of God left his throne in heaven and took a lowly place here on earth. But this is now supplemented with the thought that the death of the Son of God is a necessary part of the way in which life is made available.[18] Both truths are important for an understanding of this chapter as a whole and for an understanding of John's view of eternal life. The necessity of the death of Jesus comes out in a number of places. God's love led to his giving his Son so that people would get life (3:16), and such passages as the treatment of the Good Shepherd who gives his life for the sheep (10:11, 15, 17-18) reinforce the truth. But indeed the shape of the entire Gospel points to it. John deals with the whole of Jesus' public ministry in his first 12 chapters, but then gives over nine chapters to Jesus' last talk to his disciples, and to the death and resurrection. This is to put a tremendous emphasis on his death. For that death is central to the bringing of life.

---

feast in God's kingdom, the Eucharistic bread" (*John 6 and the Jewish Passover,* Lund, 1959, p. 23). I cannot go along with him in seeing a reference to "the Eucharistic bread", but there is certainly an important distinction between two kinds of "bread" which give no lasting life, and the bread that does, the flesh of Christ.

18. Cf. W. H. Cadman, "In interpreting the thought of the discourse as a whole it is important not to miss the significance of this twofold application of the figure of the bread. From the one point of view Jesus is 'the bread of life', 'the living bread which came down out of heaven' (*vv.* 35, 48, 51), because with His presence in the human earthly order 'life' has now become accessible to men; from the other point of view He is the 'bread of life' because He chooses to die, in order that He may make the 'life' which is in Him the actual possession of many more as well" (*The Open Heaven,* Oxford, 1969, p. 81).

In response to the difficulty the Jews found in the eating of his flesh Jesus goes further and says, "Truly, truly, I say to you, unless you eat the flesh of the Son of man and drink his blood, you have no life in yourselves. He who eats my flesh and drinks my blood has life eternal, and I will raise him up at the last day" (6:53-54). The addition of drinking the blood to eating the flesh would have made the saying even more abhorrent to the Jews, but it emphasized the reality of the death that would bring life to those who received Jesus. Jesus would bring real life to those who were so bound to this earthly life with all its values that they saw nothing from the perspective of heaven and of eternity, and he would bring this life at the cost of his own death. With this we are at the very heart of the Christian way.[19]

Having explained that life proceeds from his death, Jesus goes on to link it with the life of the Father. He speaks of "the living Father" as having sent him, and says that he lives "on account of the Father" (6:57). This probably means two things: Jesus' life is bound up with that of the Father so that he has no independent existence (cf. 5:26),[20] and further he lives to do the Father's

19. Most modern scholars hold that John is here referring to the Holy Communion. But despite the popularity of the view no one seems to have explained why Jesus should have puzzled an audience in Capernaum by referring to a non-existent sacrament (it would be another year at least before the Holy Communion would be instituted); he could not possibly have been understood. And if we say that John is not concerned with accurate history in our sense of the term but is giving his eucharistic teaching at this point in his narrative, the question arises of why John thought his readers would find no problems with eucharistic teaching alleged to have been given to a group consisting largely of unbelievers at least a year before there was any Eucharist. It is also a problem that no one partook of this Eucharist (there is no report of anyone drinking the wine that was an integral part of that sacrament). And further, in all the early accounts of the Eucharist there is a reference to Jesus' "body", not to his "flesh". Why should the terminology be changed on this one occasion? We should also take note of the strength of the language used. In verse 53 we read, "Truly, truly, I say to you, unless you eat the flesh of the Son of man and drink his blood, you have no life in you." This language is absolute. Are we to say that John taught that unless we receive the Eucharist we "have no life"? And that this is the one thing necessary for life? For all its popularity the hypothesis is flawed.

20. C. K. Barrett comments, "The life of the Son is entirely dependent upon the Father (dia ton patera); he has no independent life or authority, and it is because the Father that men may live by abiding in him" (The Gospel according, p. 300).

Best defense yet for non sacramental / appeal to John

will (in 4:34 this is his very meat). This leads on to the thought that "he who eats me, that one also will live on account of me" (6:57). To partake of Christ, to enter into the life he gives, means to begin to live a derivative life, a life bound up with Christ, and a life of service to Christ. The life that Jesus gives is never a self-centered life; it is always a life of service. Then he repeats a thought he has already given us: "This is the bread that came down from heaven, not as the fathers ate and died; he who eats this bread will live for ever" (6:58). It is important to understand that the life of which he speaks is not the life of which his opponents speak, a physical life that was sustained in the wilderness by an unusual food supply. He is referring to an eternal life, a life that can never cease. And that life is given by appropriating his death.

Jesus goes on to say, "The Spirit is the life-giver; the flesh profits nothing; the words that I have spoken to you are spirit and they are life" (6:63). In this very difficult expression we should see a reference to the Holy Spirit rather than a contrast between spirit and flesh in the human body, for the human spirit is not life-giving. That Jesus' words "are spirit and they are life" means that the Holy Spirit is involved in the teaching. The words of Jesus are not to be understood in some woodenly literal way: they are to be understood as the Spirit leads us to understand them. And understood in this way, they bring life. From another point of view Jesus is insisting that real life comes not from anything terrestrial. Peter discerned this, for when Jesus saw people defecting from him and asked the Twelve, "Do *you* also want to go off?" that apostle spoke on behalf of them all, "Lord, to whom shall we go? You have words of life eternal" (6:67-68). Already Peter has come to know that life eternal comes from Jesus.[21] It may also be said to come from the Father (5:24, 26), and now we see that the Holy Spirit is involved as well. Expressions involving any member of the Trinity bring out the point that Jesus is not referring to a form of life that is produced by human striving. He is referring to a gift of God.

---

21. He still, of course, has much to learn. R. Alan Culpepper can say, "He has grasped the importance of Jesus' words, his glory, and the life his words give. Paradoxically, the words of life may also require death, and this Peter has not yet grasped" (*Anatomy of the Fourth Gospel,* Philadelphia, 1983, p. 120).

Faith and Life

From what we have said it is plain that John puts great emphasis on the truth that life eternal is God's good gift, that normally it is seen as coming from Christ, and specifically his death is said to be involved in the process. But he does not regard the gift of life as distributed indiscriminately among the human race. It is freely available, to be sure, and available to people of every race and class. But it must be appropriated by faith. "God so loved the world," we read, "that he gave his only Son, in order that everyone who *believes* in him should not perish, but have life eternal" (3:16). It is the will of the Father "that everyone who sees the Son and *believes* in him should have life eternal" (6:40; Jesus goes on to say that he will raise him up at the last day). When he talked to Martha after the death of Lazarus, Jesus spoke of himself as "the resurrection and the life" and went on to say, "He who *believes* in me, though he should die, will live, and everyone who lives and *believes* in me will not perish for ever" (11:25-26). The life he gives believers is a life that never ends. Or this may be put very simply: "He who *believes* in the Son has life eternal" (3:36). Believing is not simply a recommended procedure—it is necessary. It is the one way by which sinners receive the gift of life.[22]

All the passages so far noted employ the "believing in—" construction, but the same truth may be expressed otherwise. In the best understanding of 3:15 we read that the Son of man must be lifted up "in order that everyone who believes may have in him life eternal." Or life may be linked with the Father, using the construction with the simple dative, "Truly, truly, I tell you that he who hears my word, and believes him who sent me, has life eternal" (5:24).[23] The importance of faith is emphasized in the simple

---

22. "Faith is the attitude whereby a man abandons all reliance on his own efforts to obtain salvation, be they deeds of piety, of ethical goodness or anything else. It is the attitude of complete trust in Christ, of reliance on him alone for all that salvation means. . . . Faith is the one way by which men receive salvation" (*IBD,* I, p. 496).

23. R. Schnackenburg comments, "The Father is heard in the Son"; on the dative he remarks, "the verb *pisteuein* with the dative does not mean 'to believe in the Father', but rather 'to believe him' who has sent the Son" (*The Gospel according to St John,* II, New York, 1982, pp. 108, 109).

statement (prefixed with the solemn "Truly, truly"), "he who believes has life eternal" (6:47). Nothing could show more clearly that we bring nothing to merit the gift. We come believing, and that is all. Believers have life eternal.

The critical importance of believing for John may be seen in the fact that he tells his readers that he wrote his Gospel in order that they might believe that Jesus is the Christ, "and that believing you may have life in his name" (20:31). Believing and life are connected in the closest fashion, and John writes to bring people to believe.

Now and then life is linked with light. This happens as early as the fourth verse (which may indicate that John considers it an important idea, even though he does not develop it fully at that point). "In him was life," we read, "and the life was the light of men" (1:4). The life that the Word gives illuminates the whole of life. It is true that the gift of life means that those who have it no longer abide in death, and it is also true that the life they live is full of light in sharp contrast to the existence in darkness of those who do not receive the light. Again, after speaking of himself as "the Light of the world" Jesus goes on, "he that follows me will not walk in darkness, but will have the light of life" (8:12). Again there is the thought of the contrast between the miserable existence of those without light and the wonderfully illuminated life of those who have it. There is also probably the thought that life and light go together: without light we do not really have life.[24]

We should not miss the further point that light sometimes has to do with judgment as much as with illumination. Thus we read, "This is the judgment (or condemnation), that the light has come into the world, and men loved the darkness rather than the light, for their deeds were evil" (3:19). Light does of course provide illumination to guide the life, and this the Gospel brings out. But it also makes clear that the coming of the light means a responsibility to profit from the light. People come under condemnation

24. Cf. Alf Corell, "Just as light is the prerequisite condition for all earthly life, so Christ is the light, the very source of life, which is the condition of all human existence." He draws attention to the significance of Genesis 1:3 (*Consummatum Est*, p. 142).

if they reject the light.[25] The coming of light does not necessarily result in life; it may result in condemnation since it shows up what should not be there.

Life Is For Ever

A feature of John's understanding of life is his insistence that it has no end. Seventeen times he has the expression "life eternal" (*zōē aiōnios*), where the adjective points us to what is endless. The word derives from *aiōn*, or "an age", and signifies "pertaining to an age". The Jews divided all time into the age before creation, the present age, and the age to come, that is, the age ushered in by the coming of the Messiah, an age that will have no end. Theoretically there seems no reason why the adjective should not be applied to any age, but in practice it meant "pertaining to the age to come". The expression "into the age" (*eis ton aiōna*) meant "forever".

"Life eternal", then, meant "the life of the age to come", "life appropriate to the coming age". It may in a given context have the significance "life without end", but John seems to have a deeper meaning than this. He refers to life that is appropriate to the age to come. He is referring to life of a particular quality rather than life of an endless quantity. He can, of course, speak of this life as endless, but for John this is clearly no more than one aspect of life eternal; it is not its essential character. Thus in Jesus' high-priestly prayer we find the words: "this is eternal life, that they may know you, the only true God, and him whom you sent, Jesus Christ" (17:3). The knowledge of God and of Christ is itself eternal life.[26] It is not that it brings eternal life: it is itself that life. Akin to this is Jesus' statement, "I know that his commandment is life eternal"

25. Cf. Barnabas Lindars, "John uses the theme of light, not simply with its expected connotation of spiritual illumination, but with the idea of showing up truth and falsehood. Thus it belongs closely with the theme of judgement and discernment"; in 8:12 "The theme of light is not developed from the point of view of the revelation of knowledge. It is again concerned with judgement, the light which reveals true from false" (*Behind the Fourth Gospel*, London, 1971, pp. 24, 67).

26. W. H. Rigg asserts "that eternal life is a divine life, and that it is essentially spiritual. It is essentially union with God. . . . It is a mutual indwelling; the believer abides in Christ, and Christ abides in him (15:4, 7)" (*The Fourth Gospel*, London, 1952, p. 84).

(12:50). He does not say that to keep God's commandment brings eternal life: he says that it *is* eternal life (cf. *Twentieth Century* translation, "Immortal Life lies in keeping his command").

With this will go the thought that what we do here and now has its effects in the life to come. Thus John records a conversation Jesus had with the disciples while the Samaritan woman he met by the well was going back to her village and in which he spoke of the fields as "white for harvest" and went on, "he who reaps receives a wage and gathers fruit to life eternal" (4:36). It may be that this means that the "wage" the reaper gets is that of seeing sinners enter eternal life, or it may mean that the reaper's reward is one that he will receive in the life to come. Either way the passage looks forward to a life beyond this world, a life in which what we do here and now has consequences. And this is in mind also when Jesus speaks of Judgment Day and says that those "who have done good things" will enter "the resurrection of life" (5:29).[27] What we do now has its effects in the life to come.

Of course, the fact that this life never ends comes out in many statements. The person who has it "will live for ever" (6:58). There is a classic statement about the resurrection at the end of this age, a resurrection that will come about because the Son calls people from the tombs. Then some will experience the "resurrection of life", which is set over against the "resurrection of condemnation" (5:29). This brings us to life in the age that has no ending and is thus life that never dies. We should deduce this also from the repeated "I will raise him up in the last day" in the "bread of life" discourse (6:39, 40, 44, 54).[28] This chapter has a good deal to say about the quality of the life that Christ brings, but it also repeats the statement that takes us into the life of the world to come.

27. "The 'resurrection of life' is not in contradiction with the Johannine concept of life, since this involves the whole man" (Schnackenburg, *The Gospel according to St John,* II, p. 118; he also says, "what really matters to the evangelist is not the future event but the present attainment of life through belief in the Son of God").

28. "The 'last day' can denote only one great period of resurrection for the whole Church of God. . . . It is not the gift of eternal life that belongs to the last day. Whosoever receives the Son at once receives in Him life eternal . . . but the day of the resurrection of the body witnesses the completion of that gift of eternal life which is now bestowed" (W. Milligan and W. F. Moulton, *Commentary on the Gospel of St. John,* Edinburgh, 1898, p. 82).

Life and the Holy Spirit

In his conversation with the Samaritan woman at the well, Jesus told her that if she knew what the free gift of God was and who it was to whom she was talking, "you would have asked him, and he would have given you living water" (4:10). The woman asks where he is going to get the living water, since the well is deep and he has no bucket. She does not ask what "living" water is, and Jesus does not explain it. But we should notice that his usage is exceptional. The Rabbis often used "water" metaphorically (mostly to bring out truths concerning the law), but "living water" is very rarely a metaphorical expression. Its ordinary use is for running water as opposed to still water, water in a pond, or the like. We find something of what Jesus means by it in the present passage if we attend to the subsequent discussion. Jesus points out that anyone who drinks from the well will in due course get thirsty again, "but whoever drinks of the water that I will give him will certainly not thirst, not ever, but the water that I will give him will be in him a fountain of water leaping up into life eternal" (4:14).[29] The reference to life eternal shows that Jesus is referring to no merely temporal gift but to that life which God alone can give.

The water metaphor is found again in the incident at the Feast of Tabernacles. On the last day, the great day of the Feast, Jesus stood up and cried out, "If anyone is thirsty, let him come to me and drink; he who believes in me, as the Scripture said, rivers of living water will flow from his innermost being." John adds an explanation, "This he said about the Spirit, whom those who believed in him would receive; for it was not yet Spirit, because Jesus was not yet glorified" (7:37-39). It can scarcely be said that this is a completely straightforward passage, but it is clear that in some way the "living water" and the Spirit are connected.[30] The Spirit in all his fulness would not be given until the consumma-

29. J. A. McClymont says that here Jesus "claims for his gift an incomparable value, as having the power to quench man's thirst not for a time only but for ever, abiding with the receiver and dwelling in him as a spring of water ever leaping up afresh with incessant energy and inexhaustible fullness" (*St. John*, Edinburgh, 1901, p. 155).

30. E. Schweizer, "the Spirit as the water of life will flow into the community in the proclamation which takes place in word and act. The new statement here, however, is that the Spirit will come only after the death of Jesus. In the first in-

tion of Jesus' earthly ministry, and he would bring deep satisfaction to the believer.

It seems that both these passages are looking at the new life Christ would bring people, a life that would be characterized by the work of the Holy Spirit within believers. This would be such a satisfaction that believers will never again thirst as they did in their unfulfilled state before they received the living water from Jesus. It is possible that we have another significant reference to water, namely the report of the observer at the cross that blood and water came out of Jesus' side when a soldier pierced him with a spear (19:34). John Lightfoot draws attention to a rabbinic passage which refers to the incident when Moses smote the rock in the wilderness and says, "Moses therefore smote the rock twice, and first it gushed out blood, then water."[31] Lightfoot held that John may well have such rabbinic teaching in mind and that he saw the significance of the water and the blood that came from the Savior's side in this way: "this is the true blood of the new covenant, which so directly answers the type in the confirmation of the old."[32]

The Dead

Now if some receive life, the corollary is that those who do not receive it are dead, and this is part of John's teaching. He records Jesus' sorrowful words to some of his opponents, "you will not come to me so that you may have life" (5:40). These people had the Scriptures and they searched them diligently, but in such a way that they did not see that the Scriptures pointed to Jesus. They thought that they had eternal life in those writings (5:39).[33] It is the greatest of tragedies when people use the word of God and

---

stance this simply corresponds to the historical facts. It acquires for John, however, a special significance, as the sayings about the Paraclete will show" (*TDNT*, VI, p. 442).

31. *A Commentary on the New Testament from the Talmud and Hebraica*, III (Grand Rapids, 1979 reprint of 1859 edition), p. 440.

32. *Ibid.*, p. 441.

33. The great Hillel said, "the more study of the Law the more life. . . . If a man . . . has gained for himself words of the Law he has gained for himself life in the world to come" (*Aboth* 2:7).

do not find the Son of God. But that was the fate of the people of that generation.

Persistently they rejected the way of life. John tells his readers that "he who believes in the Son has life eternal", whereas "he who does not obey[34] the Son will not see life, but the wrath of God remains upon him" (3:36). He does not gloss over the fact that people are faced with a real choice and that eternal issues hang on this. The unbeliever can look forward to nothing but the continuing wrath of God.

In another place John tells us that Jesus said to the people who heard him in the synagogue at Capernaum, "Truly, truly, I tell you, unless you eat the flesh of the Son of man and drink his blood, you have no life in you" (6:53). We saw earlier that this is a vivid way of speaking of the appropriation of the blessings brought by the death of Jesus, but it is an appropriation that the people addressed would not make. They would cooperate in bringing his death about, not in seeing in it the way to life. For such at the last judgment there can be nothing other than "the resurrection of condemnation" (5:29).

It agrees with the emphasis John gives to life that he often warns of death, the result of not accepting the gift of life. Thus he tells us that Jesus said to the Jews, "I am going away, and you will look for me, and you will die in your sin", and again, "I told you that you will die in your sins; for if you do not believe that I AM, you will die in your sins" (8:21, 24). Neither here nor elsewhere does he explain what "dying in sin" means, but clearly it stands for the ultimate horror.[35] It is the very opposite of that life on

---

34. The natural antithesis of "believe" would be "does not believe", but the verb *apeitheō* normally means "disobey" (so most translations, though JB has "refuses to believe" and LB "don't believe and obey"). See further chapter 5, n. 12. However we translate, there can be no doubt that the particular disobedience in this passage is the refusal to believe.

35. Cf. R. Bultmann, in John "Outside revelation in Jesus the human race is given up to death, and it is responsible for this because it is sinful. Its sin is simply that it will not understand itself in its creatureliness from the standpoint of its Creator. . . . It seeks rather to understand itself in terms of itself. This is shown in the fact that in relation to God it thinks it has criteria by which His revelation must be proved (5:31ff.; 8:13ff.), that it thinks it is free (8:33) and that instead of asking concerning God's glory it establishes its own standards of glory (5:41ff.). It is thus in sin and death (8:21-24, 34-37)" (*TDNT*, III, p. 16).

which John puts so much stress. We see this also in passages such as that in which Jesus says that those to whom he gives eternal life "will not perish for ever" (10:28), where the implication is that those who do not receive this gift will "perish for ever."

It accords with this that John has the verb *apothnēskō*, "to die", more often than anyone else in the New Testament (28 times). Often this refers to the death that Jesus would die for people, but passages like those just quoted point to the death that is the inevitable result of refusing to believe. It is not that John has a morbid interest in death. He has not. He simply draws attention to the fact that when people are offered life, there is a very serious choice before them. To refuse it is to choose death. We should all be clear on that. But John's aim is not that people choose death, but rather that they become believers and enter into that life which is life eternal.

General Index

Jesus, 147f.; as Teacher, 160f.; baptism in, 146, 149-52; born of, 24, 129, 149ff.; of truth, 154-58, 160

Synagogue, 83f., 152

Tabernacles, Feast of, 79, 112, 206
Taheb, 75
Talmud, 26
Temple, 81, 112; cleansing of, 9, 21, 24f., 138
Thirst, 60, 63
Thomas, 118, 185
Tiglath-pileser, 89
Truth, 8, 94, 118f., 145
Trypho, 81

Unbelievers, 93, 97

Vine, 119-22, 137f.

Water, 18, 61, 161, 186; into wine, 8, 22, 24f., 40, 57; living, 25-27, 206; walking on the, 20f., 32-35, 40, 46f., 123
Way, 118f.
Witness, 13, 16f., 28, 41, 66, 123, 136, 146f., 161
Wonder, 11, 13, 17, 21
Work(s), 13ff., 86, 129, 182
World, 77, 103, 141f.
Worship, 26, 70, 138-41
Wrath, 129

Zacharias, 108
Zera, R., 81

Index of Authors

215

Index of Scriptural Passages

224